The Internet and Instruction

The Internet and Instruction
Activities and Ideas

Second Edition

Ann E. Barron
University of South Florida, Tampa

Karen S. Ivers
California State University, Fullerton

1998
Libraries Unlimited, Inc.
and its Division
Teacher Ideas Press
Englewood, Colorado

For our parents:
Delwin and Frances Borhart for my lifetime investment in education,
John and Betty Ivers for my creativity, strength, and will to succeed.

LIBRARIES UNLIMITED, INC.
and Its Division
Teacher Ideas Press
P.O. Box 6633
Englewood, CO 80155-6633
(800) 237-6124
www.lu.com/tip

Constance Hardesty, *Project Editor*

Sheryl Tongue, *Design and Composition*

Pine™ is a trademark of the University of Washington.

Portions Copyright Netscape Communications Corporation, 1997. All Rights Reserved. Netscape, Netscape Navigator and the Netscape N logo are registered trademarks of Netscape in the United States and other countries.

Screen Capture from Geometry Center (http://www.geom.umn.edu) at the University of Minnesota. Used with permission.

Yahoo screen capture: Text and artwork copyright © 1998 by YAHOO! Inc. All rights reserved. YAHOO! and the YAHOO! logo are trademarks of YAHOO! Inc.

The Microbial Ecology page is copyright © Michigan State University.

Library of Congress Cataloging-in-Publication Data

Barron, Ann E.
    The Internet and instruction : activities and ideas / Ann E.
Barron. Karen S. Ivers. -- 2nd ed.
    xi, 244 p.   22×28 cm.
    Includes bibliographical references and index.
    ISBN 1-56308-613-1
    1. Teaching--Computer network resources.   2. Education--Computer
network resources.   3. Internet (Computer network) in education.
4. Computer managed instruction.   I. Ivers, Karen S.   II. Title.
LB1044.87.B37   1998
371.33'4678--dc21   98-15021
                                                        CIP

Contents

8 Language Arts Resources and Activities

9 Social Studies and Geography Resources and Activities

Figures and Tables

Preface

Through telecommunications, the typical classroom is no longer bound by four walls; it is open to include students, experts, and learning experiences from around the world. Telecommunications is changing the way students learn, when they learn, where they learn, and who teaches them. Information about telecommunications, the Internet, and the World Wide Web is appearing everywhere. The quantity of educational resources available through these sources is overwhelming, and it may be difficult for teachers and students to find the time to explore these resources and integrate them into their curricula.

The second edition of *The Internet and Instruction: Activities and Ideas* is designed for K–12 educators who are interested in tapping the Internet (particularly the World Wide Web) for instructional purposes. It seeks to demystify the technology and provide relevant, feasible, and easy-to-implement activities and ideas for the classroom. The book is designed for teachers, media specialists, and administrators who are currently employed in the educational field, as well as for those who are planning a career in education.

The overall purpose of this book is to improve the instructional process through the appropriate integration of telecommunications. It accomplishes this purpose by providing basic information about the benefits of the Internet for teachers, students, media specialists, and administrators. In addition to an overview of the hardware, software, and navigational issues involved in telecommunications, a major focus of the book is the ideas, activities, and lesson plans designed to encourage exploration and integration of Internet resources for instruction. Although many of the activities are interdisciplinary, they are categorized into the following major subject areas: Science; Mathematics; Language Arts; Social Studies; and Art, Theater, and Music.

Organization and Use

The Internet and Instruction: Activities and Ideas can be used as a resource book, as a guide for in-service education, or as a textbook. As a resource, this book provides a wealth of information. Each chapter begins with a scenario illuminating the implementation of telecommunications in an educational setting. Detailed graphics provide configurations and illustrations of hardware and software, and reproducible black-line masters are provided for activities and lesson plans. In addition, the book contains references to many educational Internet addresses and a detailed index for easy access to specific topics and information.

The book is also designed for use in conjunction with in-service training. To facilitate in-service workshops, each chapter was written to be independent of the others, although relevant topics are cross-referenced. In addition, several chapters include camera-ready activities and lesson plans that enhance the topic. These activities and lesson plans may be copied and distributed in accordance with the copyright statement on page iv.

As a textbook, *The Internet and Instruction: Activities and Ideas* is appropriate for technology courses at both the undergraduate and graduate levels. Throughout the book, emphasis is placed on the educational applications of telecommunications and relevant examples are included for teacher training. The activities and lesson plans are designed to focus on several levels of research and communications skills for a variety of grade levels and content areas.

The Internet: An Educator's Perspective

Ms. Ramirez watched as Cindy pinned the postcard from Nova Scotia on the bulletin board. The postcard had been sent by a student named John, who wrote about going ice fishing and hunting. A few weeks ago, Ms. Ramirez's third-grade class had begun a collaborative project that involved sending picture postcards to 150 elementary classes around the world. Now, as the responses arrived, the students pinned the cards on the bulletin board and used a piece of yarn to connect them to the corresponding locations on a large map.

Ms. Ramirez marveled at how this relatively simple project helped to make education more relevant and authentic for the students. They had enhanced their communications skills when they sent the postcards, and now, as postcards arrived, they learned about geography and culture.

This project would not have been possible, however, without the Internet. It was just over a month ago when Ms. Ramirez had seen the Call for Participants on an e-mail exchange. The project was called Postcard Geography, and it involved teachers who exchanged addresses via e-mail so students could send and receive *real* picture postcards. It was a perfect project for a third-grade class with only one computer!

As Ms. Ramirez reflected about this and other Internet projects, one thing was clear—the Internet had expanded her classroom and made the educational process more authentic and exciting. Her class had participated in several Internet projects, including GeoGame, the Jason Project, and Journey North.

GeoGame involved using maps, atlases, and other resources to determine the location of participating schools based on their latitude, weather, and other factors. The students also enjoyed the Jason Project, which provided ongoing dialog with researchers around the world. And the Journey North project engaged students in tracking butterflies and studying insects' habitats.

Ms. Ramirez had witnessed tremendous benefits from using the Internet, and students loved it! She was convinced that the activities provided her students with cultural awareness and information-gathering skills. The projects helped motivate students to write, challenged their analytical processes and curiosity, and opened their minds to the fact that learning was not confined to the classroom.

As Cindy returned to her desk, the discussion about ice fishing began. This was certainly a better way to learn about Canada than reading a chapter in a textbook!

GUIDELINES FOR USING THE INTERNET IN THE CLASSROOM

The Internet offers tremendous potential for education. Used appropriately, it can enhance instruction, stimulate thinking, and facilitate communication among students, educators, scientists, researchers, and others around the world. However, given a specific situation, educators must ask, "Is telecommunications the most efficient and effective medium to reach the instructional goals?" It is a constant challenge for teachers to differentiate between activities that provide high-level cognitive engagement and contrived activities that provide only exposure to technology (Ross 1995). One way to ensure a telecommunications exercise is relevant and meaningful in a given situation is to ask:

- Can I teach the goals or concepts of my lesson just as effectively (or more effectively) through another medium?

- Is there a more efficient method for obtaining the information I plan to obtain through the Internet?

- Am I taking advantage of the distance, multiple resources, and speed offered by the Internet?

- Will this activity increase students' ability to conduct information searches and retrieve relevant resources?

- Will this exercise require students to synthesize, analyze, and evaluate the information?

In addition to being appropriate, Internet activities should be instructionally significant and systematically designed. Design is an important consideration when online time needs to be optimized, when there are hardware constraints, or when time of day is a significant factor. Many Internet sites have busy peaks or periodically close for maintenance. This book presents guidelines, templates, and ideas for capitalizing on the educational potential of the Internet. Activities are also included to help familiarize students and teachers with the Internet resources.

BENEFITS OF USING THE INTERNET

Before investing time, money, and resources in a new technology, it is wise to question the potential benefits. In educational environments, telecommunications usually refers to using modems or computer networks (like the Internet) to send and receive information through telephone lines or data lines. Advantages of using telecommunications include the convenience of sending international messages at any time of the day or night; the elimination of telephone tag; the ability to save messages; the benefit of sending messages to many receivers simultaneously; the reduction of long-distance telephone charges; and access to enormous quantities of text, computer programs, and multimedia resources (Barron 1998). Research has demonstrated that telecommunications—specifically the Internet—can benefit education in many ways.

Benefits for Students

The Internet can provide students with new, exciting, and challenging resources. It opens doors to multicultural education; establishes real-world learning experiences; encourages higher-order thinking skills; helps to improve writing skills; and increases motivation, achievement, and positive behavior.

Sample Classroom Projects

The Internet offers tremendous opportunities for education. Teachers in distant locations can exchange ideas and information, and students can interact with peers and experts in various cultures, countries, and languages. In addition, international resources, including government, commercial, and educational sites, can be accessed quickly and inexpensively from school computers. This section provides a brief overview of several ongoing Internet projects that are being implemented in classrooms around the world.

Journey North
http://www.learner.org/jnorth

With the Journey North project, students track migrating butterflies, caribou, whales, and other species through reported sightings. Journey North is more than a passive exhibit, with students simply viewing a Web page; instead, they are encouraged to become actively involved through various endeavors. In the Monarch Butterfly project, students are encouraged to keep a record of the monarch sightings near their school, to calculate how far the butterflies must fly to reach Mexico City, to create a paper butterfly to send to Mexico City for display, and to build a monarch habitat in their community.

Many teachers use Journey North projects as platforms to discuss geography, weather, instinct, and other related topics. Challenge questions, provided on the Web page, help integrate the project into the curriculum. The Journey North project is sponsored by the Annenberg/CPB Math and Science Project.

See the home page for more information (or send an e-mail message to **jberger@dorsai.org**).

GeoGame
http://www.gsn.org/project/gg/index.html

The Geography Game is a very popular Internet activity designed by Tom Clauset, Winston-Salem, North Carolina. In this project, participating classes provide information about their location, including latitude, weather, geography, time zone, and population. A facilitator shuffles the information and then presents the data as a set of clues. Students use maps and other reference materials to identify the cities.

GeoGame began several years ago as an e-mail activity. Now it is available on the Global SchoolNet Web site. This activity has been used by many teachers to teach geography terms and map skills and to increase awareness of cultural diversity.

Jason Project
http://www.jason.org

The Jason Project provides interactions to help students explore the following questions: What are the earth's physical systems? How do these systems affect life on earth? What technologies do we use to study these systems?

Through interactions with researchers led by Dr. Robert Ballard, students receive live video and audio from expedition sites above and below the earth's surface. In addition, students are encouraged to participate in local research studies; locate relevant information; and expand their knowledge of geology, chemistry, physics, mathematics, geography, art, literature, and history.

Headbone Derby
http://www.headbone.com/derby

Headbone Derby provides structured Internet research adventures for students in grades 4–8. Each Derby is a story with seven episodes and a puzzle at the end. To solve the puzzle, students must conduct research on the Web and submit their answers. Each puzzle takes about 45 minutes to solve.

Headbone Derby is a free service. After you access the site, there is a sign-on process (for individuals or teams), and then the fun begins! Students are encouraged to conduct thoughtful searches (speed does not count), ask for hints if needed, and submit answers to the questions. For teachers, there are advance previews and a teacher's guide with extension activities and related off-line projects.

Multicultural Education

The demographics of U.S. society accentuate the need for understanding and tolerating cultural diversity. Banks (1994) states, "teaching from a range of perspectives will prepare students from diverse groups to work together in a truly unified nation" (p. 4). One powerful benefit of the Internet is that it offers students opportunities to exchange ideas and interact with students from backgrounds different from their own.

The Internet also offers students opportunities to increase their understanding and respect for cultural differences (Gersh 1994). Telecommunications removes the face-to-face biases that students may have or may encounter when interacting with someone of a different race, age, gender, or ability group. It provides students with the benefits of risk-free expression, greater self-esteem, and increased self-confidence (Collis 1992).

Real-World Learning Experiences

Kinnaman (1993, 86) states, "school learning is much more useful when it is grounded in authentic activities that emphasize the link between the acquisition of knowledge and its application." The Internet provides students with such activities by engaging them in interactive, real-world communications and up-to-date information. When compared to traditional methods, telecommunications offers students a more realistic opportunity to broaden their perspectives on global issues (U.S. Congress 1995).

Higher-Order Thinking Skills

One of the most highly rated incentives for using telecommunications with students is increasing students' inquiry and analytical skills (Honey and Henriquez 1993). The Internet provides a natural setting for inquiry skills, including collecting information for analysis and communicating with experts.

Writing Skills

Studies have demonstrated that telecommunications experiences can significantly increase the quality of students' writing (Cohen and Riel 1989; Wright 1991; Gallini and Helman 1993). In addition, the activities can provide students with purposeful writing experiences and can increase students' motivation to write and share their knowledge and experiences with peers (Allen and Thompson 1994). "The Internet vastly extends the audience for student multimedia publishing" (D'Ignazio 1997, 23).

Motivation

Recent research studies indicate that computer-based telecommunications can positively affect student attitudes and motivation. For example, in the evaluation of a collaborative project between students in New York state and students in Moscow, a positive effect was noted on student interest in international issues and current events (MAGI Educational Services, Inc. 1992). Likewise, Chiu (1996) found that tenth-grade students who used network resources in science demonstrated significantly more positive attitudes toward both school and science.

Achievement

Various studies that have analyzed student achievement (as measured through projects, interpretation skills, and knowledge) have noted significant increases with regard to the integration of telecommunications (Weir 1992). A study conducted by the Center for Applied Special Technology compared the work of 500 students in fourth-grade and sixth-grade classes in seven urban school districts—half with online access and half without. Experimental groups with online access attained significantly higher scores on measurements of information management, communication, and presentation of ideas (Follansbee et al. 1996).

Positive Student Behaviors

In a study that examined student participation in an electronic discussion group, Karayan (1997) found that "approximately 50% of the students were more likely to exhibit desired behaviors as a result of participating in electronic discussions" (p. 71). The positive behaviors included: think more before answering, develop a positive relationship with the instructor, learn class content, and answer peer-asked and teacher-asked questions. In another study, Riel (1992) reviewed research on the use of networking for collaboration and found evidence of improved social skills.

Benefits for Teachers

The Internet provides teachers instant access to educational research, curriculum sources, lesson plans, online experts, discussion centers, and teacher forums. This wealth of information opens doors for collaboration, encourages alternate instructional strategies, and enhances the curriculum in a manner that benefits both the teacher and the student.

Teacher Collaboration

According to Honey and Henriquez (1993), teachers report they have grown professionally by collaborating and communicating with their peers. For example, electronic forums and conferences designed for teachers offer educators the opportunity to discuss current issues and topics. These topics may include alternative assessment, school-based management, technology trends, and equity issues. The Internet also offers opportunities for continuing education for teachers.

Alternate Instructional Strategies

Telecommunications is beginning to change the way teachers teach. Honey and Henriquez (1993) report, "conducting telecommunications activities with students enables teachers to spend more time with individual students, less time lecturing to the whole class, and allows students to carry out more independent work" (p. 79). Similarly, Follansbee et al. (1996) found that teachers who integrated telecommunications into their curricula were more likely to use computers with their students to enhance achievement through gathering, organizing, and presenting information.

Enhanced Curriculum

Telecommunications also influences the curriculum: "Topics are of a more global significance ... and apply higher-level thinking skills of analysis and synthesis" (Honey and Henriquez 1993, 79). The Internet provides access to information that would not otherwise be available in classrooms. It is an ideal tool for investigative activities and collaborative writing projects. The Internet makes it possible to collect global data for an experiment and to electronically share the data with students and experts around the world much more efficiently than traditional methods (Donlan 1998). In addition, teachers and students have access to a tremendous amount and variety of resources, including online databases, experts, dictionaries, encyclopedias, educational software, books, and journals.

Benefits for Media Specialists

The Internet can provide media specialists with access to data resources, timely information, and useful tools for teaching research skills. Enhanced communications reduce geographical and emotional isolation from colleagues.

Data Resources

The Internet offers an abundance of resources, including online books, journals, searchable databases, surveys, polls, graphics, sounds, digital movies, and software. Fortunately, information acquisition can be conducted electronically, and the resources take up little storage space! Ladner and Tillman (1993) noted that using telecommunications is "a vastly more efficient way of locating information" than other methods (p. 49).

Timely Information

The Internet gives media specialists access to up-to-date information about current issues in education. Online discussions with experts make it possible to receive firsthand information, answers to specific questions, and input from a variety of perspectives. In addition, the Internet allows many libraries to link to a single master catalog or circulation system, enabling educators and students to locate resources outside of their own libraries (Kline 1994).

Tools for Teaching Research Skills

The Internet is a wonderful tool for teaching research skills (Caputo 1994). Students can practice locating, analyzing, and reporting information without expensive connect charges. Many of the online systems also feature keyword and Boolean searches. Studies have shown a significant increase in the variety of sources used and cited in student bibliographies when students use online searching (Mancall 1984; Follansbee et al. 1996).

Collegiality

In a survey conducted by Ladner and Tillman (1993, 50), the major reason media specialists used the Internet was that it provided "a convenient, timely, nondisruptive, and inexpensive mechanism for communication with their colleagues throughout the world." It can help to reduce the isolation felt by many media specialists in rural or remote schools.

Benefits for Administrators

At the administrative level, telecommunications offers flexibility and enhances the preparation and delivery of documents. It also provides an efficient and effective method for receiving up-to-date information and maintaining external contacts.

Document Management

Telecommunications offers "overall cost reduction, reduced paper handling, faster communications, improved communication effectiveness, and integration of data communication with records management" (D'Souza 1992, 22). In addition, with fewer opportunities for human error in the electronic transfers, documents tend to be more accurate (Palmer and Wei 1993). Another advantage of electronic data communication is the ability to transmit in an interchangeable format. For example, a PC can retrieve and display information sent by a Macintosh computer and vice versa.

Communication with Faculty and Community

Through e-mail and distribution lists, administrators can communicate with all of the faculty members at the same time. For example, it is easy to send notices for meetings. Likewise, administrators can quickly and easily interact with community members.

External Contacts

Telecommunications provides administrators with access to immediate, up-to-date information about educational research, conferences, and state initiatives. In addition, requests for business partnerships, grants, and other funding may be initiated using the Internet (Cheely 1995). For example, grant information is available on TeachNet at **http://www.teachnet.org**.

Benefits for the Community

Telecommunications is an excellent way to involve the community in school issues, fundraisers, class projects, special events, and volunteer activities. It is also a viable means of communicating with local business leaders, experts, and community officials who are accessible online. In addition, many community members may wish to participate in some of the online instructional programs that are designed for K–12 students.

Communication with the School

Telecommunications offers parents the opportunity to become involved electronically with their children's homework assignments, and it offers a forum for teacher/parent conferences (Golub 1994). It is possible for parents to tour a school, to view student projects, and to converse with teachers—all online.

Student–Community Activities

The Internet makes it possible for senior citizens and people lacking mobility to share their knowledge and experience with students. Many students obtain valuable tutoring from senior citizens through online communication.

Distance Learning Opportunities

Virtual high schools and other distance learning initiatives produce instructional programs accessible through the Internet. Although these programs may be designed primarily for high school students, community members may also benefit by enrolling in or auditing the programs.

CONCLUSION

More than a decade ago, Shea (1984) stated that some industry sources predicted, "within 10 years we'll be telecommunicating almost as regularly as we now use a telephone" (p. 34). In many cases, the prediction was right; in fact, some people use telecommunications *more* than they use the telephone.

The use of telecommunications is increasing in today's schools and universities. Recent reports note that roughly 40 percent of U.S. schools have at least one line to the Internet (Jacobson 1997). Telephone companies, local corporations, and government offices have taken steps to ensure that the use of telecommunications will become integral to education. NetDay, an initiative in which schools work with local corporate and community volunteers to wire schools, was responsible for connecting 20 percent of California's classrooms (Hickox 1997) and 75 percent of Connecticut's classrooms in a single day (Jacobson 1996).

President Bill Clinton and the federal government are also promoting plans to connect every classroom to the Internet by the year 2000 (Riley 1997). The Telecommunications Act of 1996 and a plan approved in 1997 by the Federal Communications Commission resulted in *e-rates*: telephone rates and other charges discounted up to 90 percent for schools. (See the U.S. Department of Education Web site at **http://www.ed.gov/** and the Federal Communications Commission site at **http://www.fcc.gov/learnet/** for more information about government initiatives.)

Through appropriate projects, the multiple benefits of telecommunications will be realized by students, teachers, media specialists, administrators, and the community. Telecommunications and other information technologies can "empower people of all ages, both inside and outside the classroom, to learn more easily, enjoyably, and successfully than ever before" (Gates 1996, 208).

REFERENCES

Allen, G., and A. Thompson. 1994. *Analysis of the effect of networking on computer-assisted collaborative writing in a fifth grade classroom.* ERIC Document ED373777.

Banks, J. A. 1994. *Multiethnic education: Theory and practice.* 3d ed. Boston, MA: Allyn and Bacon.

Barron, A. E. 1998. *Getting started with telecommunications.* Tampa, FL: Florida Center for Instructional Technology, University of South Florida.

Caputo, A. 1994. Seven secrets of searching: How and when to choose online. *MultiMedia Schools* 1(1):29–33.

Cheely, C. 1995. Search & seizure: Using your modem to find grants. *Multimedia Schools* 2(3):22–28.

Chiu, C. H. 1996. The effects of computer networks and collaboration on the development of science skills and attitudes among secondary science students in Taiwan, R.O.C., Dissertation Abstracts International 57/06-A. (Order Number AAD96-33125.)

Cohen, M., and M. Riel. 1989. The effect of distant audiences on students' writing. *American Educational Research Journal* 26(2):143–59.

Collis, B. 1992. Supporting educational uses of telecommunication in the secondary school: Part I. An overview of experiences. *International Journal of Media* 19(1):23–44.

D'Ignazio, F. 1997. Young authors at home on the Web. *MultiMedia Schools* 4(3):22–28.

Donlan, L. 1998. Visions of online projects. *MultiMedia Schools.* 5(1):21–25.

D'Souza, P. V. 1992. Electronic mail in academic settings: A multipurpose communications tool. *Educational Technology* 32(3):22–25.

Follansbee, S., N. Gilsdorf, S. Stahl, J. Dunfey, S. Cohen, B. Pisha, and B. Hughes. October 1996. *The role of online communications in schools: A national study.*

Peabody, MA: Center for Applied Special Technology.

Gallini, J. K., and N. Helman. 1993. Audience awareness in technology-mediated environments. Paper presented at the Annual Meeting of the American Educational Research Association, Atlanta, Georgia.

Gates, B. 1996. *The Road Ahead.* New York: Penguin Books.

Gersh, S. 1994. The global education telecommunications network: Criteria for successful e-mail projects. *Telecommunications in Education News* 5(4):10–11.

Golub, J. N. 1994. *Activities for an interactive classroom.* Urbana, IL: National Council of Teachers of English.

Hickox, K. 1997. 5 trends your job depends on. *Electronic Learning* 16(4):32–38.

Honey, M., and A. Henriquez. 1993. *Telecommunications and K–12 education: Findings from a national survey.* New York: Center for Technology in Education, Bank Street College of Education.

Jacobson, S. 1997. State education networks spread. *Electronic Learning* 16(6):8.

———. 1996. NYC NetDay: Where's the beef? *Electronic Learning* 16(3):6.

Karayan, S. S. 1997. Student perceptions of electronic discussion groups. *T.H.E. Journal* 24(9):69–71.

Kinnaman, D. E. 1993. Technology and situated cognition. *Technology & Learning* 14(1):86.

Kline, N. 1994. Education and the Internet: The evolution of the electronic library. *Syllabus* 8(3):14–15.

Ladner, S. J., and H. M. Tillman. 1993. Using the Internet for reference. *Online* 17(1):45–51.

MAGI Educational Services, Inc. February 1992. *Evaluation of the New York State/Moscow Schools Telecommunications Project.* Albany, NY: New York State Department of Education.

Mancall, J. D. 1984. Training students to search online: Rationale, process, and implications. *Drexel Library Quarterly* 20(1):64–84.

Palmer, B. H., and P. B. Wei. 1993. SPEEDE made easy. *College and University* 69(1):4–13.

Riel, M. April 1992. Educational change in a technology-rich environment. Paper presented at the Annual Meeting of the American Educational Research Association, San Francisco, California.

Riley, R. February 1997. Your Work and the Department's Agenda for Education. United States Department of Education. **http://www.ed.gov/ updates/970227.html** (October 20, 1997).

Ross, P. 1995. Relevant telecomputing activities. *The Computing Teacher* 22(5):28–30.

Shea, G. 1984. Information services: The new frontier of communication. *Electronic Learning* 4(2):33–34, 88–89.

U.S. Congress, Office of Technology Assessment. April 1995. *Teachers and technology: Making the connection.* Washington, DC: U.S. Government Printing Office. Document OTA-EHR-616.

Weir, S. January 1992. *Electronic communities of learners: Facts or fiction.* Cambridge, MA: TERC Communications. (ERIC Document Reproduction Service No. 348990.)

Wright, W. 1991. International group work: Using a computer conference to invigorate the writing of your students. Pages 100–103 in *The English Classroom in the Computer Age,* edited by W. Wresch. Urbana, IL: National Council of Teachers of English.

Getting Started with the Internet

For the past two years, Mr. Cronbach had been using a modem in his classroom to connect to the Internet. He remembered how excited he was to get it up and running. At first all of his interactions on the Internet were through e-mail (text-based), and it seemed like a miracle that he could connect with other teachers and students in faraway countries. Recently, however, he had become acquainted with the World Wide Web and really loved the graphics, links, and media elements he was able to access. There was only one problem—it was soooo slow! Sometimes when he clicked on a link, a minute or two would go by before he could see the Web page on his screen. This was definitely ineffective for middle school students—there had to be a better way!

At the next faculty meeting, Mr. Cronbach mentioned his frustration to the other teachers. Ms. Alpha, the technology specialist, responded that a solution was on the way. At first Mr. Cronbach thought she was talking about one of the faster modems he had seen advertised, but she said the solution was even better than that. The school was installing a LAN (local area network) that would connect all of the computers to a central server. "That's nice," said Mr. Cronbach, "but I want to be connected to the Internet, not just a server in this building!"

Ms. Alpha went on to explain that by installing a LAN and server, along with data lines connecting the LAN server to an Internet service provider, all of the computers could have direct access to the Internet. That would mean that all of the computers could be online at the same time, and they would not have to worry about having a phone line for every room. "That sounds good," said Mr. Cronbach, "but it will probably be even slower than before with all of the computers sharing one line to the Internet!" Ms. Alpha calmly explained that although they would share a line,

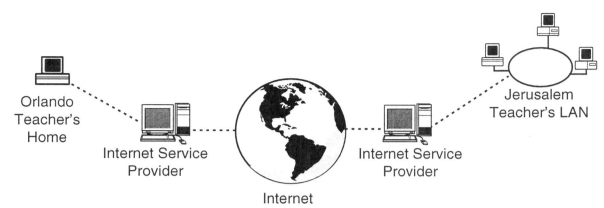

Figure 2.1   The Internet connects users around the world.

the line was much, much faster and had more bandwidth (capacity) than the regular telephone line. The eternal pessimist, Mr. Cronbach said he would believe it when he saw it.

Two months later, the LAN was connected, the Internet software was installed on each computer, and a high-speed data line connection was established. The teachers, including Mr. Cronbach, could not believe the difference. Files and pages that had taken 10 minutes to transfer now appeared on the screen in a matter of seconds. Yes, the line was more expensive for the school district, but with the special discounts for education, it was affordable. This, thought Mr. Cronbach, is the way the Internet should operate! He couldn't wait to send his students exploring on the Web for projects and resources.

The Internet is a worldwide communications system that is referred to as a "network of networks" because it connects thousands of computer networks all over the world. The backbone, or main part, of the Internet consists of data lines that can transmit computer information at extremely high speeds.

The U.S. portion of the backbone was created by the federal government in the 1960s for military and research purposes. In the 1980s, it was updated by the National Science Foundation, and in the early 1990s, it was expanded to allow commercial use. Since then, the number of people using the Internet has increased dramatically, making it a common communication tool for schools, homes, and businesses. The U.S. backbone now connects with satellites and data lines in other countries to provide rapid exchange of information all over the world.

Through the Internet, a teacher with a modem at her house in Orlando can connect to an Internet service provider that in turn connects to the Internet. Likewise, a teacher on a computer network in Jerusalem can connect to an Israeli service provider that connects to the Internet. In this way, the Internet provides the conduit to transfer information from the home in Orlando to the school in Jerusalem (see fig. 2.1).

The interstate highway system often serves as an analogy for the Internet. Both systems are designed for high–speed travel (of cars or data), and both have a multitude of inputs and outputs (on-ramps and off-ramps) to or from smaller networks or roads. Neither the Internet nor the country's system of roads is controlled or owned by a single entity, and both offer a variety of routes to get from point A to point B. Expanding on this analogy, the fee that must be paid to the Internet service provider for access to the Internet is similar to the toll required to enter certain highways. In a similar sense, the Internet has some restricted areas (where a subscription or password is required), just as some gated communities have private roads. A major difference between the highway system and the Internet is that the Internet is global, whereas the interstate

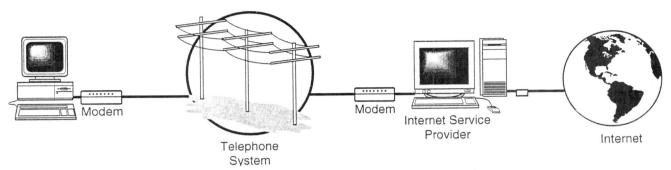

Figure 2.2 Hardware configuration for a dial-up connection.

highway system is constrained by geography (Barron et al. 1997).

GETTING CONNECTED

Internet Service Providers

In order to connect to the Internet, you must have an Internet service provider (ISP). The function of an ISP is to provide the connection (on-ramp) for Internet access. ISPs maintain computer servers and pay for high-speed links to the Internet 24 hours a day. Your service provider may be a very large company with many computers (such as America Online), an educational agency (such as a university), or a small local company.

In many cases, educators can obtain access to the Internet through a state or regional educational organization, such as the Florida Information Resource Network (FIRN) or the Texas Education Network (TENET). If your state does not provide an educational system with Internet connections, you may be able to obtain Internet access through a local university, school district, or library. Another option for Internet access is to locate a FreeNet in your community. A FreeNet is a computer network that is run by a community organization, such as a college or public library. These networks usually offer a variety of community–based services, such as local databases, class schedules, and public activities. Many FreeNets also offer full or partial Internet access for members at little or no cost.

If you cannot locate an educational system or FreeNet in your area, your best option may be to join a commercial online service, such as America Online or CompuServe. These online services offer access to the Internet, as well as electronic discussion forums, public domain software, online catalogs, and other resources. There are also many national Internet providers (which may be telephone or cable companies), such as SprintLink and WorldNet. In addition, there is a proliferation of local service providers. Most of these providers charge about $20 per month for unlimited access to the Internet (see **http://www.celestin.com/pocia/** for a list of ISPs).

Most schools have two options for connecting to the ISP's server:

- Dial-up connections with a modem and a regular telephone line

- Direct connections through local area networks and a leased data line

Each option requires a different software and hardware configuration.

Dial-Up Connections

Educators commonly use a dial-up connection to gain access to the Internet because the hardware and software are inexpensive to obtain and maintain. The hardware required for a dial-up connection consists of a computer, modem, and telephone line. These are used to connect to a remote computer (see fig. 2.2).

Advantages of Dial-Up Connections

Free or inexpensive connection charges. Many universities or educational systems offer free dial-up connections for schools. Dial-up accounts with commercial services cost about $20 per month.

Inexpensive software. Dial-up connections are relatively easy to make. Shareware telecommunications software is available, or the software may be supplied by the ISP.

Inexpensive hardware. A regular telephone line can be used, and no special arrangements are required with the telephone company. Modems are relatively inexpensive, and either Macintosh or Windows computers will work fine.

Disadvantages of Dial-Up Connections

May get busy signals. Dial-up connections require a modem at the receiving end to answer your call. Most systems have a limited number of modems; therefore, you may have to compete for time on the system. It can be very frustrating to plan a lesson around the Internet and then receive a busy signal when you try to dial in.

Slower than a direct connection. In most cases, a dial-up connection is not as fast as a direct connection through a leased data line.

Requires a fast modem. Although a 14.4 Kbps modem will work for a dial-up connection, faster modems (at least 28.8 Kbps) speed the transfer of graphics, files, and other elements.

Computer

A computer and monitor are essential. It does not matter whether you use a computer with the Macintosh, UNIX, Windows, or other operating system—all can communicate with each other through the Internet. If you plan to save a lot of files and information from the Internet, a large hard drive will be necessary. In addition, a fast computer processor will speed access and display of the information. Finally, at least 8 (preferably 16 or 32) megabytes (MB) of random access memory (RAM) are recommended. RAM serves as a buffer to accept and hold onto information from the Internet without saving it to the hard disk; if you have insufficient RAM, you will not be able to access or display the many large multimedia files the Internet offers.

Modem

Modem stands for MOdulate/DEModulate; it is a device that translates (modulates) computer data to a form that can be sent over regular telephone lines. Computer information is stored in digital form (bits and bytes), but most telephone lines transmit sound in analog form. The modem takes the digital computer information and changes it to analog form so it can be sent through the telephone system. A modem at the receiving end demodulates the analog signal back to bits and bytes so the receiving computer can display it.

Modems can be external peripherals, or they can be internal computer cards. External modems usually include small lights that indicate the status of the modem, that is, whether it is receiving or sending data. External modems connect to the back of the computer through a modem port on Macintosh computers or through a COM (communications) port on other types of computers. A telephone line connects to the back of the modem. In some cases, an optional telephone port is also available on the modem.

Internal modems are installed in a computer. Generally, they are less expensive than external modems, and they do not have status lights. An advantage of internal modems is that they do not require a separate power source—they derive their power from the computer. The telephone line connects directly to the back of the modem card.

Modems transmit data at various speeds. In the past, modems of 2,400 bits per second (bps) were common. Now, modems capable of 28,800 bps (28.8 Kilobits per second [Kbps]) are common, and modems up to 56 Kbps are available. Purchase the fastest modem you can afford, because fast modems decrease the time it takes to transmit files. Before purchasing a modem, check with your ISP to find out what speed modems are being used, because two modems of different speeds will communicate at the slower speed.

Telephone Line

Dial-up connections require a telephone line that hooks into the modem. (A telephone handset is not necessary, just the telephone line.) If you are connecting to an ISP from home, the same line that is used for your telephone can be used for the modem. Obtaining a telephone line is often the missing link for using telecommunications in the classroom. Many teachers find that enlisting the aid of the parent-teacher organization or seeking assistance from the local telephone company can bring telephone lines into the classroom. If all else fails, you may have to settle for one telephone line in the media center or another central location until you can demonstrate the benefits of telecommunications and generate enthusiasm among students, faculty, parents, and administrators.

At school, it is best to have a telephone line dedicated to telecommunications. That means you need a telephone line that does not have call waiting and is not shared by several classrooms. If the telephone line is not dedicated, you may run into problems with interruptions and disconnections. These interruptions are especially frustrating if you are trying to transfer large files or conduct an online lesson.

Telecommunications Software

In addition to the basic hardware, you will need telecommunications software to use a dial-up connection to the Internet. This software dials the telephone number and formats the data on

Advantages of Direct Connections

No busy signals. Because modems are not required for direct connections, you will not receive a busy signal.

Simultaneous connections. A major advantage of connecting a LAN directly to the Internet is that all of the student computers can access the Internet at the same time. Unlike a regular telephone line, the leased data line can transmit data from many computers simultaneously.

Less interference. There is less interference on high-speed leased data lines than there is on regular telephone lines.

Disadvantages of Direct Connections

Expense of hardware. In addition to the components of a LAN, direct connections involve the purchase of special hardware, such as a router and other communication devices.

Expense of leased lines. The expense of the leased line is a major consideration in linking a LAN to the Internet. In most areas, leased lines are available at several speeds and prices. For example, a line that transmits data at 56 Kbps may cost about $50 per month (depending on the length of the line). A T1 line that operates at 1,544 Kbps (1.544 Mbps) may cost hundreds of dollars each month.

Complexity. Obtaining and installing a direct Internet connection is complex. In addition to the LAN, router, and high-speed data line, you must contract with an ISP, assign Internet Protocol (IP) numbers to each computer, and configure the direct connection software. Before entering this arena, seek the advice of networking experts, contact other schools in your area, check with your state educational department, and call your local telephone company.

the screen. If you are connecting to the Internet through a commercial ISP, it will probably provide all of the software you need at little or no charge. If you need to supply your own software, there are many products on the market. Some of them, such as FreePPP for Macintosh and Windows Terminal for Windows, are available free or as shareware programs.

When all of the components (computer, modem, telephone line, and software) are in place, dial-up connections are made by typing the telephone number into the software program and clicking on Dial.

At this point, you will hear dial tones (if your modem has speakers), followed by a scratchy noise that signifies a connection. When the connection is complete, follow the procedure supplied by your ISP to enter your login name and password. Initially, the login name and password will be supplied by the ISP. After your first connection, you will be encouraged (or required) to change the password.

Considerations for Dial-Up Connections

When you are investigating a service provider that offers dial-up capabilities, there are some important considerations. First of all, a toll-free or local telephone number is important. If you must pay long-distance phone charges, the bill can quickly mount. Second, find out exactly what the charges will be for access or connect time (the amount of time you are connected to the system, usually measured in minutes). The best option is to find an educational network, university, or FreeNet that provides free connection time. If that is not possible, find out whether the connection fee is charged per minute or as a flat monthly fee. Some ISPs charge an extra fee for storing files (such as e-mail messages and Web pages) or for using special components and services, such as encyclopedias or airline reservation systems.

Direct Connections Through Local Area Networks

Many schools are establishing direct connections to the Internet through local area networks

(LANs). LANs consist of several computers equipped with network interface cards that are linked together with cables. Usually, a file server on the network stores all the programs and files that can be shared. Other peripherals, such as printers, scanners, and CD-ROM players, may also be connected to the network for all to use.

LANs are very popular in schools because money can be saved by purchasing network versions of software programs rather than separate programs for each computer. Also, expensive peripherals can be shared. An additional benefit of school networks is that they allow students and teachers to communicate electronically. For example, if a student is having trouble while working on a computer, he or she can send an electronic note to the instructor. In addition, there are software programs designed for student collaboration through a LAN. For example, the network program *Wagon Train 1848* by MECC allows several students at separate computers to view the same scenario and to interact through the network.

Installing a LAN requires installing cables from a central server to all of the computers. It can be a time-intensive process, but it pays off with ease of maintenance and speed of access. NetDays (specified days on which community volunteers help pull wires in schools) have become popular in the last few years. For more information about school LANs, see the *Educator's Guide to School Networks* at **http://fcit.coedu.usf.edu/network**.

Connecting a LAN to the Internet

LANs can provide each workstation with direct connections to the Internet. A school can connect its LAN directly to an ISP by leasing a high-speed data line from a telephone or cable company. When a direct connection is established, you do not need modems, and all of the computers on the LAN can connect to the Internet simultaneously (see fig. 2.3).

The hardware required for a direct connection is considerably more complex than that required for a dial-up connection. The basic components consist of computers, an Internet server, a router,

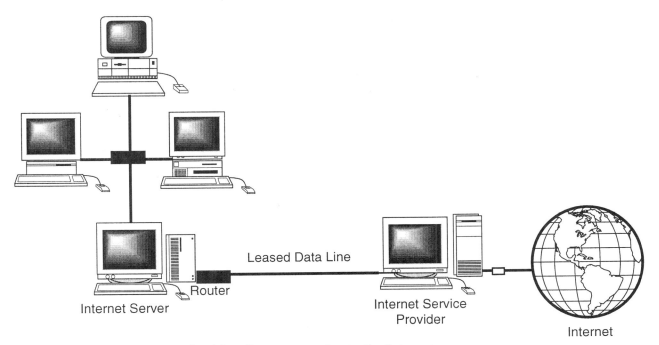

Figure 2.3 Computer network with a direct connection to the Internet.

and a leased data line. Consult a technical expert to determine the best configuration for your school.

Computers

A LAN comprises several workstations connected to a central server by cables. A typical workstation is a standard computer that has had a network interface card added to it. The LAN cable plugs into the network interface card through the back of the computer. Many new computers in both Macintosh and Windows environments now come with network cards already installed. With the correct software and cables, both Macintosh and Windows computers can share a LAN.

Internet Server

Most LANs have at least one computer that acts as the file server. This very large, very fast computer serves as the traffic director to keep all of the computers and printers working together. If you want to connect your LAN to the Internet, you can use this file server as an Internet server by installing additional software designed for Internet access.

Router

An Internet router is a small piece of hardware that is placed between the Internet server and the leased line. The router controls the messages that are going out to the Internet and receives incoming messages. Another piece of hardware (CSU/DSU) is used in conjunction with the router to convert the data for the router.

Leased Data Line

Direct connections generally make use of a leased data line to connect to the ISP. The leased line is usually a 56 Kbps line or a T1 line operating at 1.54 Mbps (see All About Bandwidth for more information about leased lines). The lines are generally leased from the local telephone company and are dedicated to Internet communications. The cost of the leased lines can range from a few dollars to several thousand dollars per month. The current initiatives by the U.S. government and telecommunications companies to establish a discounted "e-rate" for schools are designed to make leased lines affordable for schools and school districts (Brooks 1997).

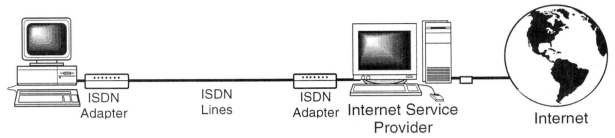

Figure 2.4 ISDN connection to the Internet.

Software for Direct Connections

The "language" of the Internet is often referred to as TCP/IP (Transmission Control Protocol/Internet Protocol). To operate a direct Internet connection, this software must be resident on all of the computers on the LAN and on the Internet server. Fortunately, because of the popularity of the Internet, this software is now installed on all Macintosh and Windows computers when you purchase the computers.

In addition to the TCP/IP software, special Internet server software must be installed on the Internet server. There is a wide range of Internet server software that can be purchased, including Netscape servers and Microsoft servers. For more information about setting up an Internet server, see **http://web66.coled.umn.edu**.

ALL ABOUT BANDWIDTH

Bandwidth refers to how fast a telephone line, data line, or other connection can transfer information. For example, a 28.8 Kbps modem can transmit data at 28,800 bits per second, and a T1 line can transmit 1,544,000 bits per second. A constant complaint about the Internet is that it is too slow. Although the backbone (main part) of the Internet consists of extremely high-speed data connections (at minimum, T3 lines that can transmit at 44,736,000 bits per second), the information may have to be funneled to your home through a slow modem.

Several options available now or in the near future will help to expand bandwidth and increase the speed of information transfer via the Internet. These options include ISDN lines, T1 lines, ADSL modems, cable modems, satellite delivery, and WebTV.

ISDN

ISDN stands for Integrated Services Digital Network. It is a digital system designed to transmit information faster than standard modems. A single ISDN line with two channels can transmit data at 128 Kbps (about five times faster than a 28.8 Kbps modem). ISDN telephone lines use interface devices (called ISDN terminal adapters or ISDN modems) to connect to the computers (see fig. 2.4).

ISDN has great potential for telecommunications because it can use some of the copper telephone wire system that is currently in place. To implement ISDN on a large scale, however, telephone companies need to upgrade their switching equipment, and homes and schools need to upgrade their telephone wiring and computer interfaces.

At present, ISDN availability and costs vary dramatically. In some areas, ISDN lines are available for almost the same cost as standard voice lines, but in other areas they are either very expensive or unavailable. Before purchasing an ISDN terminal adapter, check with your ISP to be sure that it is compatible with the service. Also, when checking on the price of an ISDN connection, be aware that some systems require a connection fee, a monthly fee, and a per-minute charge.

T1 and T3 Lines

A standard T1 line (also referred to as DS1) allows digital information to be transmitted at

Table 2.1 Comparison of Transfer Rates and Costs for Telecommunications (Feeley 1997)

Technology	Speed	Monthly Cost
28.8 modem	28.8 Kbps	$25
ISDN	128 Kbps	$80
Satellite	400 Kbps	$40
T1	1.5 Mbps	$1,500
ADSL	9 Mbps	$40
Cable modem	10 Mbps	$45

1,544 Kbps (1.544 Mbps). This transmission speed is almost 54 times faster than a 28.8 Kbps modem. Because T1 lines can be quite expensive to lease, many schools lease a "fractional" T1 line in which they have access to a portion of the bandwidth.

T3 lines are even faster than T1 lines. T3 lines can transmit data at 44.736 Mbps. This is roughly equivalent to 29 simultaneous T1 lines. T3 lines are extremely expensive. In most cases, T3 lines are used to connect parts of the Internet backbone or to connect supercomputers at government and research sites.

ADSL Modems

ADSL stands for Asymmetric Digital Subscriber Line. These lines transmit data at two different speeds: a fast speed for incoming data and a slower speed for outgoing data. ADSL modems can transmit data to users at up to 9 Mbps—about 12 times faster than ISDN modems. The return rate (outgoing data transmitted back to the ISP or Internet) is not quite as fast—only 640 Kbps. In most cases the difference in the transfer rates is acceptable, because we are most likely to receive large files from the Internet (such as graphics and video). On the other hand, we generally do not send back as much data to the Internet—perhaps an e-mail message or a command (a click on a hyperlink). Therefore the slower rate on the return segment is not detrimental.

A major advantage of ADSL is that it uses standard copper telephone lines; however, the telephone lines in many areas need to be upgraded to allow the rapid transmission of data. Several companies, including Bell Atlantic, Pacific Bell, and GTE, are promoting ADSL and plan to charge approximately $100 per month (Feeley 1997).

Cable Modems

In some areas, cable companies offer Internet access through the same cable that delivers television signals to your home. If your area has been configured for this service, you can connect a cable line to a network card on your computer. The advantage of cable modems is the speed. Cable modems can bring data to your computer roughly 400 times faster than a 28.8 Kbps modem (Salvador 1996). If you have a 10 Mbps network card in a computer, you may be able to receive information at that speed. As illustrated in Table 2.1, cable modems offer one of the fastest technologies available for Internet access (Feeley 1997).

Although cable modems are faster than most other technologies, they are not the most expensive (see table 2.1). However, to use a cable modem you must have a computer with a network card and you must purchase a cable modem (about $500). In addition, the transfer rate may be slowed if many people in your neighborhood connect to the Internet at the same time. Although

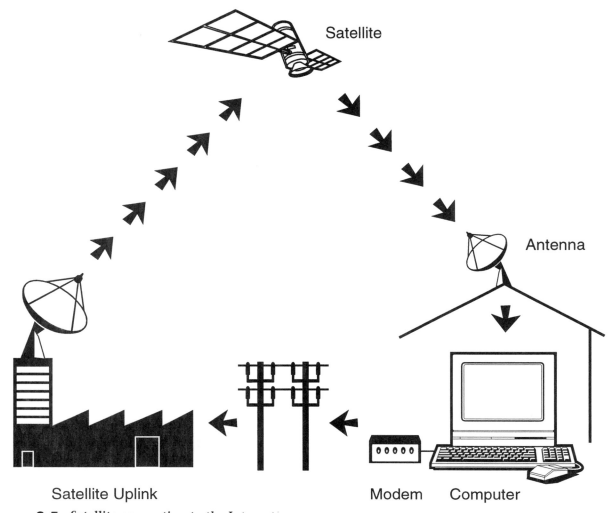

Figure 2.5 Satellite connection to the Internet.

this technology is new and the standards for cable modems are not firmly established, cable modems offer great potential for high-speed access to the Internet (Li-Ron 1998).

Satellite Delivery

It is possible to receive information from the Internet from a satellite. DirectPC is one technology that offers Internet access to satellite dishes on homes, schools, and businesses. Satellite access is relatively fast, does not require the installation of telephone or data lines, and is not affected by the number of users.

Satellite delivery, however, is usually one-way; you cannot send information back up to the satellite (not on a school budget, anyway). In most cases, a telephone line is used to send information to the Internet, and the satellite is used to receive information (see fig. 2.5). This configuration works well in most cases, because the information you send to the Internet is generally very small (a command or an e-mail message), whereas the information you receive can be quite large (audio files, Web pages, and so forth).

WebTV

It is possible to access the Internet and display it on a television set. WebTV consists of a small box that attaches to a television and a telephone line (for about $300). To log on to WebTV, you must subscribe to a WebTV service provider and pay a monthly fee.

WebTV is a great way to access the Internet if you do not have a computer. However, the resolution is not as good as a computer, causing the images and text to appear blurry. In addition, you must purchase an infrared keyboard to enter the Web addresses.

CONCLUSION

Compared to other new technologies, telecommunications hardware and software are inexpensive. The best option for you depends on the hardware available in your school, the amount of technical support available, and the services offered by your Internet service provider.

REFERENCES

Barron, A. E., K. Ivers, D. Hoffman, and L. Sherry. 1997. *Telecommunications: Ideas, activities, and resources.* Tampa, FL: Florida Center for Instructional Technology, University of South Florida.

Brooks, S. Summer 1997. The ins and outs of government funding: Tapping into the new "E-rate." *Technology & Learning*, 16.

Feeley, J. August 1997. Wideband Web. *Digital Video*, 42–48.

Florida Center for Instructional Technology. Educator's guide to school networks. **http://fcit.coedu.usf.edu/network** (January 17, 1998).

Li-Ron, Y. 1998. The need for speed. *The Web Magazine* 2(1):38–40.

Salvador, R. 1996. What's new in net connectivity? *Electronic Learning* 16(1):14.

Web 66: A K12 World Wide Web project. University of Minnesota. **http://web66.coled.umn.edu** (January 17, 1998).

3 Navigating the Internet

Mark and Juliana had finished the research for their social studies report and were considering options for presenting it to the class. The only requirement Mr. Little had mentioned was that it had to be presented electronically. They considered using PowerPoint or another presentation program, but Juliana suggested they create a Web page instead. "But we don't know HTML," said Mark, "and I've heard its quite complicated."

"We don't need to know HTML," said Juliana. "There are programs that will do all of the coding for us—we can simply enter the information, almost like PowerPoint." Mark was skeptical, but he agreed to give it a try. After all, most of their research had been conducted on the Web and it seemed logical to create a Web page that could include the links.

Fortunately, Mr. Little had just helped them to download the latest version of the Netscape browser. The new browser included a component that allowed users to create Web pages without entering any HTML codes. Mark was astonished by how easy it was to import their text, add hyperlinks to other Web sites, and embed graphics. They even added a link that would allow people to send them e-mail messages.

When the page was finished, they called the technical support person at the high school to find out how to upload the files to the Internet server. She told them they would have to FTP the files to the Web server, and explained the procedure to them. After the FTP software program was installed, it turned out to be very easy to upload the files to the server.

When it was time for their presentation, Mark asked Mr. Little if they could use a computer with an Internet connection. The class was amazed as they demonstrated their project, with active links to the White House and other relevant Web sites. "You were right," Mark admitted to Juliana. "I would never have believed that creating a Web page could be so easy!"

There are two basic interfaces, or looks, to the Internet—text-based and graphical. Text-based interfaces dominated the Internet until about 1994. These interfaces displayed text on the screen, with an occasional line of asterisks or dashes. Text-based interfaces worked well with modems of any speed. With text-based systems, telnet (remote access to other computers) and gopher (menu-based systems) were popular.

Graphical interfaces, in which you can point and click, now dominate the Internet. These interfaces require either a fast modem or a direct connection to the Internet. (Chapter 2 discusses connections.) Graphical interfaces make using the Internet much easier. In addition, graphics and colors can be displayed directly on the screen and you can play the sound files or view digital movies.

Educators and students can use the Internet to

- Collaborate and send messages using e-mail

- Participate in electronic conferences and newsgroups

- Access Web pages and documents located on computers around the world

- Create Web pages to share their information

- Transfer files from remote computers to their local host computer

- Interact with video and audio through media files or online conferences

This chapter focuses on the basic tools that help users find, view, and transfer information on the Internet. The tools include e-mail, listservs, newsgroups, World Wide Web, file transfer protocol, and conferencing.

ELECTRONIC MAIL

Electronic mail (e-mail) messages are created by a person using a computer; the messages are transmitted to other computers and read by one or more persons using computers. E-mail messages can be exchanged on a worldwide basis—students in the United States can communicate directly with students in Germany, China, and other countries. Internet e-mail is an inexpensive and expedient method for global communication because the cost of sending an e-mail message is usually the same, regardless of where (that is, how far) you are sending it.

When e-mail messages are sent, they do not go directly from the sender's computer to the receiver's computer; instead, they are temporarily stored on a remote computer server. In other words, if Monique in France (who has an account with a university in Paris) sends an e-mail message to Alex in Montana (who has an account with America Online), the message will be stored on a large computer operated by America Online until Alex signs on to read his e-mail. It does not matter where or when Alex signs on to read his e-mail message; at that point, the message will be sent to whatever computer he is using.

E-mail communications benefit education because they are inexpensive and fast, and messages can be sent at any time. Time differences are not important because, regardless of when the message is sent, it will wait for the recipient to check for messages. E-mail is making telephones and fax machines less important, and it is providing financial savings for schools.

Using E-mail

To send e-mail through the Internet, you must have

- an Internet account with an ISP

- an Internet e-mail address

- a software program to access the e-mail system

In most cases, your ISP provides your e-mail address. An Internet address may look like this: barron@typhoon.coedu.usf.edu. In this case, *barron* is the name of the person; *typhoon* is the name of the computer her account is on; *coedu* is the building (College of Education) in which the computer is located; *usf* is the institution (University of South Florida); and *edu*, the domain, indicates the institution is an educational organization.

Internet addresses for other organizations and countries look slightly different. For example, an Internet address for a government entity ends in *gov* and the address for a military entity ends in *mil*. Addresses for accounts in countries other

Table 3.1   Domains and Country Codes

Extension	Domains by Institution	Extension	Domains by Country
.edu	Education	.au	Australia
.com	Commercial Organization	.ca	Canada
.mil	Military	.de	Germany
.gov	Government Sites	.fr	France
.net	Special Network Resources	.uk	United Kingdom
.org	Nonprofit Organizations		

than the United States usually do not indicate the type of institution. Instead a country code is used, for example *uk* for the United Kingdom. Table 3.1 lists common domains and country codes.

The length of addresses may vary. For example, the U.S. president's address (**president@ whitehouse.gov**) and accounts on America Online (**nickname@aol.com**) have only two components after the @.

E-mail addresses, like postal addresses, must be unique. The most efficient way to obtain someone's Internet address is to call the person and ask.

E-mail Systems

Most ISPs supply e-mail software. Although e-mail software varies, most are menu-based and easy to use. For example, Pine, by the University of Washington, is a popular text-based system (see fig. 3.1). This public-domain software program offers spell-checking, sending to multiple recipients, and automatic forwarding of messages. Pine is a server-based system, meaning that all of your messages will remain on your ISP's server after you read them (until you manually delete them).

Some e-mail software uses a graphical interface, meaning that you can point and click to send a message. Examples include Netscape Mail (see fig. 3.2), Internet Explorer Mail, and Eudora. Graphical e-mail systems are generally client-based, meaning that your messages may be

downloaded to your computer when you read them, rather than continually stored on the remote computer.

Creating E-mail Messages

Students can create e-mail messages using e-mail software or word processing software. When students write their message using word processing software, they can cut and paste the message into the e-mail software in order to send it. In most cases, when the message is pasted into the e-mail software, all of the text is converted to ASCII characters (basic text without styles, such as bold or italic). Thus, students can create a message in a word processor that contains bold characters, various sizes, etc. However, when the message is pasted into the e-mail system, it will be converted to basic text (without bold, sizes, etc.). To produce an e-mail message that will be easy to read on the computer screen as well as easy to print, certain guidelines should be followed.

Write clearly and concisely. Encourage the students to send several concise messages rather than one long, rambling message.

Use a descriptive phrase in the subject line. Most e-mail programs display only the sender and subject line of each message in the recipient's in box. Indicating the topic of the message on the subject line allows the user to sort mail, either manually or with the help of a search-and-retrieve feature in the e-mail software.

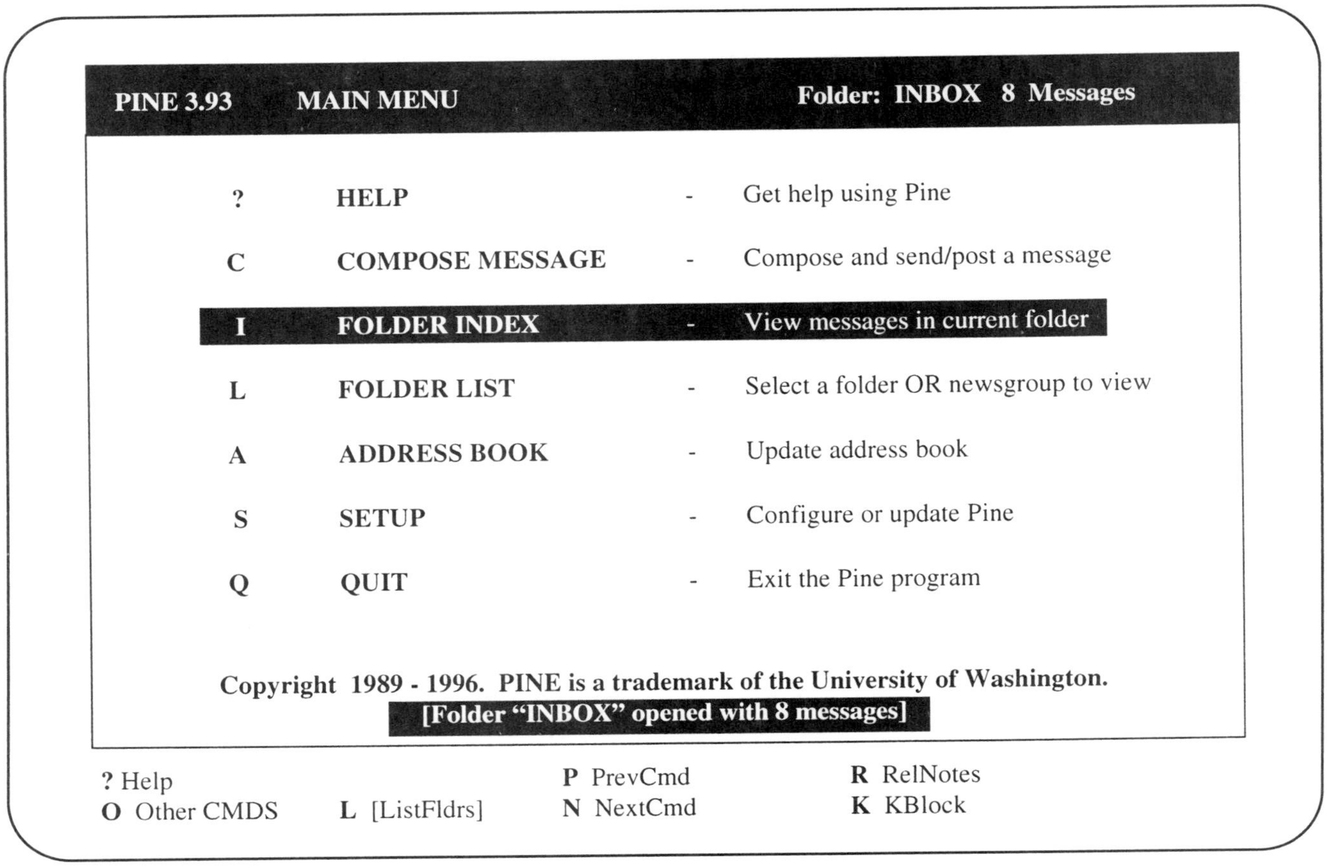

```
PINE 3.93        MAIN MENU                    Folder: INBOX  8 Messages

         ?      HELP               -    Get help using Pine

         C      COMPOSE MESSAGE    -    Compose and send/post a message

         I      FOLDER INDEX       -    View messages in current folder

         L      FOLDER LIST        -    Select a folder OR newsgroup to view

         A      ADDRESS BOOK       -    Update address book

         S      SETUP              -    Configure or update Pine

         Q      QUIT               -    Exit the Pine program


   Copyright 1989 - 1996.  PINE is a trademark of the University of Washington.
              [Folder "INBOX" opened with 8 messages]

? Help                         P PrevCmd        R RelNotes
O Other CMDS    L [ListFldrs]  N NextCmd        K KBlock
```

Figure 3.1 Pine e-mail interface.

DO NOT USE ALL CAPS. This is the equivalent of shouting.

Use a default text style. Remind the students that fancy fonts or text styles may not be legible on all recipients' computers.

Use narrow margins and short lines. Keep the line length under 65 characters to avoid inappropriate line breaks and word wraps when the document is read, printed, or forwarded.

Double space between paragraphs. Tabs and indents are lost in most e-mail programs. Putting an extra space between paragraphs (and capitalizing headings) helps recipients see the structure of the message.

Eliminate tables and columns. The formatting will be lost and the text may be jumbled.

Convert smart quotes to regular inch and foot marks. Smart quotes may be converted to ASCII text characters, such as R or S.

Classroom projects centered on e-mail messages are common. Students can send messages to peers around the world to discuss food, entertainment, sports, and other topics. They can communicate with experts, work with tutors, or interact with others to investigate global issues. Chapters 6–10 provide suggestions for e-mail activities for various subject areas and grade levels.

LISTSERVS

A listserv is a computer program that automatically posts, or sends, e-mail messages to a list of people who subscribe to the service (see fig. 3.3). If you subscribe to a listserv, you receive every message that is posted to the listserv address, and every message you post to the listserv address is sent to all of the other subscribers.

Listserv messages appear as incoming e-mail messages. Because you receive all messages posted

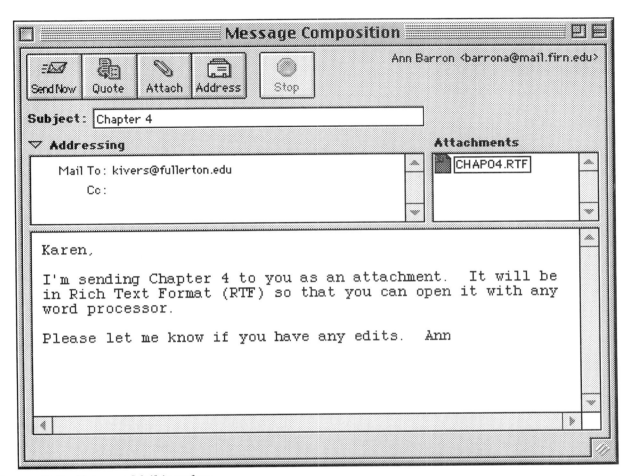

Figure 3.2 Netscape Mail interface.

to the listserv address, you may receive hundreds of messages in a short time. This can create problems if your ISP limits the number of messages it will store for you or if it charges for message space.

To subscribe to (or join) a listserv, you send a simple e-mail message to the listserv administrator. Computers handle most listserv management functions; for this reason, the format of subscribe messages is fairly standard and must be typed correctly. Following is a subscribe message for HILITES, a popular educator's listserv. Note that the subject line is blank.

```
To: majordomo@gsn.org
Subject:
Message Text: subscribe hilites
```

Within a few days, listserv messages will begin to arrive. After you begin to receive messages, you can contact other people on the list and collaborate on projects. To contact other people on the list directly, use the person's private e-mail address, which usually appears somewhere in the message header. Remember, if you send a message to the list, everyone will get a copy!

Listservs have two different e-mail addresses. One address sends messages to the list administrator; this is the address you use to subscribe, unsubscribe, or ask questions of the system administrator. The other address is the operational address; this is the address you use to send messages to other subscribers.

If you decide to discontinue the list, you must unsubscribe. This procedure is very similar

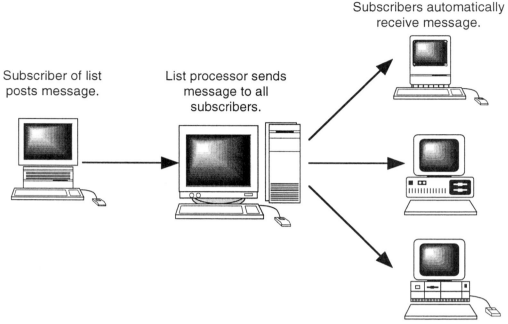

Subscriber of list
posts message.

List processor sends
message to all
subscribers.

Subscribers automatically
receive message.

Figure 3.3 Path of messages posted to listservs.

to subscribing—simply send a message to the administrative address and type **unsubscribe** in the body of the message.

Most listservs send a short introductory message or "user's manual" to new subscribers. Keep this message. It reminds you how to contact the system administrator, how to unsubscribe, and how to send special commands that can help you manage messages. For example, the digest command collects or summarizes all messages for a day, so that you get only one message per day, rather than many; other commands allow you to put your subscription on hold while you are on vacation.

Educational Listservs

Two of the most popular K–12 listservs, HILITES and Kidsphere, provide a convenient way to connect with hundreds of educators who use telecommunications in the classroom.

HILITES is the oldest listserv devoted to classroom projects. It is a moderated list, which means that all of the messages are screened to ensure they meet certain criteria before they are sent to subscribers. To subscribe to HILITES, send a message

to **majordomo@gsn.org**. Leave the subject line blank. In the body of the message, type **subscribe hilites** (see example on page 25).

Kidsphere is a very popular educational listserv. Most of the subscribers are classroom teachers, and it has many international participants. To subscribe to Kidsphere, send an e-mail message to **kidsphere-request@vms.cis.pitt.edu**. Enter the following:

```
To: kidsphere-request@vms.cis.pitt.edu
Subject:
Message Text: subscribe Kidsphere your
name
```

NEWSGROUPS

Newsgroups are similar to listservs in that they consist of e-mail messages. However, newsgroups do not send messages to you. Instead, newsgroups act as a central repository where people can leave messages, ask questions, and respond to inquiries. Messages are posted for anyone to access, like bulletin boards (see fig. 3.4).

Newsgroups are stored on their sponsors' computers. You do not subscribe to newsgroups; you

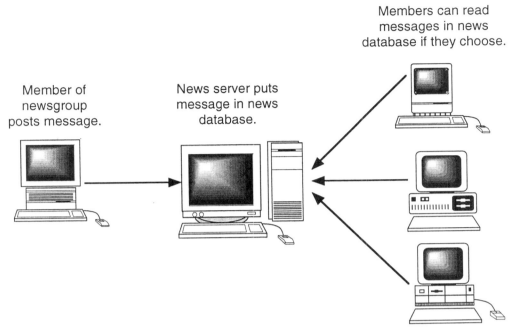

Members can read
messages in news
database if they choose.

Member of
newsgroup
posts message.

News server puts
message in news
database.

Figure 3.4 Path of messages posted to newsgroups.

access them using newsgroup reader software
(which is provided by your ISP or included in
commercial Internet software suites, like Internet
Explorer or Netscape). When you access a newsgroup, you will have options to read, print, reply
to, or post messages. In addition, you can send a
private note to the author of any message by using
the author's return address in the message header.

Access to newsgroups is regulated by your ISP;
it may provide you with restricted access (to some
newsgroups) or full access (to all newsgroups on
the Internet). To find out which newsgroups you
can access, contact your ISP or connect to your
ISP and open your newsgroup reader software.

Newsgroups are organized into categories.
Some of the main areas are:

alt	Special-interest topics
comp	Various topics related to computers
k12	Elementary and secondary education
rec	Recreational activities and hobbies
sci	Related to the sciences
soc	Social issues
talk	Debates and conversations

Many newsgroups focus on developments in
education. You could join the **misc.education.
multimedia** newsgroup to keep up with developments and activities in multimedia, or you could
subscribe to **K12.lang.art** for discussions of language arts curricula. The **k12.chat.junior** newsgroup facilitates conversations among middle
school students.

Participating in newsgroups is an excellent
way to stay current and exchange information.
However, if students use newsgroups for research
and information, be sure to caution them to check
the reliability of the source. Newsgroups are open
to all, and the information must be taken with
healthy skepticism. Also, be aware that many
newsgroups are not moderated and may be
inappropriate for classroom use.

WORLD WIDE WEB (WEB)

In 1991, researchers at CERN (the European
Laboratory for Particle Physics) conceived the idea
for the World Wide Web (Web)—an Internet environment in which documents are linked to other
documents or files by commands embedded in the

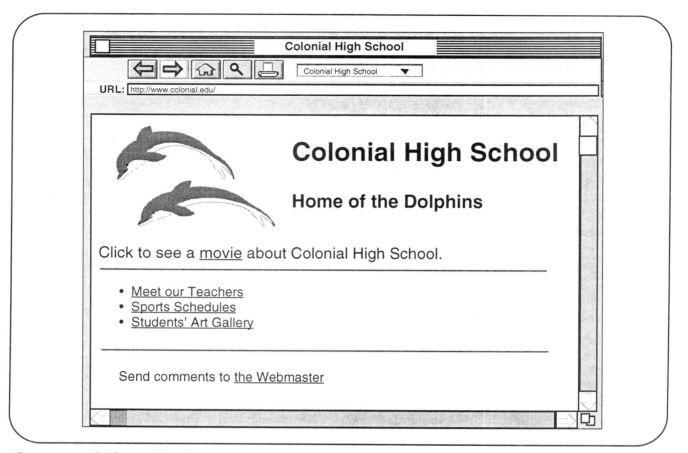

Figure 3.5   Web page for a fictitious high school.

files themselves. A Web document (often referred to as a page) is illustrated in figure 3.5.

The options that are underlined (and usually highlighted in color) are linked to other documents. By clicking on the links, the user is immediately transported to the corresponding page, file, or directory, which may be on a computer in another part of the world. In many cases, graphics also contain invisible buttons (called image maps) that can link you to a new page when they are clicked.

Uniform Resource Locators

Each page or resource on the Web has a unique location. These locations (including the address, path name, and file name) are written as URLs (Universal Resource Locators). Some sample URLs are shown in table 3.2. Note that the address may be a series of numbers rather than

letters and that although many URLs begin with www, some do not.

URLs for Web sites begin with http (HyperText Transfer Protocol) followed by a colon, two slashes, and the address for the Web page or site. (Note that the domains used in URLs are the same as those used for e-mail addresses: org, gov, and so forth.) Following the address, another slash may appear, followed by a path and file name (see fig. 3.6). For example, **http://www.jason.org/expedition.html** will take you to a document titled expedition.html at the Jason site.

Browsers

To view Web documents, you must have a browser. A browser is a software program that displays Web documents and navigates the Internet. Several graphical browsers, such as Netscape

Table 3.2 Sample Universal Resource Locators

Web Site	Uniform Resource Locator
Jason Project	http://www.jason.org/expedition.html
Microsoft	http://www.microsoft.com/
NASA Home Page	http://www.nasa.gov/
Florida Center for Instructional Technology	http://fcit.coedu.usf.edu/
Create Your Own Newspaper	http://crayon.net/
Patch American High School	http://192.253.114.31

Figure 3.6 Anatomy of a URL.

Navigator/Communicator and Internet Explorer, have been developed. These browsers are free to educators and can be downloaded from the Web. Most ISPs supply a browser to get you started. You can keep that browser or use it to download another browser you prefer.

Graphical browsers run on Macintosh, PC, and UNIX computers. Like most graphical interfaces, they provide a point-and-click environment built around a menu bar. These menus allow you to perform various operations: back up to the last Web page you viewed, return to the home page, set a bookmark, type a URL. Most browsers also provide a link to Internet search engines that allow keyword searching of Internet resources.

Plug-Ins for Browsers

Plug-ins are small programs that expand the capabilities of your browser by allowing it to display or play files in various formats. Plug-ins are often needed to view video files, display files created using Adobe Acrobat, and play games.

You can download some plug-ins when you download your browser. For example, when you download Netscape, you can also download a plug-in called LiveAudio that enables the browser to play sound files. Another option is to download plug-ins as the need for them arises. If you connect to a Web page that requires you to have a plug-in, a note will appear on the Web page, along with a link to the appropriate plug-in file. In most cases, you simply click on the link and the plug-in is downloaded to your computer. After they are downloaded and installed, plug-ins are stored in a special folder on your hard drive.

Text-Only Browsers

Graphical interfaces do not work well for users with slow modems or text-only connections. For these users a text-only browser, such as Lynx, provides access to Web documents. With Lynx, you will not see graphics or hear sounds, but you can read the text and link to

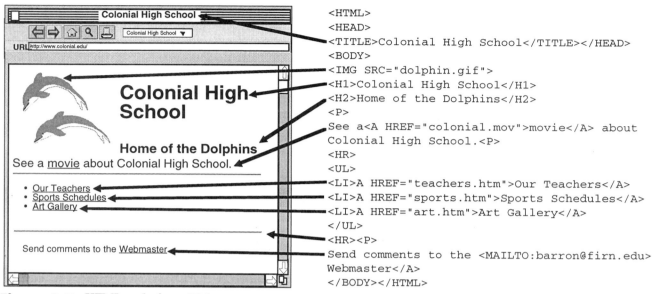

Figure 3.7 HTML code for a Web page.

CREATING DOCUMENTS ON THE WEB

All Web documents are created in a common format called HTML (HyperText Markup Language). HTML consists of simple text documents with embedded commands. The commands are placed within angle brackets. The commands within brackets, called tags, are used to format the Web page. For example, to make a word appear in bold, the tag <B> is placed in front of the word and the tag </B> after the word. <B>This is easy!</B> displays as **This is easy!** The first tag turns the style on, and the second tag turns the style off.

HTML documents can be created with a standard word processor; with HTML editors available as freeware or shareware; or with commercial packages, such as Adobe PageMill. Figure 3.7 shows HTML text and the resulting Web page.

About 50 HTML tags are commonly used in Web documents. HTML codes may appear confusing at first, but students and teachers soon discover that creating an HTML document

other documents and sites. Instead of a mouse, text-based browsers are controlled with the keyboard.

is not much more difficult than writing a paper. Some sample HTML tags and guidelines for Web design appear at the end of the chapter. To learn more about HTML and creating your own Web page, visit one of the many tutorials on the Web, such as A Beginner's Guide to HTML at **http://www.ncsa.uiuc.edu/General/Internet/ WWW/HTMLPrimer.html** or HTML Tutorial at **http://www.coedu.usf.edu/inst_tech/ publications/html/**.

Finding a Web Server for Your School

After you have created a Web page, you must place it on a Web server (a computer with special software that is running 24 hours a day) in order for interested users to access it. Many schools or school districts have a Web server for class and student projects, or a local university or college may provide this service for K–12 schools. Your ISP may provide a limited amount of server space, or you may be able to get space on a community (city or county) server. Remember, the server does not need to be local; if you are building a small Web site, you may be able to find a free server to host it. A list of free servers appears in the Resources section at the end of this chapter.

Thousands of K–12 schools now have their own Web pages. Some provide extensive sites with school newspapers and information about community events and school functions, as well as class projects. For a list of schools on the Web, visit Web66 at **http://web66.coled.umn.edu/**.

The World Wide Web allows students to "read" interactive storybooks, tour museums, control remote robot arms, and take part in instructional lessons. Chapters 6–10 contain information about Web sites useful to K–12 educators.

Multimedia on the Web

It is quite easy to create a link to an audio or video file. The problem is that these files are generally quite large and can take several minutes to download and play. For example, a 1-MB file that plays a 20-second video clip can take more than 10 minutes to download. One solution is to "stream" the files, that is, to play them as they are transferring. A media file that contains a streaming format will begin to play almost immediately and will continue to play as it transfers. In this way, you can listen to radio stations or concerts, or you can hear a live presidential address (with a short delay).

To play streaming files, you need a plug-in that can decipher the format. Several plug-ins designed to work with the most common browsers (Netscape and Internet Explorer) are available for free. For examples of streaming files, visit the RealAudio site at **http://www.realaudio.com** or the VDOlive site at **http://www.vdonet.com/**.

▓FILE TRANSFER PROTOCOL

On the Internet, software and other files can be transferred quickly and inexpensively from one computer to another. A process called file transfer protocol (FTP) was developed many years ago to allow users to examine remote directories and move files and programs to or from a remote computer. With a graphical interface, FTP is very easy. You simply point and click, and the files are transferred to your computer. With a text-based interface, a few basic commands achieve the same result. A list of educational FTP sites appears at the end of this chapter.

Downloading Files

To use your Web browser to download files from public FTP sites, first access the site by typing the site's URL in the Location area of your Web browser. For example, to access the files at the University of South Florida FTP site, you would type **ftp://typhoon.coedu.usf.edu**. When you are connected to that site, you will see a series of files and folders. At that point, you simply click to download the files you want and select a folder on your hard drive for the transfer.

Large files usually are stored in compressed form and must be decompressed before they can be used. Some files decompress automatically; others must be decompressed manually, using decompression software. Shareware decompression software is available for downloading. Visit Shareware.com at **http://www.shareware.com** to locate software.

Uploading Files

Uploading files (sending them to a remote site) generally requires special FTP software, as well as access (via a password) to the remote site. For example, if you have created a file for your Web site and want to transfer it to the district server, you could use Fetch (Macintosh), CuteFTP (Windows), or several other FTP programs to transfer the file.

To use Fetch to upload a file, begin by connecting to the Internet. Then open your FTP software and enter the address for the remote site. Note that to transfer files to another site you will need a password and login for that site. (Some sites allow you to login as **anonymous**.) After you are logged in, you will be able to see the file structure of the remote site (see fig. 3.8). Select the folder on the remote server that you want to transfer the file into, then select the file on your computer that you want to transfer, and click "Put file…"

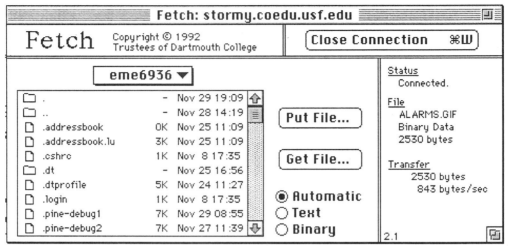

Figure 3.8   Uploading a file using Fetch.

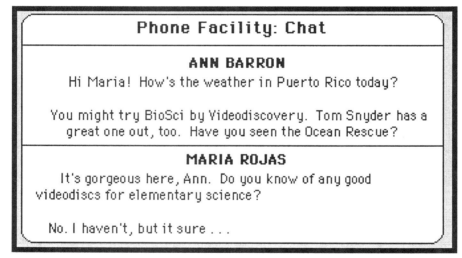

Figure 3.9   Internet chat screen.

CONFERENCING

Most communications on the Internet take place in asynchronous mode, for example, you can send an e-mail message and it "waits" until the recipient reads it at a later time. It is also possible to communicate in synchronous mode, in which all parties are online at the same time and communicate in real time. The basic forms of conferencing on the Internet include Internet chat, audio conferencing, and video conferencing.

Internet Chat

Chatting on the Internet refers to an interactive message exchange among remote computer users who are online simultaneously. All the participants in the chat see what you type as you are typing it, and you see what they type as they are typing it. Figure 3.9 shows the textual exchange between two people (one in Alaska and one in Florida).

Many online services (such as America Online) provide chat rooms for subscribers. Chat is also available on some educational Web sites. For example, Cyberkids offers chat areas that are restricted to students. To participate, access **http://www.cyberkids.com** and fill out the registration form.

There are also chat rooms open to almost everyone who has an e-mail account; these are accessed using IRC (Internet Relay Chat). Caution: Always closely supervise students participating in online chats. Unfortunately, unscrupulous people spend a great deal of time in chat rooms, often impersonating someone else.

Audio Conferencing

If you have a fast connection (at least 28.8 Kbps), it is possible to participate in limited audio conferencing—the Internet equivalent of a telephone call. Using audio conferencing software, a computer, and a microphone, it is possible to make international calls for a fraction of the cost of a long-distance phone call. Both parties must have a relatively fast connection, and both must log onto the Internet at a prearranged time. After they are connected to the Internet, they can "dial" each other by entering the IP (Internet Protocol) number of their computer or their e-mail address. At that point, they can talk to each other, almost as if they were connected by telephone. This technology for audio conferencing is new, but it holds great promise. You can download trial versions of telephony software at **http://WWW.vocaltec.com** or **http://WWW.emagic.com**.

Video Conferencing

The most popular software for video conferencing on the Internet is CU-SeeMe, which was developed at Cornell University. CU-SeeMe makes it possible for you to see and talk to as many as seven people at one time. The software is still in development, the images are small, and the sound sometimes breaks up, but it is free and it works!

Another popular video conferencing program is Net Meeting by Microsoft. This free software includes a chat board (to share written notes), a shared whiteboard (to draw or cut and paste objects and text), and a collaboration feature (to share a computer application that is available on one of the computers).

CU-SeeMe and Net Meeting are generally used to connect two points, as in a one-on-one teleconference. To participate in a video conference, you need a direct Internet connection (usually through a LAN), and your workstation must have a microphone and a video digitizing device. If more than two sites are to be involved in a conference, an additional computer with software called a reflector is needed. The reflector software usually runs on a powerful UNIX workstation that coordinates the streams of data from and to the multiple sites.

CONCLUSION

The primary uses of the Internet include e-mail, newsgroups, listservs, file transfers, and the World Wide Web. These features vary slightly, depending on the software and type of connection you use to access the Internet. Although the Internet may seem overwhelming at first, with practice you will soon be surfing the 'Net like a pro!

Resources

Web Page Development Tools

Adobe PageMill • 800-833-6687
http://www.adobe.com

Claris Home Page • 800-544-8554
http://www.claris.com

Microsoft FrontPage • 800-426-9400
http://www.microsoft.com

Netscape Composer
http://www.netscape.com

Personal Web Page Designer • 800-755-9036
http://www.pacificasoftware.com

Sunburst's Web Workshop • 800-321-7511
http://www.nyhsunburst.com

Webmaster • 800-638-1639
http://www.wentworth.com

Web Page Wizard • 800-999-8911
http://www.web2000.com

WebPublisher • 800-448-6543
http://www.asymetrix.com

Web Workshop • 888-484-8438
http://www.vividus.com

Web Sites That Will Host Web Pages for Schools

Classroom Connect
http://www.classroom.net/classweb/

Schools on the Web
http://www.gsh.org/fetc/design.htm

Vive Web Connections
http://www.vive.com/connect/

Geocities
http://www.geocities.com/

America School Directory
http://www.asd.com

Basic HTML Commands

Essential Parts:
```
<HTML>
<HEAD><TITLE>...</TITLE>
</ HEAD >
<BODY>...</BODY >
</HTML>
```

Formatting Text:
    Headings:
    <H1>...</H1> Most prominent heading
    <H2>...</H2>
    <H3>...</H3>
    <H4>...</H4>
    <H5>...</H5>
    <H6>...</H6> Least prominent heading

    Physical Styles:
    Boldface: <B>...</B>
    Italics: <I>...</I>
    <u>Underline</u>: <U>...</U>

    Format a Paragraph:
    Display preformatted text: <PRE>... </PRE>
    Block quoted text: <BLOCKQUOTE>...</BLOCKQUOTE>
    To separate paragraphs (Same as a carriage return):
    Horizontal ruler: <HR>
    Paragraph: <P>...</P>

Making Lists:

Unordered List:	**Ordered List:**
<UL>	<OL>
<LI>List #1	<LI>List #1
<LI>List #2	<LI>List #2
</UL>	</OL>

Hypertext Links and Anchors:
    Hyperlinks: <A HREF="http://whereto.domain">...</A>
    E-mail links: <A HREF="mailto:name@my.domain">...</A>

Displaying an Image/Movie/Sound:
    Display a picture: <IMG SRC="image.gif" ALT="[Alternate Text]">
    Show a movie: <A HREF="file_name">...</A>
    Play a sound: <A HREF="file_name">...</A>

Web Design Guidelines

The following guidelines can help to make your Web pages more user-friendly for the visitors to your site.

General

Carefully plan your pages before you create them.
Place a descriptive title on the top of all pages.
Include the date of the last revision on the pages.
Limit the length of Web pages to screens.
Test the pages with several different browsers and computers.
Spell-check and grammar-check all pages.

Graphics

Make sure the graphics are relevant to the page.
Limit the file size of the graphics to less than 30K each.
Limit the number of graphics on each page.
Use GIF graphics for line drawings and simple graphics.
Use JPG graphics for photographs.
Limit the width of graphics to less than 470 pixels.

Text

Make sure there is high contrast between background and text.
Limit the length of text lines.
Include blank space between paragraphs.
Limit the use of blinking text.

Media: Audio and Video

Use audio and video only when necessary.
Include information about audio and video file sizes.
Include information about format (wav, avi, quicktime, etc.)

4
Internet Activities for Students: Communication and Research

Brenda was working on her chemistry project about iodine clock reactions. The experiment was complete, but she still had to write the report and have it ready for the morning. It was a good thing the library had direct Internet access for students!

Her first step was to conduct a search on the Web for information about kinetics. She went immediately to InfoSeek (one of her favorite search engines) and typed in *kinetics* for the search word. In a matter of seconds, she had more than 1,500 hits—far too many to look at in the short time she had. She quickly refined the search by entering *+kinetics +iodine +clock*. This time the result was only eight hits—a perfect number for a student with a deadline!

Brenda looked through the list of hits and found a couple she could use. The first one was a link to the *Journal of Chemical Education*. The abstract about iodine clock reaction would be a nice reference. Another link led to a high school

lesson plan that focused on an experiment similar to hers. She also found an article written by two high school teachers about iodine clock reactions.

To augment the written report, she needed to construct diagrams of the reaction. Her teacher had mentioned students could download the chemical drawing program ISIS/Draw they had used in class. Finding the program was easy; Brenda merely typed in the search string *+ chemistry +ISIS +draw* to obtain a list of sites that mentioned the software. She clicked on one called Steven's List of Chemistry Software on the WWW. There she found a link to the MDL Information Systems, Inc., Web page, from which she could download ISIS/Draw.

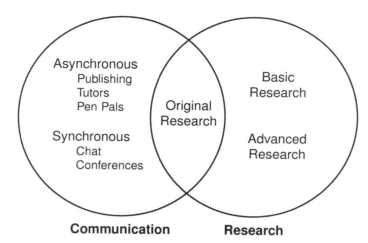

Figure 4.1 Communication and research activities.

Brenda found the download link for her computer type, clicked on Download, and waited for the program to transfer to her computer. Within 20 minutes, she had downloaded the drawing program, extracted it from its compressed form, and checked it for computer viruses. Adding the molecules representing the chemical reactions to her report was a snap!

Finally, though it was getting late, she took the time to save her report as a Web document. That way, she could e-mail it to her teacher in case he wanted to check out the Web sites in her reference list. Thank goodness for the Internet!

The educational applications of the Internet can be divided into two very broad areas: communication and research. The communication category includes asynchronous communications that involve a time lag between messages (such as e-mail and electronic publishing) and synchronous communications that take place in real time (such as chat rooms, audio conferencing, and video conferencing). The research category includes basic, advanced, and original research. Original research contains aspects of both communication and research (see fig. 4.1). Some activities involve simple exchanges or transfer of information; others involve high-level problem-solving and synthesis. This chapter investigates both communication and research. Specific activities and lesson plans are given in chapters 6–10.

ASYNCHRONOUS COMMUNICATIONS

Asynchronous communications are often described as time shifted, meaning a student may send a message and receive an answer two minutes or two days later. Compared to the postal system, the time delays can be short. The speed at which an answer arrives depends on when the receiver responds; it does not depend on mail carriers. In addition, the cost is minimal; in many cases, there is little or no charge to educators for sending messages, whether they go across the street or around the world.

Many Internet communication projects in schools are accomplished using e-mail or Web documents. Common projects involve electronic pen pals, peer-to–peer tutors or mentors, appearances and personifications, collaborative stories, student galleries, and publishing Web pages.

Electronic Pen Pals

Perhaps the most common and least perplexing form of telecommunications projects is electronic pen pals (also referred to as key pals). Like traditional pen pals, electronic pen pals exchange personal thoughts, stories, ideas, questions, and experiences. Each person has an individual mailing address.

Electronic pen pals offer students the opportunity to express themselves and learn from others in a risk-free environment, within and beyond their communities. This form of electronic messaging enables students to overcome stereotypes, practice written communication skills, become aware of other cultures, and make new friends. Pen pal exchanges also provide a forum for practicing a different language.

Electronic pen pals may be arranged with peers in another school, state, or country. This allows students to compare and contrast their cultures and social environments. Cross-age pen pals may be arranged, with older students paired with younger students, or with senior citizens or other adults sharing their lives and experiences with students.

In some cases, pen pals can provide eyewitness reports that are unavailable from other sources. For example, during the Gulf War, students in Washington state communicated with children in Israel daily. Through e-mail messages, the U.S. students received firsthand accounts from the Israeli children about how it felt to go to school with gas masks (Golub 1994).

Although penpal activities can be informal and individual, it is often more efficient to engage in these activities as a class or small group (Harris 1995). If telephone lines are limited or you pay a fee for connect time, it may be necessary to write some of the messages off-line (while not connected to the Internet). In other words, one or two students may be responsible for checking the e-mail account for new messages each day and printing or capturing the incoming messages. The class or small groups can then write responses to the messages using a word processing program. Finally, students can quickly send their responses to their key pals.

Structure helps to make an ongoing e-mail exchange successful. It may be fine to converse about hobbies, but it is best to have a time line for interactions that meet a curricular objective. (Chapter 5 offers guidelines for setting up telecommunications projects.)

Electronic Tutoring and Mentoring

Using e-mail for tutoring and mentoring links students with other students or adults who provide one-on-one assistance and guidance on a routine basis. This approach is especially beneficial with home-based students for whom face-to-face meetings may not be possible. E-mail allows students and mentors to exchange messages at their convenience or on a schedule.

In some cases, online tutoring takes place solely through messages—students send messages and receive answers at a later date or time. In other cases, a chat or conferencing system may be used for real-time communication. Mentoring also may take place on an as-needed basis. Many sites on the Web encourage students to submit questions to experts in various fields (see table 4.1), including astronomy, biology, chemistry, computer science, engineering, mathematics, and physics. In most cases, the answers are supplied in less than two days, and they are free!

Appearances and Impersonations

Electronic networks can bring students into direct contact with notable people. For example, famous authors may participate in chat rooms at prearranged times, or scientists may participate in Internet-based video conferences. America Online offers forums in which individuals can address electronic messages to contemporary authors.

In some cases, someone answering e-mail may impersonate a famous author, character, or person. For example, Virginia's educational network (VAPEN) sponsored a forum entitled the Electronic Village. In this village, students could send messages to Willy Wonka and other fictional characters. Teachers or graduate students answered the questions from Willy's perspective (Bull et al. 1989). Other examples of impersonations include the portrayal of folklore characters, such as the Easter Bunny, and historical characters, such as George Washington.

Collaborative Stories

Collaborative or round robin stories are an example of informal publishing on the Internet. In this approach, a participating class may start a story with a few paragraphs. The story starter is then sent to another class. Students in the second class add a new paragraph to the story. Then the

Table 4.1 Online Experts

Site	URL
AskAsia	http://www.askasia.org
Ask a Scientist	http://ippex.pppl.gov/ippex/pages/Ask_an_expert.html
Ask an Expert Sources	http://www.etc.bc.ca/tdebhome/int_expert.html
Ask Dr. Math	http://forum.swarthmore.edu/dr.math/dr-math.html
AskERIC	http://ericir.syr.edu
Mad Scientist Network	http://medschool.wustl.edu/~ysp/MSN
ProfNet	http://time.vyne.com/profnet/ped/ed.acgi
Pitsco's Ask-an-Expert	http://www.askanexpert.com/p/ask.html

story goes to a third class, which adds to the story variation. This cycle continues until the story reaches the last class in the round.

In like manner, students may collaborate as a class or in small groups to write poems, music, or other material. When the composition is complete, it may be posted on a Web page, distributed to each participating class, or submitted for formal publication.

Student Galleries

The Web offers a wonderful forum for students to share their stories, art, and other productions with the rest of the world. Several Web sites welcome student submissions. Table 4.2 provides a list of Web sites that encourage others to submit their products. (Submission requirements and procedures are listed on each site.)

Publishing Web Pages

Many schools have created Web pages to publish information. For example, Patch American High School, in Germany, produced a Web page devoted to D-Day (see fig. 4.2). Students at Patch accumulated graphics, text, video, and sounds about D-Day and made them available at this site (**http://192.253.114.31/D-Day/**). In the first six months, more than 70,000 people visited the site.

Creating Web documents is not difficult (see chapter 3). To view K–12 schools that currently have Web pages, visit the Web66 Schools Registry at **http://web66.coled.umn.edu/Schools.html**.

Although it is impossible to determine the exact number of student-produced Web pages on the Internet, more than 10,000 schools are registered at the Web66 site. The Web pages provide a wide variety of features, including background information, community news, class projects, current events, and online school newspapers (Barron and Ivers 1997).

SYNCHRONOUS COMMUNICATIONS

Synchronous communications take place in real time, with all participants online at the same time. In many ways, synchronous communications are similar to telephone conversations, but they cost less. A 30-minute call to Europe would be far beyond the budget of most schools, but having a text-based chat with a partner in Europe does not cost any more than sending an e-mail message.

The type of synchronous communications used—text chats or audio or video conferencing—depends on the connection speed, software, and hardware available at the participating sites (see chapter 3). Some common synchronous projects

Table 4.2 Web Sites That Publish Student Projects

Site	URL	Focus
CyberKids	http://www.cyberkids.com	Art, stories
CyberTeens	http://www.cyberteens.com	Art, stories
The Diary Project	http://www.diaryproject.com	Student diaries
Global Show-n-Tell Museum	http://www.telenaut.com/gst	Art
KidNews	http://www.vsa.cape.com/~powens/Kidnews.html	Stories
KidPub	http://www.kidpub.org/kidpub	Stories
Kids' Space	http://www.kids-space.org	Art, stories, music
Kids' Space Connection	http://www.KS-connection.com	Student Web pages
Kids' Web	http://www.lws.com/kidsweb/links.htm	Art
Young Composers	http://www.youngcomposers.com/	MIDI music
IPL Youth Division Writing Contests	http://www.ipl.org/youth/PutMyStory/	Writing contests

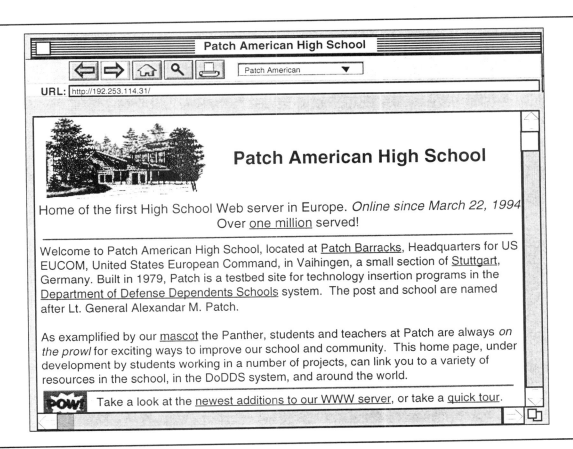

Figure 4.2 D-Day information from Patch American High School.

include idea exchanges, foreign language practice, and interactive mentoring or instruction.

Idea Exchanges

Many synchronous communications focus on informal exchanges of ideas. In these forums, students are encouraged to interact with their peers, discuss topics of interest, and express their feelings. Two live chat rooms for students are CyberKids (**http://www.cyberkids.com**) and CyberTeens (**http://www.cyberteens.com**). Many commercial Internet service providers also offer chat rooms for members. Most of these areas are not moderated. Caution students against chatting with unknown people as you would caution them against talking with strangers.

Foreign Language Practice

The Internet has opened up a whole new realm of possibility for students to practice a foreign language. In the asynchronous mode, they can read foreign newspapers or visit Web sites developed in another language. Even more powerful is direct interaction with students who speak another language. With the proper hardware and software, it is not difficult to arrange an audio or video conference with native speakers in the United States or abroad. Students can talk and possibly see each other as they practice their language skills.

Interactive Mentoring or Instruction

Imagine having a mentor or instructor from another country or location make a live appearance in your classroom. This, and other interactive exchanges, are useful applications of synchronous communications. For example, a mentor might establish virtual office hours during which he or she is online and available for a chat session or conference. Likewise, a guest speaker could make an appearance to a class and engage in questions and answers with the students. For example, the Florida Commission of Education participated in a 20-minute interactive chat session with students in a classroom hundreds of miles away. The students were able to type questions and view immediate answers.

RESEARCH

Conducting research on the Internet is similar to conducting research in a huge, well-stocked library. Students may know exactly which book they want and where it is located, or they may conduct an intense search to locate the best resources. Also, the outcome of the research may vary. Students may accomplish their instructional objective simply by locating the correct book, or they may be required to locate several sources and produce a product or solve a problem that demonstrates they can analyze and synthesize the information they found.

Things to Consider Before Going Online

It is easy to collect information on the Internet, but it is also easy to get sidetracked by irrelevant data. "Online is the best thing to come down the line in years in the educational field, because it teaches kids to think. For the first time, they have to ask themselves what it is they're really looking for" (Basch 1993, 184).

Alternative media. Before conducting research on the Internet, students should determine whether the Internet is the best tool for the research (Thome 1996). In many cases, especially for young children, a CD-ROM may be a better alternative. CD-ROMs designed for elementary students often provide a better interface, and they contain content that is tailored to young learners. Likewise, if an investigation requires reviewing lots of video, a videodisc or videotape may be the most appropriate source. Finally, one characteristic of Internet information is its currency; if you are studying the 1920 elections, other sources may be better.

Evaluating sources. "The Internet is far from perfect. Largely unedited, its content is often tasteless, foolish, uninteresting, or just plain wrong" (Elmer-DeWitt 1995, 10). Students often believe if they see something in print or on the computer, it must be true. Instead of blindly accepting and reporting information, students must learn to investigate its source and validate the information.

Table 4.3 Factors Related to the Validity of Internet Information Sources

	Newsgroups	Listservs	Databases	Electronic Journals		FTP Sites
Source	Individuals	Individuals	Organizations	Publishers		Individuals
Edited?	No	No	Usually	Usually		No
Refereed?	No	No	Sometimes	Usually		No
Available in print?	No	No	Sometimes	Usually		No

The issues of accuracy, authority, objectivity, currency, and coverage are used to ascertain the quality of print sources. These criteria can be applied to Internet sources. An evaluation checklist with questions related to the five issues appears at the end of this chapter.

In some cases, the type of source offers clues about the validity of the information. For example, most newsgroups are unmoderated and messages may reflect opinions rather than facts. Table 4.3 matches data sources on the Internet with important questions to consider in evaluating their validity. If the information is not edited, refereed, and available in print, students should be encouraged to validate the data by checking with experts or cross-checking the information with other valid sources. Inaccurate, incomplete, or questionable data should be rejected. A worksheet that provides guidelines for students investigating Web sites appears at the end of this chapter.

A Web site's domain (gov, com, edu) may also offer some clues as to the validity and reliability of the information. Sites in the government (gov) domain are maintained by the federal government, and the information is likely to be validated. Because lack of funding may preclude subsequent research to update the information presented, however, information is typically less dynamic. Internet addresses for sites in the government domain are usually quite stable.

Sites in the commercial (com) domain may be associated with marketing organizations. They usually contain more technical, leading-edge

information and are maintained by trained Web masters. The information content in this domain may be biased with an emphasis on commercial interests.

Sites in the educational domain (edu) vary greatly in the quality and appearance of information presented. Most of these sites have very few resources to devote to creating and maintaining Web sites. In addition, they may not be electronically sophisticated, and most of their faculty and staff may lack the technical expertise necessary to establish a sophisticated Web presence. Information (research papers, home pages, and so forth) is commonly moved without leaving a forwarding address, and dead-end links are common.

Additional Web evaluation materials are available at the following sites:

http://www.library.cornell.edu/okuref/ research/skill26.htm

http://www.albany.edu/library/internet/ evaluate.html

http://www.capecod.net/shrockguide/eval.htm

The Internet Research Cycle

An adaptation of the six-step research cycle to information problem–solving (Eisenberg and Berkowitz 1990) is appropriate for Internet searches. As indicated in figure 4.3, the steps in the cycle may be repeated as necessary. The steps are

Questioning. Before students go online, they should structure their research questions and determine their topics of interest. This helps students

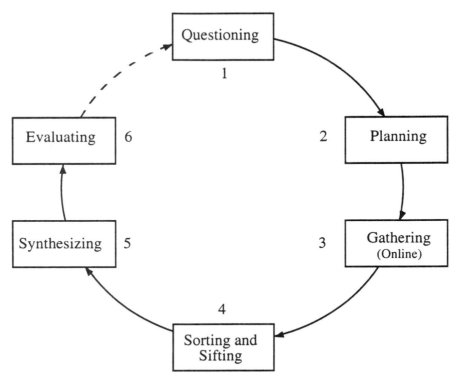

Figure 4.3 Internet research cycle.

develop a clear picture of the types of information they are seeking. Students should be encouraged to write detailed questions, identify related topics, and outline primary areas of interest.

Planning. Using their research questions, students develop a list of sites to investigate. With careful planning, students can make the most of their time online. To help students, a planning guide appears at the end of this chapter.

Gathering. Students go online to retrieve the information they need. Skill in downloading and capturing files is beneficial during this stage. Students should be cautioned to quickly assess the relevance of information before downloading it to avoid acquiring mountains of unimportant data.

Sorting and sifting. After students have logged off, the analysis phase begins as students cull the data. Depending on the amount of information that was collected, this stage can take a substantial amount of time as the information is categorized and accepted or rejected.

Synthesizing. Students integrate the information that addresses the research questions and draw conclusions.

Evaluating. Finally, students seek to determine whether the research question has been adequately addressed or whether additional research is necessary. In many cases the cycle starts over, with a revised research question and additional sites to search (McKenzie 1995). An Internet research rubric, used to assess students' skills in the research cycle, appears at the end of this chapter.

Information Skills

Information literacy empowers students to be independent learners, recognize relevant information, use technology when appropriate, and communicate using multiple media. Information literacy skills are useful in adult life and pertinent to all careers.

The American Association of School Librarians (AASL) and the Association of Educational Communication and Technology (AECT) are working together to develop guidelines that pertain to information literacy for school library media programs. The guidelines address the following abilities:

- Access information efficiently and effectively

- Evaluate information critically and competently

- Use information effectively and creatively

- Pursue information related to personal interests

- Appreciate and enjoy literature and other creative expressions of information

- Strive for excellence in information seeking and knowledge generation

- Recognize the importance of information to a democratic society

- Practice ethical behavior in regard to information and information technology

- Participate effectively in groups to pursue and generate information (AASL/AECT Vision Committee 1997)

The Colorado Educational Media Association (1994) developed Model Information Literacy guidelines for students. The guidelines require students to:

- Construct meaning from information

- Create a quality product

- Learn independently

- Participate effectively as group members

- Use information and information technologies responsibly and ethically

Integrating the Internet into educational curricula can enhance students' information skills. Students develop information-seeking strategies, locate information, analyze information relative to need, communicate with a wide audience, work independently or as part of a group, and use the information effectively and appropriately.

Chapters 6–10 address specific information skills to illustrate those that can be learned using the Internet.

Research Levels

Students may conduct basic, advanced, or original research on the Internet. Although these levels may overlap, they serve as useful distinctions based on the number of sites visited, the sources used, and the complexity of research questions.

Basic Research

Basic research involves finding, comparing, and reporting facts from one or more preselected sources. In most cases, students' initial uses of the Internet involve basic research. They may participate in an Internet hunt designed by their teacher to practice browsing the Web, or they may use a preselected source, such as the online *CIA World Factbook*, to write a research report.

Basic research skills are important prerequisites to more advanced research. Time invested in the teaching and practice of these skills pays off later, especially for young and inexperienced researchers. Several worksheets for basic research activities appear at the end of chapters 6–10. These worksheets can be incorporated as class activities or used for individual practice.

Advanced Research

Advanced research differs from basic research in that it includes a wider variety of sources (such as several Internet sites in addition to print or CD-ROM sources). Another difference is that the sources are not preselected; the students must select the source or sources to investigate.

To conduct advanced research activities, students must first determine the best sources of information and then select a strategy for conducting the research. At this level of research, students should be familiar with search techniques (see pages 47–49).

In addition to locating the correct information, students should be encouraged to analyze the results of their searches, compare facts, and report them appropriately. Students should begin to question and compare data, rejecting poor, incomplete, inaccurate, and inconsequential facts. Analysis and extension are very important for Internet research. Students must realize that some of the information available on the Internet is not accurate. They should learn to be especially suspicious of information gathered from newsgroups, listservs, and personal Web pages unless they can verify the validity of the sources.

Internet research projects can result in concrete benefits. Pease Middle School in San Antonio, Texas, participated in air-quality studies conducted by Global Lab. As a result of the studies, the school's ventilation system was improved and the parents and administrators gained new respect for students' input (Berenfeld 1993).

Original Research

The Internet is an excellent place to conduct original research using surveys and collaborative experiments. Students may use e-mail to conduct surveys collecting and comparing the prices of food (or other items) in various locations around the world. After the information is compiled, it can be graphed, analyzed, and reported.

Collaborative experiments can also be conducted. Students in various locations may plant the same kind of seed on the same day and follow the same directions for care of the plants. As the plants grow, students measure the plants and send data to other participants. The data are used for graphing, analysis, and drawing conclusions.

When conducting collaborative experiments, it is important to ensure that all factors influencing measurements are controlled. For example, some locations have better access than others to scientific instruments and computers. If you plan to compare water samples, it might be best to send the same testing kit to all locations. Involving local experts and insisting on the use of common instruments will also minimize variables. Because various countries use different systems of measurement (English system and metric system, for example), all measurements must be converted to a common gauge.

Another type of original research may pit students against data sources on the Internet and in print. Students may gather original data and then compare them to what others have found and reported. Such projects may lead to students' questioning and correcting data sources, even when these sources are considered highly authoritative.

Citations for Internet Research

Conducting research on the Internet raises the question of the appropriate way to cite electronic sources.

The basic information that students should record for each citation includes:

- Title of work

- Subtitle of work

- Author's name

- Original publication date (as shown)

- Date of Internet access

- Protocol (http, telnet, FTP, etc.)

- URL with complete path. Remind students that some URLs are case sensitive; therefore, the punctuation and capitalization should be recorded exactly as it appears on the Web page.

- Author's Last Name, Author's First Name. "Title of work: Subtitle." (Original date of publication or latest version). Protocol and URL, (Date of message or visit).

Examples:

Walker, Janice. R. "Columbia Online Style: MLA-Styles Citations of Electronic Sources." Nov. 1997. http://www.cas.usf.edu/english/walker/mla.html (28 Nov. 1997).

Barron, Ann E. "Advantages of Web-Based Training." barrona@mail.firn.edu (18 Nov. 1997).

Two of the most common citation formats are MLA (Modern Language Association of America) and APA (American Psychological Association). The preceding examples are presented in MLA format. Information about citations that conform to these formats can be found at:

http://www.cas.usf.edu/english/walker/mla.html

http://www.cas.usf.edu/english/walker/apa.html

http://owl.trc.purdue.edu/files/110.html

http://www.baker.edu/library/mla.html

http://www.pitsco.inter.net/p/cite.html

http://clever.net/quinion/words/citation.htm

Because Web materials may disappear or change at any moment, students should take special precautions to preserve their sources. To start, students should print any page they cite; that way, they can refer to the printed copy if the online version disappears. For future reference, students should set the preferences in the Web browser so the URL appears on each page as it prints.

SEARCHING THE WEB

There are more than 50 million pages of text on the Internet, making it extremely difficult to locate specific information. It is not uncommon for a student to type in a search word or phrase and obtain 265,000 or more hits. To reduce the frustration and increase the success rate, it is important to teach a few techniques for searching the Web.

The tools that are used to search the Web consist primarily of subject directories and search engines. Both of these methods appear to work the same way—you access a search site on the Web and type in a word or phrase. Within seconds a list of related sites appears.

Subject Directories

Subject directories are catalogs that organize topics by categories for people who want to browse a list (see fig. 4.4). Yahoo and Magellan are the most popular subject directories. With Yahoo, you can type in a search word or find the information you want by clicking on various

If a search produces too many hits...

Use more specific search words (enter *Thunderbird* rather than *car*).

Use multiple search words.

Capitalize proper nouns (such as names).

Look for a "Search These Results" option that narrows the first search.

Use one of the search directories, like Yahoo, that manually reviews the sites before they are listed.

If the search produces too few hits...

Check your spelling.

Read the "search tips" related to the search tool you are using.

Use synonyms and variations of the words.

Try a search engine, like Excite or AltaVista, that conducts full-text searches.

topics and subtopics. All of the sites listed on Yahoo must be submitted and are reviewed by people before they are added to the directory.

Search Engines

Search engines use software programs to index thousands of Web sites, and the indexes are updated almost continuously. When you enter a keyword into a search engine, you receive a list with the number of hits, or links to related sites. The number of hits may vary among search engines because some of the engines create their indexes based on the titles of Web sites, and others are based on the full text of the Web sites. Also, some of the engines index more than

Figure 4.4   Subject directories in Yahoo.

Table 4.4   Addresses for Search Programs

Site	URL
AltaVista	http://www.digital.altavista.com
Excite	http://www.excite.com
HotBot	http://www.hotbot.com
Infoseek	http://www.infoseek.com
Lycos	http://www.lycos.com
Magellan	http://www.magellan.com
WebCrawler	http://www.webcrawler.com
Yahoo	http://www.yahoo.com

30 million documents (such as AltaVista) and some index fewer than 1 million (such as WebCrawler).

To access a search engine, you can click on the Search button on the menu bar of the Web browser, or you can type in a URL. After the search program is displayed, simply type in the keyword or words.

Many search engines and search directories are available on the Web. Most of these can be used free of charge. See table 4.4 for the addresses of some of the popular search tools.

Search Techniques

As previously stated, search tools index thousands of Web sites, and many searches result in thousands of hits. Several techniques can be used to help narrow searches and limit the number of hits. Common commands include the following:

"..." Using quotation marks indicates specific phrases involving more than one word.

"physical fitness" will locate only articles with the words next to each other.

+ Adding a + sign before a word means that it *must* be at each site listed.

+chemistry +experiments will find articles that include both words.

– Adding a hyphen before a word means that it will *not* appear on sites listed.

+probability -gambling will find articles that include the word *probability* but do not include the word *gambling* in the title.

* Asterisks can be used for wild cards in some search engines.

Mexic* will find articles with Mexico, Mexican, etc.

The best way to learn to search the Web is to practice; a search practice worksheet appears at the end of this chapter.

Search Engines for Children

A few search engines are designed for children (see table 4.5). These engines either provide a list of child-safe sites or search a database that has preselected sites for students. Using one of these engines will help to keep students from wandering into adult materials.

Metasearch Engines

If you get tired of using one search engine after another to find your topic, you will be glad to know about metasearch engines. A metasearch engine submits your request to several Web engines or directories at the same time. The results are then put in a single list, often with a relevance score based on the number of times your word or phrase appears in the Web document. Several metasearch tools are listed in table 4.6.

CONCLUSION

Communication activities offer an inexpensive means for students to collaborate on projects, mentor (or be mentored), publish their compositions, and interact with students and experts throughout the world. Research activities challenge students to become aware of other cultures; collect, compare, and analyze information sources; and question the validity of the data. Important skills for students now include the ability to use the Internet to access, analyze, filter, and organize multidimensional information sources.

REFERENCES

AASL/AECT Vision Committee. 1997. Information standards for student learning. **http://www.ala.org/aasl/stndsdrft5.html** (November 28, 1997).

Barron A. E., and K. S. Ivers. June 1997. *Web Pages and K–12 Education: A study of the patterns of use.* Proceedings of the National Educational Computing Conference, Seattle, Washington.

Basch, R. 1993. *Secrets of the super searchers.* Wilton, CT: Eight Bit Books.

Berenfeld, B. 1993. A moment of glory in San Antonio. *Hands On!* 16(3).

Table 4.5 Search Tools for Students

Search Tool	URL	Description
AOL NetFind for Kids	http://www.aol.com/netfind/kids	Based on kid sites from Excite
Magellan	http://www.magellan.com	Green light indicates safe site
Lycos Kids Guide	http://www.lycos.com/kids	Features a Just for Kids site
Xplore Kids	http://www.xplore.com/xplore500/medium/kids.html	Rotating list of 500 sites
Yahooligans	http://www.yahooligans.com	Eight categories for kids

Table 4.6 Metasearch Tools

Search Tool	URL	Description
All-In-One	http://www.albany.net/allinone	200 search tools
cinet	http://www.search.com	250 Web searchers
Inference Find	http://m5.inference.com/ifind/	Searches and categorizes
Internet Sleuth	http://www.isleuth.com/	Thousands of databases
Metacrawler	http://metacrawler.cs.washington.edu:8080	Searches 9 services
Savvy Search	http://guaraldi.cs.colostate.edu:2000	23 databases
UseIt!	http://www.he.net/~kamus/useen.htm	Business, news, computer databases, etc.

Bull, G., J. Harris, J. Lloyd, and J. Short. 1989. The electronic academical village. *Journal of Teacher Education* 40(4):27–31.

Colorado Educational Media Association. 1994. *Model information literacy guidelines*. Denver: State Library and Adult Education Office.

Eisenberg, M., and R. Berkowitz. 1990. *Information problem-solving: The big six skills approach to library and information skills instruction*. Norwood, NJ: Ablex Publishing.

Elmer-DeWitt, P. 1995. Welcome to cyberspace. *Time* 145(12):4–11.

Golub, J. N. 1994. *Activities for an interactive classroom*. Urbana, IL: National Council of Teachers of English.

Harris, J. 1994. *Way of the ferret: Finding educational resources on the Internet*. Eugene, OR: International Society for Technology in Education.

McKenzie, J. 1995. Direct connect: Beforenet and afternet. *MultiMedia Schools* 2(3):6–8.

Thome, R. 1996. The fourth R is research. *Electronic Learning* 16(2):58.

Analyzing Web Resources

Answer the following questions to evaluate Web resources.

Accuracy

Are sources listed for the facts?	Yes	No
Can information be verified through another source?	Yes	No
Has the site been edited for grammar, spelling, etc.?	Yes	No

Authority

Is the publisher reputable?	Yes	No
Is the sponsorship clear?	Yes	No
Is there a phone number or postal address?	Yes	No
Is there a link to the sponsoring organization?	Yes	No
Is the author qualified to write on this topic?	Yes	No

Objectivity

Does the sponsor have commercial interests?	Yes	No
Is advertising included on the page?	Yes	No
Are there obvious biases?	Yes	No

Currency

Is there a publication date listed?	Yes	No
Is there a date listed for the last update?	Yes	No
Is it a topic that does not change frequently?	Yes	No

Coverage

Are the topics covered in depth?	Yes	No
Does the content appear to be complete?	Yes	No

Fact or Fiction

Because anyone can create a Web page, it is important to try to determine if the information that is presented is true or not. Fill out this form for Web sites that you are including in your project.

Web Site 1

Title of Site _____

Address (URL) _____

Author _____

Date last modified _____

Clues that help to determine if the information is Fact or Fiction

_____

Web Site 2

Title of Site _____

Address (URL) _____

Author _____

Date last modified _____

Clues that help to determine if the information is Fact or Fiction

_____

Web Site 3

Title of Site _____

Address (URL) _____

Author _____

Date last modified _____

Clues that help to determine if the information is Fact or Fiction

_____

Web Planning Worksheet

Developing a research question and planning a strategy are key elements to successful Internet research. Use this Web Planning Worksheet to help define your research.

Research Question

Write a short, concise research question.

_____

_____

Related Topics

List at least four topics that may be related.

1. _____   2. _____

3. _____   4. _____

Other Sources of Information

Place a checkmark in front of other sources of information that may be helpful for this research.

☐ CD-ROM   ☐ Videodisc   ☐ Encyclopedia

☐ Newspaper   ☐ Magazine   ☐ Person

Keywords or Phrases for Searching

List at least four keywords for the search.

1. _____   2. _____

3. _____   4. _____

Potential Web Sites

List at least two potential Web sites.

1. _____   2. _____

Internet Research Rubric

	1 inc.	2 poor	3 fair	4 good	5 excellent
QUESTIONING Formulates clear research question.					
PLANNING Selects relevant Web sites and search terms.					
GATHERING Collects and organizes relevant information.					
SORTING Creates structure with retrieved information; inaccurate information is rejected.					
SYNTHESIZING Reorganizes information and formulates conclusion.					
EVALUATING Translates findings to answer research question. Decides if additional research is necessary.					
Total _____					

Search Practice

Fill in the following charts to practice your search skills on the Web. Type the words in the search box of each search engine. Then record the number of hits and compare the results. As you search, note the different strategies that are used for different combinations of words.

Yahoo	http://www.yahoo.com
Infoseek	http://www.infoseek.com
Excite	http://www.excite.com
Alta Vista	http://www.altavista.digital.com

Combinations of words (both words must appear in the result)

Words	+listening +strategies	+listening +strategies	listening AND strategies
Engine	Yahoo	Infoseek	Excite
Results			

Combinations of words (one word must NOT appear in the result)

Words	+probability -gambling	+probability -gambling	+probability AND NOTgambling
Engine	Yahoo	Infoseek	Excite
Results			

Combinations of words (two words appear adjacent to each other)

Words	"physical fitness"	"physical fitness"	"physical fitness"
Engine	Yahoo	Infoseek	Excite
Results			

Teaching in a Classroom Without Walls: Strategies and Resources

Ms. Martin sat at her desk in the sixth-grade classroom and logged onto her Internet account. She had about 15 minutes before the students would arrive, and she planned to spend the time catching up on her e-mail messages and double-checking the online activities for the day.

She responded quickly to an e-mail message from Alex's mother regarding the assignments he had missed because of his appendectomy. Since Ms. Martin had established the homework Web page last semester, it was easy for parents and teachers to check on assignments. Ms. Martin found it required only a few minutes each day to fill out the form on the Web page listing the day's assignments.

A message from the principal reminded all teachers about the in-service training program on Wednesday. Ms. Martin was glad the district provided ongoing training and support for teachers. Keeping up with the changes in technology required substantial time and energy. The district workshops were worthwhile and welcome because they focused on relevant, hands-on materials for immediate use in classrooms.

Next, Ms. Martin sent an e-mail message to the media center requesting the use of two computers with Internet access and a certain CD-ROM for next Tuesday. It was so nice not to have to fill out paper request forms and walk to the media center! She knew the message would be processed today and, unless there was a conflict, the computers would be rolled into the classroom at the requested time.

Finally, Ms. Martin checked the Web sites she planned to use in class today to make sure the addresses hadn't changed. They were studying the newly independent states of the former Soviet Union. Using the Internet, students could obtain up-to-date information about the countries, investigate the currency exchange rate, and correspond with students in Russia. One of their projects focused on nuclear power, and the newsgroup in

Chernobyl, Ukraine, provided many insights into the aftermath of nuclear explosions.

Ms. Martin logged off the system as the students started to arrive. It would be another exciting day in the classroom. Thank goodness the classroom included the rest of the world!

IMPLEMENTATION TECHNIQUES

The Internet is a virtual gold mine for educators. Never before have we had such inexpensive access to so many valuable resources—most of which are free. In addition to files, databases, and libraries, there are many resources and projects designed for teachers. Several techniques can be used to facilitate implementation of Internet projects. Be aware, however, that "innovation takes time" (Sandholtz, Ringstaff, and Dwyer 1997). Following are some considerations to keep in mind when implementing telecommunications.

Practice first. Before using telecommunications in your classroom, spend some time practicing with the computer and the systems you plan to use. Remember Murphy's Law: Anything that can go wrong, will. The more comfortable you are with the hardware, software, and systems involved, the better prepared you will be to deal with the unexpected. Many resources on the Web are designed for teachers. You can access these resources and use them to become familiar with the Internet before directly involving students.

Focus on the curriculum. Use the Internet as a tool to enhance the curriculum, not as an end in itself. Begin by examining the goals of instruction, looking at all sources of content and selecting the best source to accomplish the lesson's objectives.

Preview Internet resources on all computers that will be used to view them. Shortly before you use a site with students, preview it. First, double-check the path to be sure it has not changed. Then, preview the site on each computer that may be used to view it. This ensures that all of the computers have the hardware and software (including plug-ins) needed to support the site. (Chapter 3 discusses plug-ins.) This preview also allows you to spot possible problems with incompatibility among Web browsers and among various versions

of a particular browser. Some Web pages that display correctly in Netscape 4.0 will not display in Netscape 2.0, and some pages that are fine in Netscape 4.0 will cause the computer to crash if run in Internet Explorer 4.0. Likewise, some complex programs written in Java or JavaScript may not run on a Macintosh.

Make alternate plans. With telecommunications, many variables are difficult or impossible to control. First, if you are using a dial-up connection, the receiving modem may be busy. Or, the system you plan to use may be off-line or refusing connections. Many systems, such as NASA, can accept only a limited number of connections. During school hours that limit is likely to be reached, and you may receive a "too many connections" response. These and other potential barriers require you to have alternate plans if your use of telecommunications is constrained to a particular time period. Alternatives might include using other Internet sites or alternate media, such as a CD-ROM or videodisc.

Provide instruction in basic computer and Internet skills. If students are required or encouraged to use the Internet, they require basic instruction on its use, as well as basic computer skills. Table 5.1 provides a continuum of Internet skills that should be included in the instruction. More advanced levels can be added as mastery of the basic skills is achieved.

Conduct some activities off-line. If students plan to post a message or a story (to key pals, listservs, newsgroups, or a Web page), have them write the story using word processing software before making the online connection. This will minimize online time (which may save money), give students time to carefully assess their writing before sending it, and provide them with more powerful editing tools (like spell-check or cut-and-paste) than e-mail software provides. After students write and edit their work, they can cut and paste it into the e-mail software.

Monitor student work. Some resources on the Internet are unsuitable for children. Several filtering programs can limit access to unsuitable sites. Most of these programs contain a list of blocked

Table 5.1 Levels of Internet Skills

Internet Skill	Level I	Level II	Level III
Browsing the Web	Follow embedded hyperlinks	Enter URLs	Create or set bookmarks
Locating information	Conduct keyword searches using one search tool	Conduct searches using Boolean logic and one search tool	Conduct advanced searches using multiple search tools
Communicating	Create and read e-mail messages	Create distribution lists	Participate in an online conference (chat, audio, or video)
Publishing on the Web	Upload to an external site, such as CyberKids	Create a basic Web page with text and graphics	Create multiple Web pages with hyperlinks

Table 5.2 Filtering Software

Site	URL	Company
Net Nanny	http://netnanny.com	Net Nanny, Ltd.
Net Shepherd	http://www.shepherd.net	Net Shepherd, Inc.
Specs for Kids	http://www.newview.com	PlanetWeb, Inc.
Cyber Patrol	http://www.cyberpatrol.com	Microsystems Software
Cybersitter	http://www.solidoak.com	Solid Oak Software
SurfWatch Software	http://www.surfwatch.com	Spyglass, Inc.
Safe Search	http://www.safesearch.com	InterGO Communications, Inc.

sites; they also allow teachers and administrators to specify additional sites that should not be accessed (Novelli 1996). Some filtering programs are listed in table 5.2.

Many schools require students and parents to sign an acceptable use policy (AUP) before students are allowed to use the Internet. These AUP agreements outline the proper use of the Internet and include penalties for violations.

An AUP is used to make parents aware of the potential risks of students obtaining objectionable material. The policy should emphasize that the use of the Internet "is a privilege and not a right, and outline the penalties and repercussions of violating the AUP" (How to write an acceptable use policy, 1995). Most AUPs also emphasize the need to protect Internet passwords and advise against illegal access to computers.

AUPs generally require several signatures: Students sign to indicate they have read and understand the document; parents sign to verify they are aware that their child could access

Sources for Acceptable Use Policies

Academic Computing Policy Statements	http://www.eff.org/pub/CAF/policies/
K–12 Acceptable Use Policies	http://www.erehwon.com/k12aup/
Legal and Educational Analysis of K–12 Acceptable Use Policies	http://www.erehwon.com/k12aup/legal_analysis.html
Creating Board Policies for Student Use of the Internet	http://fromnowon.org/fnomay95.html
TIES Internet Acceptable Use Policy Links	http://www.ties.k12.mn.us/accept

inappropriate material; and teachers or administrators sign on behalf of the school. Sample AUPs and guidelines for creating them can be found at the sites listed in the box above.

Protect students' identities. Tell students to avoid revealing their addresses, phone numbers, or other identifying information in all messages they send to anyone on the Internet. E-mail messages, whether private or posted to listservs and newsgroups or even relayed in online chat rooms, can be forwarded beyond their initial destinations. Also, it is impossible to know the background and intention of everyone on the Internet. In many cases, students may use a generic classroom name rather than their own name to protect their identities.

Respect the rights of others. Some people believe anything available on the Internet is in the public domain. Although many resources may be free, many of the publications, graphics, sounds, programs, and movies are copyrighted by their creators or sponsors. Always check the copyrights before downloading and distributing materials. Although copyright law does allow the fair use of copyrighted materials in connection with non-commercial, curriculum-based learning activities (if credit is provided), these materials must be used in a secure network (not the Internet). For more information about copyright and fair use, visit the Creative Incentive Coalition Web

site at **http://www.cic.org**. Links are provided to several other sites that focus on copyright (Milone 1997).

CLASSROOM MANAGEMENT: GROUPING STUDENTS

The Internet can add a new dimension to the classroom. However, it also requires careful consideration of classroom management. One of the most important considerations is grouping of students. Students may work individually, in small groups, or as a class. The best grouping to use for any given project depends on the amount of hardware available, the age of the students, and the goals of the instruction.

Individual Projects

Individual projects can be conducted in or out of the classroom. If your school has a computer lab connected to the Internet through a LAN, students can conduct individual research, design their own Web pages, or communicate with other students.

Individual projects allow students to work at their own pace and free them from dependence on others. However, such arrangements require enough hardware for each student to complete the project. In addition, individual work does not reflect real-world learning or promote cooperative problem-solving.

When assigning individual Internet projects, begin by instructing the students about Internet use. Be sure to demonstrate procedures for connecting to the Internet and conducting efficient searches. Also provide clear guidelines, requirements, and deadlines for the project.

With the growing popularity of the Web, many students may have access to the Internet on a home computer. Resist the temptation to assign Internet projects that require home access. If even one student does not have a computer (or access to the Internet), you could create an inequitable situation.

Small Group Projects

Telecommunications projects offer an excellent opportunity to implement cooperative learning groups. "Cooperative learning takes place when students work together to accomplish shared goals" (Ivers and Barron 1998). Cooperative learning groups support positive interdependence, individual accountability, group processing, peer responsibility, and heterogeneous membership (Johnson and Johnson 1991). Students learn from each other and share responsibilities. Whether working with a small group within a single classroom or working with a group comprising students all over the globe, cooperative learning can help to support real-world learning. However, teachers and students must be careful to ensure that everyone in the group contributes to the project.

The size and composition of cooperative groups can vary. The number of students in each group depends on the students' abilities, the number of computers available, time constraints, project requirements, and other variables. In most cases, a group size of three or four is optimal in that it provides sufficient interaction among group members and sufficient accountability for each group member. Table 5.3 lists several techniques that can be used when implementing cooperative learning groups (Slavin 1987, 1990)

Implementing cooperative learning groups in a classroom requires careful planning and continuous monitoring. In a publication from the National Education Association, Lyman (1993) provides 11 steps to help ensure a successful cooperative learning project:

1. Choose your context.
2. Assign heterogeneous groups.
3. Teach group roles.
4. Assign the task.
5. Move into groups.
6. Give directions.
7. Monitor groups.
8. Provide closure.
9. Evaluate the process.
10. Maintain classroom management.
11. Plan for review.

Frequently, when students work on telecommunications projects in small groups, finishing the project takes much longer than anticipated. It may be wise to ask students to monitor their time with a kitchen timer and, where appropriate, to rotate their roles from keyboarder to recorder to planner and so forth (Ivers and Barron 1998).

Whole Class Projects

In some cases, especially with younger students or limited Internet connections, you may conduct whole class projects. In this case, all telecommunications could take place outside of the classroom, or if an Internet connection is available in the classroom, then the computer display could be projected for the entire class to view.

Whole class projects make it easier to maintain a schedule and to control access to Internet sites. However, they require either extensive use of resources outside the classroom or in-class access to the Internet plus hardware to project what is on the computer screen so that all students can see it. The most serious disadvantage of whole class projects is that they provide less hands-on experience for students than individual or small group projects.

Table 5.3 Cooperative Learning Techniques

Cooperative Group Technique	Description
Student Teams Achievement Divisions (STAD)	Students learn something as a team, contribute to the team by improving their own past performance, and earn team rewards based on their improvements. Teams earn points based on each student's improvement from previous quizzes.
Teams Games Tournament	Similar to STAD, except that weekly tournaments replace weekly quizzes.
Team-Assisted Individualization	Students are placed in groups but work at their own pace and level. Team members check each other's work and help one another with problems. Teams earn points based on the individual performance of each member in the group.
Jigsaw	A method of cooperative group learning that assigns each group member a particular learning task. Each member chooses a topic and is responsible for teaching his or her team members "all that there is to know" about that topic. Team members meet with members of other groups to form "expert groups" to discuss and research their topic. Following research and discussion, the students return to their own teams and take turns teaching their teammates about their topic. Afterwards, students take individual quizzes and earn a team score.
Group Investigation	Similar to the Jigsaw method, except that students do not form expert groups. Student teams give class presentations of findings rather than taking tests.
Learning Together	Heterogeneous student groups work on a single assignment and receive rewards based on the group product.

Projects for Classrooms with No Internet Connection

Several whole class projects can be completed with minimal Internet connect time. Teachers who do not have Internet access at school have found innovative ways to make up for the lack by using their own Internet accounts at home or by using an account at a local public library or university. For example, in the Save the Beaches project, students help to clean up a nearby shoreline and report the types of trash collected. This project does not require an Internet connection in the classroom, yet it is a relevant, worthwhile project that is enhanced by Internet communications.

Projects that can be used in classrooms without an Internet connection include those involving asynchronous communications, such as e-mail, in which you can report your findings once a week, rather than daily; projects that focus on noncomputer activities, such as the postcard exchange or GeoGame projects mentioned at the beginning of chapter 1; and ongoing projects that list activities and provide teacher resources on the Web, such as Journey North.

Another option for a classroom without an Internet connection is to download a Web page, save it on a floppy disk, and take the disk to the classroom. The software program Web Wacker (from Blue Squirrel) has become a popular tool for this procedure. Although government sites can be copied without permission, always keep copyright issues in mind when saving a Web page or graphic on disk. For more information, visit the Blue Squirrel site at **http://www.bluesquirrel.com**.

Projects for Classrooms with One Connection

If you have one computer in your classroom or media center, you may conduct whole class projects by projecting what appears on the screen so the whole class can view it together. (This requires special hardware.) Such projects might focus on reviewing the content of Web pages, conducting research, or communicating via audio or video conferences.

When conducting a "one-computer" Internet lesson, it is important to plan ahead and to consider all possible options and distractions. If the projected text is too small for students to read or the graphics do not project well, the lesson will not be effective. To avoid these problems, increase the size of the text to at least 24 points and select sites that have high contrast between the text and the background. Both Netscape and Internet Explorer allow you to change the size of type, and some browsers allow you to override the text colors to increase the contrast.

In addition, follow standard precautions, such as reserving the hardware you will need, double-checking paths just before using them to be sure they are still active, making sure all the necessary hardware and software (such as speakers and audio software) are installed on the machine you will be using, printing pages that contain text or content central to the theme of your lesson, and having backup plans.

FINDING COLLABORATIVE PROJECTS

Where can you find cooperative projects or teachers with whom to collaborate? To locate online educators and projects, check listservs, newsgroups, and Web sites devoted to educational projects.

Listservs

These electronic mailing lists (discussed in detail in chapter 3) provide an excellent means of locating others who are interested in participating in collaborative projects. When you find an interesting person or project, you can send a message directly to the individual who posted the message about the project. (In most cases, the individual's address appears on the message header.) Look for listservs in the content area and age level of interest to you.

Online Conferences and Discussion Groups

Another method of locating teachers for collaborative projects is to review the messages posted to online conferences or discussion groups. Many Web sites feature discussion groups that focus on education.

For example, if you access the Teachers.Net site at **http://www.teachers.net/** you will find a lesson exchange area, a chat area, and a "curriculum maximizer" that allows teachers to search for various curricular ideas. Additional teacher-oriented forums are listed in table 5.4.

Web Sites Devoted to Online Projects

Extensive lists of teachers who are interested in telecommunications projects are available on the Web. These free lists are compiled by organizations to assist teachers in locating projects and other teachers who want to collaborate.

Intercultural E-mail Classroom Connections (IECC)

Intercultural E-mail Classroom Connections provides information and lists to help teachers locate partners in other countries and cultures. This service includes e-mail addresses for classroom pen pals and project exchanges. It can be accessed at **http://www.stolaf.edu/network/iecc/**.

There are various areas of interest on the site. IECC (K–12) is intended for teachers seeking partner classrooms for international and cross-cultural electronic mail exchanges, not individual pen pals. IECC-PROJECTS is an electronic mailing list teachers may use to announce or request help with classroom projects that involve e-mail. IECC-SURVEYS is a forum for students and teachers to post requests for help with projects, surveys, and questionnaires.

Table 5.4 Teacher Resource Sites

Site	URL	Features
Access Excellence	http://www.gene.com/ae	Scientists and resources for biology teachers
Mighty Media Teachers Lounge	http://www.mightymedia.com/	Resources for environmental issues, human rights, arts; forums for teachers and students
Teachers Helping Teachers	http://www.pacificnet.net/~mandel/	Teaching tips, new teaching ideas, Teacher Chat, lesson plans
Teachers.Net	http://www.teachers.net/	Web-page maker, lesson plans, "curriculum maximizer"
Education Webpage	http://www.aleducation.com	Lesson plans, software, chat rooms, job board
Eduzone	http://www.Eduzone.com	Lesson plans, chat rooms, teaching tips
Internet Teachers Network	http://www.well.com/user/teaching	Internet links and training sites
Teacher's Edition Online	http://www.feist.com/~lshiney	Teacher-2-teacher mailing list
Well Connected Educator	http://www.gsh.org/wce	Technology for teaching
A Teacher's Home Page	http://pluto.njcc.com/~harris	Links and resources
Schoolhouse Site	http://www.nwrel.org/school_house	Lesson plans, resources

To submit a request, choose "Submit a request to IECC." You can search the database for existing requests or post your own request. If you choose to search other people's requests for a partner, classroom, or project, you will be prompted to fill out a form that asks about the level of your students, the country or culture with which you would like to participate, the language to be used, time frame, and other details (see fig. 5.1).

If you are posting a request for partners to join in a project you are planning, you will be prompted to fill out a form with your name, e-mail address, location, and level of your students. In addition to that information, provide a concise, complete description of the project you are planning, with specific objectives and time lines.

Global SchoolNet

The Global SchoolNet provides an Internet Projects Registry area sponsored by Walden University. Using the database at this site, teachers can locate projects based on starting date, subject area, or other criteria. They can also add their projects to the database and seek collaborating classrooms.

The Global SchoolNet also sponsors a listserv for teachers called HILITES. This listserv allows teachers to post messages about upcoming projects. Each message contains information about the grade level, subject area, and project parameters. To subscribe to HILITES, send an e-mail message to **majordomo@gsn.org**. In the body of the message, type **subscribe hilites**.

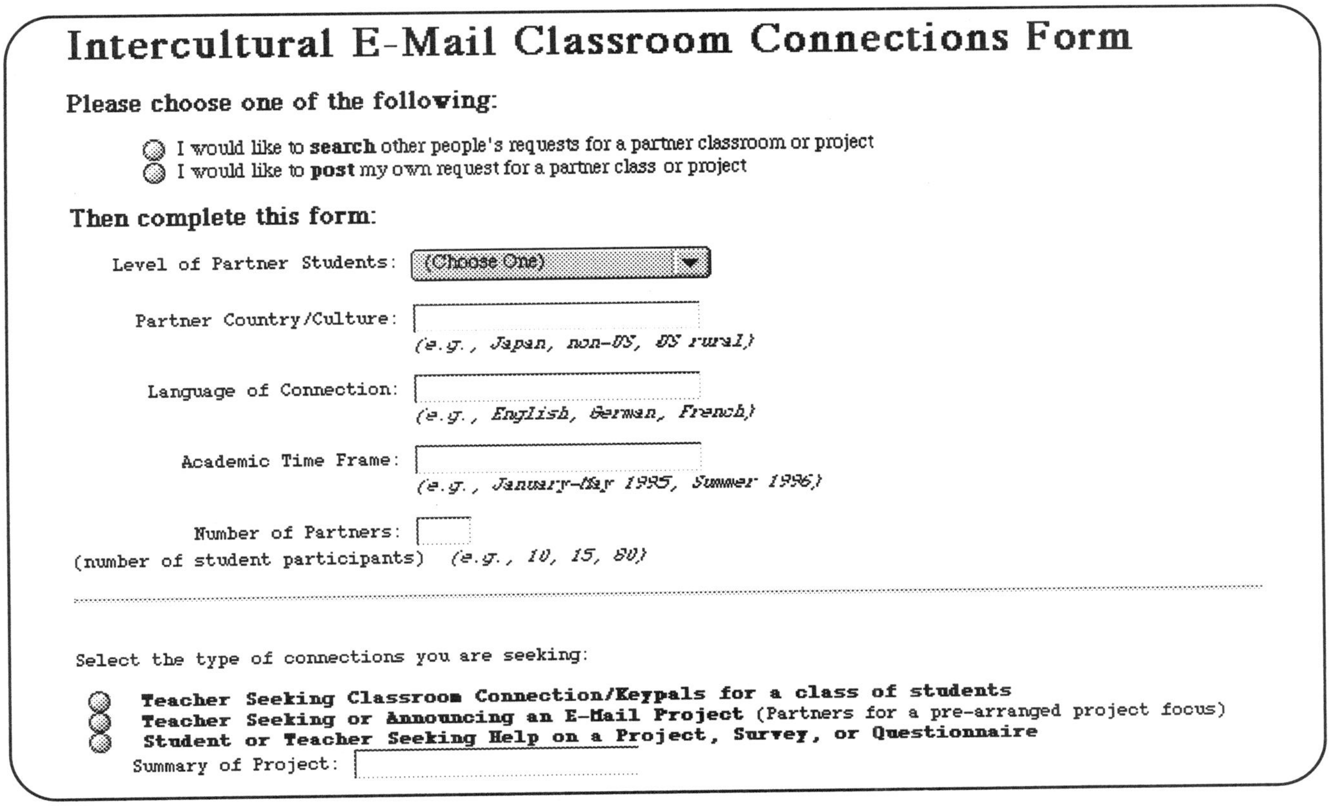

Intercultural E-Mail Classroom Connections Form

Please choose one of the following:

○ I would like to **search** other people's requests for a partner classroom or project
○ I would like to **post** my own request for a partner class or project

Then complete this form:

Level of Partner Students: [(Choose One) ▼]

Partner Country/Culture: [   ]
(e.g., Japan, non-US, US rural)

Language of Connection: [   ]
(e.g., English, German, French)

Academic Time Frame: [   ]
(e.g., January-May 1995, Summer 1996)

Number of Partners: [   ]
(number of student participants) *(e.g., 10, 15, 80)*

Select the type of connections you are seeking:

○ **Teacher Seeking Classroom Connection/Keypals** for a class of students
○ **Teacher Seeking or Announcing an E-Mail Project** (Partners for a pre-arranged project focus)
○ **Student or Teacher Seeking Help on a Project, Survey, or Questionnaire**
Summary of Project: [   ]

Figure 5.1 IECC interface.

Guidelines for Successful Online Projects

You will soon discover there are more online projects and ideas than you can possibly take part in. The following guidelines will help you determine which projects are likely to be successful. These guidelines can be beneficial whether you are organizing a project or considering whether to participate in a project organized by someone else.

Start small. Your first project does not have to be with 100 teachers in Russia. In fact, it may be best to begin with a project that involves a few colleagues or teachers in nearby schools. If your first project is small and local, you can interact off-line as well as online to troubleshoot technical problems and discuss project design (Barron et al. 1997).

Make projects relevant to students. "The most successful learners learn best when they are solving their own problems" (Caputo 1994, 32). Focus on topics that are of real and immediate interest to students. If possible, encourage students to help design and define the topics and research questions.

Formulate clear goals and outcomes. In general, the more specific the goals of a project, the better its chance for success (Rogers 1994). An informal project, such as an e-mail exchange, will soon lose its sense of purpose if there are no clear goals for communication. Also, if a project's goals are clearly stated, it is easy for other educators to assess the project's relevance for their curriculum.

Define beginning and ending dates. A clear time line provides the structure needed to keep a project on track (Gersh 1994). This time line should be established before beginning the project, and it should take into consideration the participants' school and cultural calendars.

Allow plenty of lead time. If you are seeking maximum participation, allow plenty of lead time. Access to telecommunications can be extremely expensive for some schools, and teachers may be unable to investigate the potential for online projects often. Post the initial call for participation at least six weeks before the starting date, and repeat the announcement two weeks before the starting date (Rogers 1994).

Look for or supply specific information. Whether you are setting up a project or joining one, be sure to provide basic information, including

- Contact person
- Contact addresses (e-mail addresses and postal addresses)
- Grade levels of desired participants
- Time line
- Project goals and objectives
- Number of participants
- Complete project outline
- Examples of student input (such as writings or data collections)

Have realistic goals and equipment requirements. Many online projects require the participating schools to have specific equipment. For example, schools in various countries may conduct similar evaluations of air quality or water quality. You cannot assume all schools have access to the same type of equipment for the same cost. It is best to be realistic in requiring hardware and software—or plan to ship the required equipment to participating schools (Walker 1995).

Assess the project. When you plan the project objectives, also develop a plan for assessing the project. Be aware, however, that the overall effectiveness of the project may be more appropriately measured by increased student motivation and cultural understanding than by multiple-choice test scores (Barron and Orwig 1995).

Share the results. Share project results with all participants as well as local support groups, such as parents' organizations. If the project involved publication of stories or other writing projects, print a hard copy and send it to all participants. Be sure to send copies to your principal, superintendent, and board of education.

FINDING LESSON PLANS

The Internet offers a multitude of lesson plans that vary in quality, content, and detail. Some provide step-by-step instructions; others serve as starting points for creating your own plans. Sources of lesson plans are listed in table 5.5.

In addition, the Internet provides access to actual course content, course outlines, reference materials, and registration procedures. Course content can provide information, interactivity, and multimedia components to teach basic concepts and skills. Online course content has other substantial benefits as well: the content can be continuously updated and the materials can be used on any type of computer (cross-platform delivery). Table 5.6 (page 68) lists some sources of online lessons.

SUBSCRIPTION-BASED INSTRUCTIONAL RESOURCES

In addition to the wealth of publicly available resources on the Web, there are a growing number of resources that are available only by subscription. If you subscribe to one of these services, you may have fewer worries about students accessing inappropriate materials because most sites are carefully monitored and the links are checked to screen such materials. These services generally provide a variety of instructional resources, such as lesson plans and Internet activities. For example, Scholastic Network offers curriculum materials that are correlated to national standards in math, language arts, science, and social studies; connections to authors, scientists, historians, and celebrities; and a directory of more than 2,000 teacher-reviewed Web sites. See table 5.7 (page 69) for additional sites.

CONCLUSION

As teachers trade in their chalkboards for keyboards, they are discovering the massive resources on the Internet. Never before have so many up-to-date educational materials been available at so little cost. From lesson plans to online experts, the educational resources on the Web are almost unlimited.

Table 5.5 Sources of Lesson Plans

Site	URL	Content
Awesome Library	http://www.neat-schoolhouse.org/lesson.html	Cross-curricular
Armadillo WWW Resources	http://riceinfo.rice.edu/armadillo/Rice/Resources/learn.html	Classroom aids and resources
Busy Teacher's Web Site	http://www.ceismc.gatech.edu/BusyT/TOC.html/	Cross-curricular
Connections+	http://www.mcrel.org/connect/plus/	Cross-curricular
Collaborative Lesson Archives	http://faldo.atmos.uiuc.edu/TUA_Home.html	Cross-curricular
Historical Documents of the U.S.A.	http://www.yu.edu/acdl.edu/InSci/Projects/USSourceDocs.html	Social studies
Holden's Hands-On Science Experiments	http://www.infi.net/~holdenj/	Hurricanes, geotropism
Houghton Mifflin Education	http://www.hmco.com/school	Cross-curricular
K–12 Resources of Music Educators	http://www.isd77.k12.mn.us/resources/staffpages/shirk/k12.music.html	Music
Library-in-the-Sky	http://www.nwrel.org/sky/Library/Materials_Search/Language_Arts.htm	Language arts
NCSS Online	http://www.ncss.org/online/	Social studies
Possibilities! Integrating the Internet into the Science Classroom	http://kendaco.telebyte.com/billband/Presentation.html	Science education
Secondary Mathematics Assessment	http://cq-pan.cqu.edu.au/schools/smad/smad.html	Math
Teachers.Net	http://teachers.net/lessons/	Cross-curricular
TeachNet	http://www.teachnet.org/	Language arts
Technology Lesson Plans	http://fcit.coedu.usf.edu/tnt	Technology
The Incredible Art Department	http://www.artswire.org/kenroar/lessons/lessons.html	Fine arts

Table 5.6   Online Lessons

Site	URL	Content and Notes
Anatomy of an Eye	http://www.netscape.com/comprod/products/navigator/version_2.0/frames/eye/index.html	Tutorial about eyes (requires frames)
Draw and Color (for K–3)	http://www.unclefred.com/	How to draw cartoons
Gamelan using Java	http://www.gamelan.com	Educational programs
HTML Tutorial	http://www.coedu.usf.edu/inst_tech/publications/html/	Interactive HTML primer
Iconos	http://www.iconos.com	Glue, dinosaurs (require plug-in)
Interactive Frog Dissection	http://teach.virginia.edu/go/frog/	Tutorial about dissecting a frog
Language Tutorials	http://www.travlang.com/languages/	Foreign language for travelers: many languages available
Netscape Frames	http://www.newbie.net/frames/	Advanced features in Netscape
New Technologies	http://www.coedu.usf.edu/inst_tech/publications/NewTech	Tutorial on videodiscs, CD-ROM, QuickTime, Photo-CD
Newton's Apple	http://ericir.syr.edu/Projects/Newton	Antibiotics, brain, electricity, floods, gravity, earthquakes, etc.
Science Education Gateway	http://cea-ftp.cea.berkeley.edu/Education/SII/sii_modules.html	Earth and space science
School Networks	http://fcit.coedu.usf.edu/network	Tutorial on installing a school network
Teacher's Guide to the Holocaust	http://fcit.coedu.usf.edu/holocaust/	Resources for Holocaust education
Tutorial Gateway	http://www.civeng.carleton.ca/~nholtz/tut/doc/doc.html	Instructions for creating interactive lessons on the World Wide Web

Table 5.7 Educational Networks Available by Subscription

Site	URL	Focus
Biology Place	http://www.biology.com	Curriculum projects
Britannica Online	http://www.eb.com	Encyclopedia
Chemistry Place	http://www.chemplace.com	Curriculum projects
Computer Curriculum Corporation	http://www.cccnet.com	Curriculum materials
The Curriculum Resource by NewsBank	http://www.newsbank.com	Information resources
Educational Structures	http://www.educationalstructures.com	Curriculum resources
Electric Library	http://www.elibrary.com	Online references
Information Quest	http://www.eiq.com	Online journals
Psychology Place	http://www.psychplace.com	Psychology resources
Scholastic Network	http://scholasticnetwork.com	Curriculum projects
TRO Learning	http://www.tro.com	Curriculum materials

REFERENCES

Barron, A. E., and G. W. Orwig. 1997. *New technologies for education: A beginner's guide.* 2d ed. Englewood, CO: Libraries Unlimited.

Barron, A., K. Ivers, D. Hoffman, and L. Sherry. 1997. *Telecommunications: Ideas, activities, and resources.* Tampa, FL: Florida Center for Instructional Technology, University of South Florida.

Caputo, A. 1994. Seven secrets of searching: How and when to choose online. *MultiMedia Schools* 1(1):29–33.

Gersh, S. 1994. The global education telecommunications network: Criteria for successful e-mail projects. *Telecommunications in Education News* 5(4):10–11.

Ivers, K. S., and A. E. Barron. 1998. *Multimedia projects in education: Designing, producing, and assessing.* Englewood, CO: Libraries Unlimited.

Lyman, L., H. C. Foyle, and T. S. Azwell. 1993. *Cooperative learning in the elementary classroom.* Washington, DC: National Education Association.

Milone, J. N. 1997. Fair use guidelines for educational multimedia. *Technology & Learning* 17(5):50.

Novelli, J. 1996. Safe surfing for the classroom. *Electronic Learning* 16(3):45.

Rogers, A. 1994. How to design an online project that works. *Classroom Connect.*

Sandholtz, J. H., C. Ringstaff, and D. E. Dwyer. 1997. *Teaching in high tech environments: Classroom management revisited, first–fourth year findings.* **http://www.research.apple.coom/ go/acot/full/acotRpt10full.html** (November 28, 1997).

Slavin, R. E. 1990. *Cooperative learning: Theory, research, and practice.* Englewood Cliffs, NJ: Prentice-Hall.

———. 1987. *Cooperative learning: Student teams.* Washington, DC: National Education Association.

Walker, D. 1995. Making an Internet project work. *MultiMedia Schools* 2(1):28–35.

Science Resources and Activities

The thought of dissecting a frog turned Seymour's stomach. He was relieved to discover he could complete his assignment using the Internet. His instructor, Miss Timassy, introduced the students to The Anatomized Frog, an interactive tutorial on the Web. Using the online tutorial, students could work at their own pace, interact with online experts, repeat procedures, and access additional information about frogs.

Seymour appreciated not having to touch or smell a dead specimen. Angela, on the other hand, looked forward to the hands-on experience. Unlike Seymour, Angela was considering a career in medicine and wanted the opportunity to manipulate the tools, make the precise incisions, and handle the frog's internal organs. Miss Timassy addressed the needs of both students. She explained the benefits of learning about frog anatomy using the online tutorial and how online experts and other sources of information could enhance the students' learning.

"Learning is an ongoing process that requires us to continually investigate a variety of sources; to evaluate, weigh, and synthesize information; and to apply what we have learned so that we can formulate new questions," she explained. Students would have the opportunity to apply what they learned from The Anatomized Frog and their Web research to one of three different class projects—one of which was dissecting their own frog. The Internet would provide Angela with background information and practice for dissecting her own frog, and it would provide Seymour with the information he needed to complete a multimedia report about frog anatomy.

The Internet is a natural forum for scientific inquiries, investigations, and exchanges. It provides students opportunities to share research; construct online databases; examine existing data; and apply knowledge gained from online tutorials, simulations, and content-specific Web sites. In addition to the many scientific databases and Web sites on the Internet, students can access and communicate with online experts in a variety of subject areas, including chemistry, biology, physics, and geology. The Internet provides students with the opportunity to learn about the sciences from personal and social perspectives.

This chapter features Web and telnet sites that address environmental science, astronomy, meteorology, bugs and worms, other animals, geology and paleontology, and health. For each topic, the chapter provides one or two instructional ideas for two or more sites. These ideas and skills are not comprehensive; instead, they serve as starting points for exploration and activities. Following the highlighted sites is a list of other sites related to the topic; these sites are briefly described. The chapter ends with a list of general science sites and e-mail activities.

Note: Each site's current URL is given, but because the Internet is extremely dynamic, addresses and paths may change.

ASTRONOMY

The Internet provides educators and students with access to real-time video and current events taking place in space, numerous archives of space-related information, online experts and databases, and more. In addition to viewing and reading about current events, students and educators can obtain information about the solar system, careers in space, former and current astronauts, and shuttle missions.

NASA Spacelink
http://spacelink.nasa.gov/home.index.html

NASA Spacelink offers an abundance of space-related information, including National Aeronautics and Space Administration (NASA) news, projects, and instructional materials. Students can investigate NASA launch dates, news releases, television schedules, and status reports. They can also use NASA Spacelink to research aeronautics, human space flight, satellites, comets, the hole in the ozone layer, and careers. Teachers can download software, pictures, video and activity guides, and other curriculum materials. Sample lesson plans include Living in Space, Crystal Growth, Spacecraft Design, and Exploring Infrared Light.

Careers

Students research the qualifications for careers in aerospace and enter their findings into a class database. From Spacelink's main menu, choose Library, Instructional Materials, Careers, and then Careers in Aerospace (or enter URL **http://spacelink.nasa.gov/Instructional.Materials/Careers/Careers.in.Aero space/.index.html**).

[Text Version]

Hot Topics

Cool Picks

The Library

Search

Site Map & Information

1988 - 1998

Space Link 10th Anniversary

An Aeronautics and Space Resource for Educators Since 1988

THE LIBRARY

- Educational Services
- Instructional Materials
- NASA Projects
- NASA News
- NASA Overview
- Frequently Asked Questions

HOT TOPICS

Heard something about NASA in the news? Hot Topics is one of our more popular areas in which current events related to NASA science, technology, and education are highlighted.

NASA Spacelink home page.

After reviewing careers related to space, students work together to download and summarize the educational requirements, experience, and other significant factors related to one career. Careers in aerospace include engineering, astronomy, geology, mathematics, and meteorology. Students input their information into a class database. When the student projects are complete, combine them into a single file for printing or presentation. Discuss with students why they would choose a particular career. Students may contact scientists in their field of interest through NEWTON's Ask A Scientist service or by contacting the offices provided by NASA Spacelink.

Information skills: Categorize information, construct a database, analyze data, and seek information from professionals.

Proposed Shuttle

Student groups present a proposal and a model for a new shuttle. Using the site's Shuttle pages, student groups gather background information about Crew Safety, Living and Working on the Shuttle, Propulsion Systems, Second Generation Computers FAQ, and other topics. Students create drawings or 3-D models of their shuttles. Student presentations address research and their proposed ideas. From Spacelink's main menu, choose NASA Projects, then Human Space Flight, then Shuttle (or enter the URL **http://spacelink.nasa.gov/ NASA.Projects/Human.Space.Flight/Shuttle/.index.html**).

Information skills: Collaboratively define specific information needs; locate, select, and evaluate information from a variety of sources; communicate in a persuasive manner; represent ideas in a 2-D or 3-D art format.

Views of the Solar System
http://bang.lanl.gov/solarsys/

This site provides an educational tour of the solar system. It is an outstanding resource for older students. It is extremely well organized and contains excellent photos, movies, and text.

News in Review

Student groups create videotaped news broadcasts of an Apollo mission. Information about Apollo missions can be found at **http://bang.lanl.gov/ solarsys/history.htm** under Spacecraft Mission Summaries. After researching an assigned mission, students "go back in time" to create a news broadcast as if the event were currently happening.

Information skills: Read for significant details and concepts; assemble and communicate information in a meaningful manner.

Robotic Spacecraft

Student groups research and construct models of robotic spacecraft. Each group presents its spacecraft and background information about it to the class. Information about robotic spacecraft can be found at **http://bang.lanl.gov/ solarsys/history.htm** under Spacecraft Mission Summaries.

Information skills: Locate and organize information about a specific topic; communicate information in a meaningful manner.

Additional Sites for Astronomy

Astronomy Hot Links
http://www.kalmbach.com/astro/HotLinks/HotLinks.html

This site offers current press releases, graphics, and links to a variety of astronomy Web sites.

The Nine Planets
http://www.seds.org/billa/tnp/

An excellent site for student research, this multimedia tour of the solar system (including moons) features outstanding graphics, interesting facts and data, and audio.

Science Online: Solar System Resource Kit
http://www.cea.berkeley.edu/Education/sol/solarsyst/sol_solarsyst_solarsyst.html

This site includes an abundance of images, text, and tools to use in solar system projects as well as ready-to-use activities and a link to Ask An Astronomer.

Space Telescope Science Institute
http://www.stsci.edu/

This site contains current information about the Hubble telescope, pictures taken with the telescope, and a wealth of lesson plans and resources for teachers.

StarChild
http://heasarc.gsfc.nasa.gov/docs/StarChild/StarChild.html

This learning center for young astronomers provides information at two levels about the solar system, the universe, and "space stuff." Interactive activities and a glossary are included.

BUGS AND WORMS

These sites give *computer bug* a new meaning. The squeamish may gag, but bug and worm enthusiasts will delight in the movies, close-up images, dissections, and fascinating facts. This section is dedicated to the many "buggy" sites on the Internet. Other animals are covered in another section.

Iowa State's Department of Entomology
http://www.ent.iastate.edu/

This site provides information about a variety of insects. Students can access photographs and videos of insects in the entomology image gallery. The site also provides many links to other resources, including recommended K–12 sites.

Bug Grub

The class discusses and charts students' favorite things to eat. Students tell about times they accidentally or purposely ate a bug. Students discuss their feelings about eating bugs and why people may eat bugs. Student groups research and report nutritional information about bugs, recipes that include bugs, and cultures that eat bugs regularly (including the kinds of bugs eaten). As a culminating activity, students make and eat a food containing bugs or else a bug-themed treat that does not contain bugs. Choose Insects as Food from the main menu to access bug recipes, nutrition facts, and links to more information about foods containing bugs. Katerpillars & Mystery Bugs (**http://www.uky.edu/Agriculture/Entomology/ythfacts/entyouth.htm**) provides more instructional ideas, information about people who eat bugs, and bug-themed treats (see Bugfood!). More recipes are available from Ask Orkin Insect Recipes (**http://www.orkin.com/bugrecipes.html**). Additional information may be gathered from other Internet sites and off-line resources.

Information skills: Chart and compare information; locate, organize, and evaluate information from a variety of sources; communicate results.

Visually Speaking

Student groups choose an insect or spider to research and create multimedia projects using HyperStudio or another authoring tool. Groups incorporate images, videos, and sound clips into their projects using Iowa State's entomology gallery (**http://www.ent.iastate.edu/imagegallery/**) and additional resources (see The Yuckiest Site on the Internet at **http://www.nj.com/yucky/index.html** and Bugwatch at **http://www.bugwatch.com/**). Information about insects and spiders is available on Iowa State's Department of Entomology Web site (choose Iowa Insect Information Notes from the main menu). Additional resources can be accessed through the main menu's K–12 educators link.

Information skills: Locate, organize, and evaluate information on a specific topic from a variety of sources; integrate text with images, videos, and sound clips in a meaningful manner.

The Yuckiest Site on the Internet
http://www.nj.com/yucky/index.html

The Yuckiest Site on the Internet invites students to e-mail questions to Wendell, an expert on the strange and gross aspects of the world. The Yuckiest Site provides links to Wendell's Bug World, Worm World, Your Gross and Cool Body, and two forums where students can read and post stories and messages. Students can submit artwork and poetry to Worm World and Bug World, too.

Cockroach Commercials

Student groups create a videotaped documentary or commercial featuring roach removal techniques, roach anatomy, roach facts, or types of cockroaches. To begin, students review their background knowledge by taking the Roaches in Review quiz, available on the main menu of Bug World. Following the quiz, student groups select and research a topic for the video. In addition to Wendell's Bug World (**http://www.nj.com/yucky/roaches/**), students can find cockroach information at Iowa State's Department of Entomology Web site (**http://www.ent.iastate.edu/**).

Information skills: Collaboratively define topics and identify specific information needs; locate, select, and evaluate information from a variety of sources; communicate findings in a meaningful format.

Worm Waste

Working in groups, students investigate worms as recyclers, build a worm bin, and track worms' activity. Students learn about worms as recyclers from Worm World, which is accessed from the main menu of the Yuckiest Site. Students read about worm experts, submit questions, view videos and graphics, locate instructions for building a worm bin, build the bin, and track their worms' recycling activity. Finally, students present a report about worms as recyclers; as part of their report, they display their worm bins. (Students may collect or buy worms for their bins; Worm World provides resources for purchasing worms.)

Information skills: Read for significant details and concepts; seek information from professionals; assemble information in a meaningful manner.

The Yuckiest Site on the Internet home page

Additional Sites for Bugs and Worms

Ask Orkin
http://www.orkin.com/orkin.html

Ask Orkin is an outstanding Web site for learning basic facts about a variety of bugs and pests. It includes facts, myths, homeowner tips, and links to additional bug-related sites. Students can submit questions about bugs and pests to Dr. Bug or Orkin.

B-Eye
http://cvs.anu.edu.au/andy/beye/beyehome.html

This interactive site allows students to see how things may look to a bee.

Bugwatch
http://www.bugwatch.com/

Bugwatch features summaries and pictures of a variety of insects.

Katerpillars & Mystery Bugs
http://www.uky.edu/Agriculture/Entomology/ythfacts/entyouth.htm

> This Web site for students and teachers, maintained by the University of Kentucky Entomology Department, features information about bugs, bug activities, and teacher resources.

Minibeast World of Insects and Spiders
http://www.tesser.com/minibeast/

> This site features teacher and student resources, information about becoming an entomologist, information about insects, and opportunities to ask questions of experts.

ENVIRONMENTAL SCIENCE

> Environmental issues affect everyone, making this an especially fertile topic area for international collaboration. Students and teachers can learn more about the effects of pollution, depletion of natural resources, and extinction by using the Internet to exchange ideas, projects, knowledge, and solutions for protecting the environment.

Environmental Defense Fund
http://www.edf.org/

> The goal of the Environmental Defense Fund (EDF) is to find solutions to environmental problems. Topics covered on this Web site include endangered species, forest preservation, and activism. The site also provides a search engine and links to educational resources. (The address for the list of educational resources is **http://www.edf.org/heap/resources.html**.)

Facts on Recycling

Students work in groups to research and present information on recycling. Group topics may include anti-recycling myths, precycling, compost, why we should buy recycled products, what to recycle in schools, curbside recycling, how to recycle the family car, and waste reduction. Online articles for these topics can be found via the Environmental Defense Fund search engine. Resources related to recycling can also be found at **http://www.edf.org/heap/recycle_list.html**. Final presentations can be made to the community.

Information skills: Locate and organize information on a specific topic; communicate information in a meaningful way.

Global Warming

Create a class chart with two columns headed What We Know and What We Want to Know. Ask students what they know about global warming and write their responses on the chart. Next, ask students what they would like to learn about global warming and write those responses on the chart. Organize students into groups and give them time to research three different articles about global warming using the Environmental Defense Fund page (**http://www.edf.org/ issues/GlobalWarming.html**). Have each group keep a record of the articles read. Using these articles, students attempt to (1) answer their own questions about global warming and (2) record new information. After each group has finished its research, students share what they learned by discussing their findings and writing them on the class chart. As a follow-up activity, students write a poem about global warming and submit it to the Earth to Kids page at the EDF site (**http://www.edf.org/Earth2Kids/**).

Information skills: Brainstorm and specify required information for a particular topic; locate, select, evaluate, and synthesize appropriate research articles; organize and communicate results; evaluate and respond to information.

National Wildlife Federation
http://www.nwf.org

The National Wildlife Federation (NWF) Web site provides information, links, and student activities focusing on endangered species and habitats, water quality, wetlands, land stewardship, and international issues. Teacher resources, project ideas, online tours, and interactive quizzes are available.

Cool Tours

Cool Tours provide students with an additional resource for learning about water, wetlands, endangered species, and our public lands. Cool Tours are available at **http://www.nwf.org/nwf/kids/cool**. Tour quizzes are also available, allowing students to test their knowledge by taking a pretest and posttest for each tour. Following the tours and quizzes, students can create information booklets about what they learned, create a multimedia project that teaches about a related topic, or participate in a class Jeopardy game about the tours. Students take notes during the tours.

Information skills: Read for meaning, take notes, and apply what has been learned.

Issues and Action

Students select a topic from the menu given on the NWF home page. Using this site and its links to other resources, students research the current status of their topics; identify problems (e.g., shrinking wetlands); and recommend actions to prevent, mitigate, or remedy environmental damage. Students create a class presentation of their findings and recommendations. Recommended sites to support this project are Earth Force Kids (**http://www.earthforce.org/ kidspage.html**) and the Environmental Defense Fund (**http://www. edf.org/**).

Information skills: Locate, organize, and evaluate information about a specific topic from a variety of sources; inform others of findings and recommendations.

The Rainforest Workshop

- Visit the Tropical Rainforest

- Visit the Temperate Rainforest

- Visit our Educational Resources. We have lesson plans and resource materials.

The Rainforest Workshop was developed by Virginia Reid and the students at Thurgood Marshall Middle School, the Olympia School District, in Olympia, Washington.

Animals Plants

Rainforest Workshop home page.

The Rainforest Workshop Home Page
http://mh.osd.wednet.edu/Marshall/rainforest_home_page.html

The Rainforest Workshop provides information about temperate and tropical rain forests as well as animals of the rain forest. Links to other rain forest sites are provided, as are lesson plans and activities, graphics, and articles to facilitate student research.

People of the Rainforest

Students list how they obtain food, where they sleep, how they are educated, what they do in their free time, how they care for the Earth, and other details about their lives. Then they research similar details about the lives of people who live in a rain forest. Students compare and contrast their lives with those of people who live in various rain forests. Students may also note similarities and differences among the rain forest people. Resources to support this activity can be found at **http://mh.osd.wednet.edu/Marshall/homepage/people. html** and at the Rainforest Action Network's Kids' Corner (**http://www.ran.org/ran/kids_action/index.html**).

Information skills: Locate, organize, and evaluate information from a variety of sources; compare and contrast; consider facts from a variety of perspectives.

Rain Forest Calendar

Students work in groups of four to create a 12-month calendar about rain forest animals. Each student selects three animals. Students research their animals, then write a paragraph and draw a picture of each one. The paragraphs and pictures are used to create calendars. Information about rain forest animals can be found at **http://mh.osd.wednet.edu/Marshall/homepage/animals.html**.

Information skills: Collaboratively define topics and identify specific information needs; locate and select appropriate information; communicate what has been learned through writing and drawings.

Additional Sites for Environmental Science

Earth Force
http://www.earthforce.org/

Designed for grades 5–9, Earth Force features a Youth in Action section that lists things children can do to save the environment. The site provides information about air pollution, drinking water, wildlife, and habitats.

Earth Island
http://www.earthisland.org/ei/index.html

Earth Island features projects for the conservation, preservation, and restoration of the global environment. Students can search the site for information. Projects include protecting rain forests, habitats for whales and dolphins, sea turtle nesting beaches, and sacred lands. Other projects promote organic agriculture and ecological paper fiber alternatives.

Econet
http://www.igc.org/igc/econet/index.html

Econet provides current newsgroup headlines about environmental issues as well as a search engine. Links to other environmental Web sites can be found at **http://www.igc.org/igc/en/en.other.html**.

EnviroLink
http://envirolink.org/

EnviroLink claims to be one of the largest online environmental information resources on the planet. Its news section features daily reports from correspondents around the world, an environmental events calendar, e-mail lists, boycott listings, and more. Links to educational and governmental sites are provided. An art section offers images of nature, the wilderness, and the earth. The site also includes a search engine.

Environment School Kit
http://www.iinet.net.au/~ecwa/info/skoolkit.html

Designed for secondary school students, the Environment School Kit includes topics such as pollution, deforestation, the ozone layer, energy, endangered species, and the greenhouse effect. Additional resources and links are also included.

Rainforest Action Network
http://www.ran.org

This site provides information about the rain forest as well as advocacy events, such as campaigns and demonstrations. The Kids' Corner contains information about the animals, plants, and native people of the rain forests as well as a glossary and resources for teachers and students. Kids' Corner also includes a gallery of student artwork. Links to related resources are provided.

GEOLOGY AND PALEONTOLOGY

It's impossible for students to visit the many interesting and remote regions they study. The Internet provides the next best thing: virtual tours. In addition to tours, many Web sites feature online experts, e-mail activities or projects, interactive environments, and information on geology and paleontology.

Volcano World
http://volcano.und.nodak.edu

Volcano World features images of volcanoes, information about current and recent eruptions, online experts, lesson plans, and links to other resources. It publishes students' volcano pictures.

Current Eruptions

Students research and create models of currently erupting volcanoes. Students present their findings and models to the class and compare data. Students identify the name and location of their volcanoes on a class map and on an eruption time line. Students can submit research questions to Ask a Volcanologist. (Ask a Volcanologist and Currently Erupting Volcanoes links appear on the Volcano World home page.) To obtain information about constructing volcano models, choose Kids' Door on the main menu, then Volcanic School Project Ideas, then Make a Volcano.

Information skills: Locate, organize, and evaluate information about a specific topic from a variety of sources; organize information in chronological order; analyze and compare data; locate information about a map; seek information from professionals; display findings using a 3-D art format.

Zoom Dinosaurs
http://www.EnchantedLearning.com/subjects/dinosaurs/

Zoom Dinosaurs is an outstanding dinosaur Web site that is maintained by Enchanted Software. Zoom Dinosaurs contains short summaries, hypertext links, and pictures to assist student understanding. Links include All About Dinosaurs, Mesozoic, Species and Classification, Extinction, Fossils, Dino-Birds, Geologic Time Chart, Dino Fun, and Classroom Activities.

Dinosaur Survey

Using the dinosaur myth and not-a-dinosaur information from Zoom Dinosaurs, the class creates a survey questionnaire to measure the community's knowledge of dinosaurs. Students survey people of various ages, then record their findings on a chart. The data from each student's chart are then combined on a class chart. Students may create additional charts to display results by age group. Students use the class findings to identify areas of misinformation, then create brochures and posters to convey little-known dinosaur facts. The brochures and posters may be duplicated and distributed through the school office, community library, and so on.

Information skills: Construct a questionnaire; read for significant details and concepts; record, categorize, and compare information using charts and graphs; communicate findings in a meaningful manner.

Additional Sites for Geology and Paleontology

Ask-a-Geologist
http://walrus.wr.usgs.gov/docs/ask-a-ge.html

This Web site invites students to submit questions to an online expert. Questions may be about volcanoes, earthquakes, mountains, rocks, maps, groundwater, lakes, or rivers.

Dinosaurs in Hawaii!
http://www.hcc.hawaii.edu/dinos/dinos.1.html

This is an online exhibit of dinosaur fossils.

U.S. Geological Survey
http://geology.usgs.gov/

This Web site provides links to Ask-a-Geologist, research, earthquake information, and information about geology by region.

The Virtual Cave
http://www.goodearth.com/virtcave.html

Students can tour the mineral wonders of a cave environment with outstanding photographs and definitions.

HEALTH

Nutrition, disease, drug awareness, and physiology are covered in several sites on the WWW.

The Digital Learning Center for Microbial Ecology
http://commtechlab.msu.edu/ctlprojects/dlc-me/

This site is designed to help teachers and students learn more about microbial ecology. Topics include the Microbe Zoo, Microbes in the News, and Microbial Ecology.

Heroes and Villains

Student groups read and evaluate articles about microbes and present their findings to the class. As a follow-up activity, students collect newspaper and magazine articles about microbes and classify the microbes as heroic, dangerous,

What is the Digital Learning Center for Microbial Ecology?

Microbe of the Week

Take a look at the newest addition to the Microbe Zoo's specimen collection. (Click **here** to view previous Microbes of the Week.)

The Microbe Zoo

Images and descriptions of microscopic organisms and the habitats in which they live.

The Digital Learning Center for Microbial Ecology home page.

ancient, or strange. Choose Microbes in the News from the main menu. Articles are divided into categories including Heroic, Dangerous, Ancient, and Strange. Additional articles appear under Late Breaking News. Each category allows students to e-mail questions to experts.

Information skills: Locate, organize, and evaluate information about a specific topic; seek information from professionals; inform others of findings.

Microbe Zoo Books

Student groups research a topic in the Microbe Zoo and create a book that illustrates and describes their findings. Students share books and discuss how different microbes can be helpful and harmful. Students create posters of their favorite microbes. Choose The Microbe Zoo from the main menu. Students can e-mail their questions to microbe scientists (see How to Contact Us and other e-mail links available throughout the Web site).

Information skills: Locate, organize, and evaluate information about a specific topic; seek information from professionals; categorize information; communicate findings using pictures and text.

Food and Drug Administration
http://www.fda.gov/

The Food and Drug Administration Web site provides links to information about various health-related issues. Topics include FDA News, Food, Children and Tobacco, Cosmetics, Toxicology, and much, much more.

Cosmetic Reality

Student groups create a fact sheet based on research into cosmetic safety, product information, and packaging. Next, the class creates a questionnaire to survey why people do or do not wear cosmetics and what they know about cosmetic safety, product information, and packaging. Students survey a variety of age groups. Results are compiled on a class chart and discussed. Additional charts can be made to display results by age group. Next, student groups create a "consumer-report"-type magazine based on their findings and fact sheets. Students share their magazines and make them available in the school library. As a follow-up activity, students discuss or debate whether beauty magazines impose an artificial standard of beauty against which people consistently measure girls and women and how this might affect their self-esteem.

To find additional information about cosmetics and teenagers, choose Cosmetics from the main menu and scroll down to Cosmetics of Interest to Specific Groups.

Information skills: Read for significant details and concepts; design a questionnaire; chart, analyze, and compare data; assemble information in a meaningful manner.

Food Labels

Student groups research information on food labeling and use their new knowledge to analyze and discuss labels on a variety of food products. Groups present their findings to the class. As a follow-up activity, groups create a "Did You Know?" booklet about food labeling to share with other classes. Information about food labeling is available on the Food and Drug Administration Web site by selecting More Choices from the main menu, then selecting Food Labeling. Additional information and links can be found on the National Food Safety Database Web site at **http://www/foodsafety.org/clabel.htm**.

Information skills: Locate, organize, and evaluate information on a specific topic from a variety of sources; analyze and compare information; communicate findings.

The National Food Safety Database
http://www.foodsafety.org/

The National Food Safety Database Web site provides information for consumers, the industry, and educators/trainers. In addition to articles in those categories, the site answers frequently asked questions and invites users to submit questions. Access is facilitated with an index and search engine.

Eating Out?

After reading the Online Food Safety Training Manual, students take a test to evaluate their knowledge of food safety. Next, students brainstorm observable signs of food safety (such as smell or color) and create a checklist of these signs. Students get a copy of the checklist and use it to record their observations each time they eat out for a specified period of time, for example, one month. (You may specify that "eating out" includes eating in the school cafeteria.) After the time expires, students compile, share, and compare their results with the class and discuss their reaction to food safety in restaurants, fast food places, the school cafeteria, and their homes. To access the Online Food Safety Training Manual, choose Browse The National Food Safety Database from the main menu, then choose Educator/Trainer-Related Materials, then Resources, then Training Resources, and then On-line Food Handler Training Manual, or enter the URL **http://www.foodsafety.org/train/toptrain.htm**. Then select Browse the Online Food Safety Training Manual and read each article. Students may take the quizzes at the end of each section to test their knowledge as they go. The final quiz is available at **http://www.foodsafety.org/train/toptrain.htm**. As a follow-up activity, students create posters related to food safety. Samples are located at **http://www.foodsafety.org/train/trainpot.htm**.

Students can also use e-mail to compare the results of their checklists to the results of students' checklists in other parts of the country.

Information skills: Read for significant details and concepts; brainstorm ideas based on facts; record information on a checklist; compile, analyze, and compare data; relate findings to real-world situations.

Food for Thought

Using the National Food Safety Database and other online and offline resources, student groups construct a health magazine containing articles on food topics of interest. Topics may include food safety, nutrition, foodborne illness, food myths, and so on. Magazines may include a related crossword puzzle, graphics, and other food-related information. Student groups can research topics using the National Food Safety Database search engine by accessing Topics That Everyone Should Be Aware Of from the main menu. Students can also access additional sites at **http://www.foodsafety.org/otherweb.htm**. Students share their magazines with their classmates and place them in the school library.

Information skills: Specify a topic of interest; locate and select appropriate information from a variety of sources; evaluate and compare resources; organize and share findings in an established format.

Additional Sites for Health

Cells Alive
http://www.cellsalive.com/

Cells Alive provides text, pictures, and movies about cells and infections.

HealthFinder
http://www.healthfinder.gov/

Sponsored by the U.S. government, this site is an outstanding resource for locating specific health information, support groups, and information about health through links to other sites.

Healthwise
http://www.columbia.edu/cu/healthwise/

Healthwise is produced by the Health Education and Wellness program of the Columbia University Health Service. The site contains a database of more than 600 health-related questions posted to an online expert. Students can ask the expert (called "Alice") questions about health and can search the database for specific topics.

Heart: An Online Exploration
http://sln2.fi.edu/biosci/preview/heartpreview.html

Students can make this online exploration of the heart, which features hypertext links and graphics. The site also offers resource materials, enrichment activities, and a glossary.

International Food Information Council
http://ificinfo.health.org/

This Web site provides a wealth of information about food safety and nutrition as well as lesson plans and resources for educators.

Neuroscience for Kids
http://weber.u.washington.edu/~chudler/neurok.html

Designed for students and K–12 educators, Neuroscience for Kids is a great site for learning more about the nervous system. It includes experiments, activities, resources, additional links, and more. It is sponsored by the University of Washington.

METEOROLOGY

As a real-world learning tool, the Internet provides students with opportunities to track and analyze weather conditions throughout the world, keep up-to-date on current storm activities, and obtain information about other topics related to weather. Weather sites provide current weather information; storm updates; forecasts; and information about earthquakes, tornadoes, and hurricanes.

The Tornado Project Online
http://www.tornadoproject.com/

This site is maintained by a small company that publishes books, videos, and posters about tornadoes. The Web site features facts, stories, myths, and safety tips.

Five Years of Tornadoes

Each student selects a different state and creates a time line of the date, place, and F-scale of tornadoes in that state within the last five years. Time lines may also include the number of deaths and injuries and the time of each tornado. Students look for patterns within their own time lines and publish their findings. Students compare their findings with other students' research. Discussion questions may include which state had the most tornadoes, which state had the most deaths and injuries, why some states have more tornadoes than others, whether tornadoes tend to occur at a certain time of day, what time of year tornadoes appear the most and why, and so on. Students can learn about the F-scale by selecting The Fujita Scale of Tornado Intensity from the main menu. State tornado information is accessible from the All States link on the main menu.

Information skills: Organize information in a chronological format; analyze and compare data; communicate and reflect on findings.

Storm Chasers

The class creates a list of questions about tornadoes and storm chasing. Questions may include: how old were the storm chasers when they started chasing tornadoes, what prompted them to do it, where and when did they see their first tornado, what is the scariest thing about tornadoes, where have they chased tornadoes, and what is the most powerful tornado they have seen. Working in groups, students e-mail the questions to selected storm chasers. Students compare the storm chasers' answers and discuss their own thoughts about tornadoes and storm chasing. (To reach a storm chaser's Web page or to obtain the storm chaser's e-mail address, choose Storm Chasing from the main menu and then select a storm chaser.)

Information skills: Brainstorm and specify required information for a particular topic; categorize and compare information; seek information from professionals.

Weather Underground
telnet://madlab.sprl.umich.edu:3000

Weather Underground provides information about weather conditions, hurricanes and earthquakes, and other topics. Students can compare weather conditions in various parts of the world. They can also track hurricanes, plot earthquakes, and graph and compare ultraviolet light forecasts.

Note: This is a telnet site; after you connect, press *m* to reach the main menu.

Earthquakes and Hurricanes

Students chart earthquake reports and hurricane advisories over a period of time. Using maps and charts, they plot the activity of the disasters, monitor changes on a daily or weekly basis, note the areas of the world at most risk, and discuss the implications for building construction. Access "Latest earthquake reports" and "Hurricane advisories" from Weather Underground's main menu.

Information skills: Create and evaluate charts, tables, graphs, and maps for analysis.

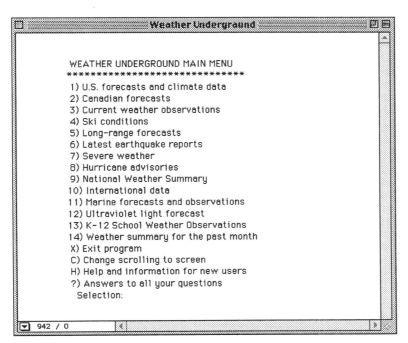

Weather Underground main menu.

Additional Sites for Meteorology

Federal Emergency Management Agency: Tornado Safety Tips
http://www.fema.gov/fema/tornadof.html

This site contains tornado facts and safety tips as well as links to additional weather resources.

Hurricane Storm Science
http://bird.miamisci.org/hurricane/

Designed for elementary students and maintained by the Miami Museum of Science, this site provides information about hurricanes, hurricane survivors, and weather instruments. The site also includes links to current hurricane data and teacher resources.

National Weather Service in San Diego
http://nimbo.wrh.noaa.gov/Sandiego/nws.html

In addition to reporting current weather conditions in California, this Web site provides links to national and international weather reports. Weather maps, tide information, and a storm tracker are available.

Rainbows
http://covis.atmos.uiuc.edu/guide/optics/rainbows/html/rainbow.html

This site provides information about rainbows. Students can learn about the types of rainbows and how they are formed and explore other rainbow-related topics. Links to related sites are provided.

Wild Weather Page
http://www.whnt19.com/kidwx

Created by a television weatherman, the Wild Weather Page is an interactive site for kids. The site addresses many topics and provides links for more information. Students can e-mail their weather questions to the creator of the Web site. Questions and responses are posted on the site. Many teacher resources are available.

OTHER ANIMALS

In addition to bugs and worms, the Internet contains a wealth of information about mammals, fish, amphibians, birds, and reptiles. Many Web sites contain animal graphics, movies, and audio clips that can be included in student multimedia projects. Students can also access online experts.

The Froggy Page
http://frog.simplenet.com/froggy/

The Froggy Page is a one-stop resource for almost anything a student or teacher wants to know about frogs. The Froggy Page contains sounds, pictures, and videos, as well as links to frog tales, science facts, online dissections, songs, home pages, research, species information, and more.

Declining Populations

Student groups research and chart declining frog populations throughout the world by accessing the Declining Amphibian Populations link on the Scientific Amphibian page (choose Scientific Amphibian from The Froggy Page main menu). Student groups e-mail experts (located at several sites) for more information. Students combine and compare their findings on a class chart, discuss projects designed to protect frog populations, and brainstorm their own solutions.

Information skills: Locate, organize, and compare information; seek information from professionals; effectively use charts and graphs; brainstorm ideas based on facts.

A Variety of Frogs

Students research different species of frogs and create a multimedia report that contains species information, pictures, and sounds of frogs. Students access frog sounds and pictures from The Froggy Page main menu and select various sites to research by selecting Scientific Amphibian from the main menu (scroll down the page to find links to species information). Students share their research findings.

Information skills: Teach students how to locate, organize, and evaluate information on a specific topic from a variety of sources; integrate text with images, videos, and sound clips in a meaningful manner; communicate research findings.

The FROGGY Page

Ribbit.

Ribbit! Welcome to the **Froggy Page**! This corner of the net is home to all kinds of virtual frogginess, from the silly to the scientific. Check out the menu below to find more frog fun.

New! | Froggy Pictures | Froggy Sounds | Froggy Tales | Songs of the Frog
Scientific Amphibian | Famous Frogs | Net.Frogs | Other Froggy Stuff

The Froggy Page home page.

NetVet
http://netvet.wustl.edu/

NetVet's main menu offers two categories: NetVet Veterinary Resources and the Electronic Zoo. The former focuses on veterinary medicine, education, careers, etc.; the latter has links to resources about various animals. The site has links to many veterinary search engines and maintains a search engine for the site itself.

Career Opportunities

Students research a veterinary field of interest (for example, zoo animal medicine, equine sports medicine, wildlife medicine, aquatic animal medicine) and report their findings. Students access career information by choosing Veterinary Resources from the main menu, then clicking on Careers. See also the Care for Pets Web site at **http://www.avma.org/care4pets/morecare.htm**. Students may submit questions to Ask a Vet (**http://www.pawprints.com/ VETCONNECT/askthevet.html**).

Information skills: Locate, organize, and evaluate information about a specific topic; seek information from professionals; communicate findings.

Caring for Pets

Student groups create a brochure on a specific pet that includes health and safety tips for caring for the animal. Students share their findings and brochures with the class and their community. Student groups use NetVet's search engine options to find resources to compare and include in their brochures. Students can also access pet safety and health information on the Care for Pets Web site (**http://www.avma.org/care4pets/**).

Information skills: Teach students to use a search engine, read for significant details and concepts, compare and evaluate information from a variety of sources, and share information in a meaningful manner.

Additional Sites for Other Animals

Animal Information Database
http://www.bev.net/education/SeaWorld/homepage.html

The Animal Information Database, maintained by SeaWorld and Busch Gardens, is designed for educational purposes. Topics include What's New, Animal Information, Career Information, and Educational Resources.

Birmingham Zoo
http://www.birminghamzoo.com/

The Birmingham Zoo offers many resources for learning about various animals. In addition to indexed topics, the site includes its own search engine, links to other animal Web sites, teacher resources, animal videos, and a graphical African safari. Students can submit questions to Ask a Zookeeper.

Cow's Eye Dissection
http://www.exploratorium.edu/learning_studio/cow_eye/

Students can take an online tutorial about dissecting a cow's eye.

International Wolf Center
http://www.wolf.org

The International Wolf Center site contains links, educational resources, images, and more.

Marine Biology Laboratory Phylum Index
http://www.mbl.edu/html/MRC/HTML/phylum.html

The Phylum Index is a visual database that provides a wealth of information about phyla.

WhaleNet
http://whale.wheelock.edu

Students, teachers, and researchers from around the world collect, compile, and share their data for interdisciplinary curricular activities and student research.

GENERAL SCIENCE RESOURCES ON THE WEB

Online Magazines and Newsletters

Best Friends
http://www.bestfriends.org

ION Science Magazine
http://www.injersey.com/Media/IonSci/index.html

Quantum
http://www.nsta.org/quantum/

Ranger Rick
http://www.nwf.org/nwf/lib/rr/index.html

Star Facts
http://www.ccnet.com/odyssey/welcome.html

Yes Mag: Canada's Science Magazine for Kids
http://www.islandnet.com/~yesmag/homepage.html

Other Science Sites

Bubbles
http://www.exploratorium.edu/ronh/bubbles/bubbles.html
Learn all about bubbles. The site includes links to other bubble sites.

Computer Museum
http://www.tcm.org/
The Computer Museum provides customized interactive exhibits (choose kid, student, adult, or educator), information about computers, and related resources.

Dr. Rabbit's No Cavity Clubhouse
http://www.colgate.com/Kids-world/main.cgi
Geared for young students, Dr. Rabbit's Web site is filled with fun facts and games about teeth.

ExploraNet: The Exploratorium's World Wide Web Server
http://www.exploratorium.edu/
ExploraNet features online exhibits, experiments, teacher resources, and a variety of science-related links.

Forensic Files
http://forensicfiles.bc.sympatico.ca/
The Forensic Files is an interactive, mystery adventure game with multiple paths. It helps students learn more about forensic science. Students must solve

a variety of puzzles to solve the case. The story features hands-on experiments and activities that help make forensic science understandable and relevant to children. They can receive advice during the game by using Ask Newton. Students can save their place with a bookmark.

Healthy Refrigerator
http://www.healthyfridge.org

The Healthy Refrigerator provides information about nutrition, heart disease, and other health topics.

Imagination Factory
http://www2.hsonline.net/homepages/kidatart.html

This Web site provides information and art activities for recycling trash.

Inner Learning On-line
http://www.innerbody.com/

Inner Learning On-line features interactive tutorials about the human body and other topics.

Mad Scientist Network
http://medinfo.wustl.edu/~ysp/MSN/

This site features an assortment of activities, ideas, and links, including Ask-a-Scientist and online experiments.

MooMilk Web Site
http://www.moomilk.com/moove/moove.htm

MooMilk includes a virtual tour of the milking process, facts about milk, and opportunities to e-mail questions about milk.

National Science Teachers Association (NSTA)
http://www.nsta.org/

This is the official Web site of the NSTA. It provides articles about current news and legislation concerning science in schools, information about upcoming events, online resources, and more.

Online Experiments
http://129.82.166.181/Experiments.html

This site offers a variety of online experiments and brainteasers.

Ontario Science Centre Interactive Zone
http://www.osc.on.ca/

This Web site features scientific fun facts presented through Macromedia movies.

Optical Illusions
http://www.lainet.com/illusions/

This Web site offers an enormous collection of optical illusions and puzzles. It includes links to recommended books, online puzzles, and resources.

Pitsco Ask An Expert

http://www.askanexpert.com/askanexpert/

This is an outstanding site for locating experts in a variety of fields. It is an excellent resource for any subject!

Science Fair Projects

http://www.fi.edu/qanda/spotlight1/spotlight1.html

This Web site offers information and resources for conducting a science fair.

Science Learning Network

http://www.sln.org/sln.html

The Science Learning Network is an excellent science resource for teachers and students. It provides a wealth of resources and links to many activities.

Thinking Fountain

http://www.sci.mus.mn.us/sln/

The Thinking Fountain provides ideas and activities that present students with surprising, gross, funny, and personal connections to science.

UT Science Bytes

http://loki.ur.utk.edu/ut2kids/

This site is designed for elementary and secondary school students and teachers. Topics include botany, geology, entomology, and careers in science.

Welcome to Energy Quest™

http://www.energy.ca.gov/education/

Energy Quest™ provides information about various types of energy and science projects.

Why Files

http://whyfiles.news.wisc.edu/index.html

Funded by the National Science Foundation, the Why Files explore questions about science.

E-MAIL EXCHANGES

One of the greatest advantages of using the Internet is the ability to communicate with people around the world. This allows students to gain real-world data, firsthand accounts, and opportunities to share findings and results.

Noting Nutrition

Students exchange a seven-day meal record with students in another country. Students record what they eat and drink for breakfast, lunch, dinner, and snacks. Older students may include information about calories, fat, and other nutritional values. Students compare their eating habits to those of students from another country. Students ask their online partners about unfamiliar foods. In addition, students exchange recipes and information about food prices and favorite places to eat. Students may also investigate how climate and agricultural conditions affect diet.

Outdoor Exchanges

Students list and photograph rocks, plants, insects, birds, domestic animals, and wildlife from the school environment, then exchange these lists with similar lists from students in other states and countries. Students compare the lists and investigate why some items are the same and some are different. Students might consider geography, climate, ecosystems, and the impact of human populations.

Scientific Challenges

Students exchange scientific challenges (such as making an egg bounce, using a cabbage to determine pH, making water appear to run uphill, and so on) with other students. Students demonstrate, explain, and compare their solutions. A Web site can be created to share students' challenges and solutions.

Grade Levels	Mission to NASA	Research Level
4-8		Basic

Educational Goals

To access, use, and become familiar with NASA Spacelink

To work cooperatively to analyze and interpret clues to locate a specific piece of information

Procedure

Students form cooperative groups. Introduce Mission to NASA as a problem-solving adventure that will help students become familiar with the information on NASA Spacelink. Distribute copies of the activity sheet to each group. Read the first frame aloud. Demonstrate how to find the answer to Nancy Newland's question (frame 2) by logging on and comparing the main menu titles with Nancy's information. Nancy notes that she recently read an overview of NASA. Based on this clue, *Overview of NASA* is the logical menu choice. Her other comments suggest you "review what happened in 1994." Select *The Years in Review*, then *1994 in Review*. Encourage students to list the paths. Note that Prof. Puzzle uses NASA's search engine. Allow groups to decipher the remaining clues and answers using NASA Spacelink. After everyone has had a chance to solve the mystery to the ignition sequence (frame 1), discuss the students' answers, strategies, and paths with another class demonstration.

Answers   (Ignition sequence = 167)

Nancy Newland: *Path: NASA Overview•The Years in Review•1994 in Review* (http://spacelink.nasa.gov/NASA.Overview/The.Years.in.Review/ 1994.in.Review) **Answer: 4**

Prof. Puzzled: *Use the search engine to search for "program names." Select NASA Program Names.* (http://www.hq.nasa.gov/office/pao/ QandA/names.html) **Answer: 2**

Sandy Scout: *Path: Instructional Materials•Careers•Student Wants to Be Astronaut* (http://spacelink.nasa.gov/Instructional.Materials/Careers/ Student.Wants.to.Be.Astronaut) **Answer: 123**

Captain Jane T. Kurk: *Path: NASA News•NASA News Releases•Previous News Releases•93 News Releases•93-02 News Releases•93-02-01* (http://spacelink.nasa.gov/NASA.News/NASA.News.Releases/ Previous.News.Releases/93.News.Releases/93-02.News.Releases/ 93-02-01) **Answer: 30**

Rocky Rigardo: *Path: NASA Projects•Human Space Flight•Apollo Lunar•New on the Moon* (http://spacelink.nasa.gov/NASA.Projects/ Human.Space.Flight/Apollo.Lunar/New.on.the.Moon) **Answer: 8**

Extension Activity

1. Groups create newspapers related to what they found especially interesting during their investigation of NASA Spacelink.

MISSION TO NASA

Greetings, Space Cadets. Headquarters is looking for cadets worthy of flying a top-secret spacecraft. Your mission is to navigate through the Internet to NASA Spacelink's library and find answers to headquarters' questions. In addition to questions, headquarters personnel will provide clues to the paths where you will find the answers. All of the answers are numbers. Add the numbers together to find the ignition sequence to the top-secret spacecraft.

NASA Spacelink's library address is: http://spacelink.nasa.gov/xh/library.html

Hello, I'm Nancy Newland, and I recently read an overview of NASA. I learned a lot by reviewing different areas of information. In fact, if you review what happened in 1994, you may discover the answer to this question: How many Space Shuttle flights were dedicated to various studies of the planet in 1994?

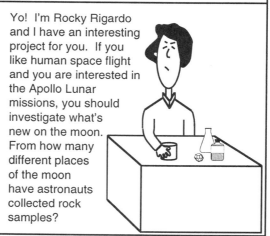

Greetings. My name is Prof. Puzzled, and I have been conducting re**search** on NASA **program names**. If you knew what I knew, you'd know how many astronauts flew on each Gemini mission. How many?

Hey there! I'm Sandy Scout, and my hobby is creating instructional materials. For my career, I'd like to be an astronaut. First, I have to finish school. I guess you could say I'm a student who wants to be an astronaut. By the way, how many of the former and present 195 astronauts were in Scouting?

I am Captain Jane T. Kurk of the Starship Expedite. My mission is to boldly read the NASA News Releases before 1994. My question addresses star date 93-02-01. What day of the month did Gene Roddenberry, creator of the *Star Trek* television series, posthumously receive NASA's Distinguished Public Service Medal?

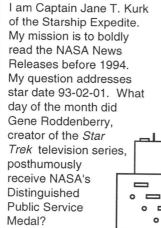

Yo! I'm Rocky Rigardo and I have an interesting project for you. If you like human space flight and you are interested in the Apollo Lunar missions, you should investigate what's new on the moon. From how many different places of the moon have astronauts collected rock samples?

Grade Levels		Research Level
4-8	**Climb It!**	Basic

Educational Goals

To access and use Internet resources for geography and weather

To discover relationships between elevation and temperature

Procedure

Students work in pairs to find U.S. cities at the elevations listed on the Climb It! activity sheet. Various answers are possible. When everyone has filled out the activity sheet, students share their answers by marking the cities on a class map of the United States. Construct a graph with their data. Note patterns or trends. Consult the local newspaper to see whether the weather conditions match what the students found. Compare the results. Does the rule of thumb that temperature falls 5 degrees Fahrenheit for every 1,000-foot gain in elevation hold true? Point out that the correlations may be less straightforward than they seem. At some times of the year, a city with a higher elevation may well have a higher temperature than a city at a lower elevation.

Resources

Geographical Name Server (telnet:// martini.eecs.umich.edu:3000)
Weather Underground (telnet://madlab.sprl.umich.edu:3000)
Geographic Names Information Server (http://www-nmd.usgs.gov/www/gnis/gnisform.html)
WeatherNet (http://cirrus.sprl.umich.edu/wxnet/)

Extension Activities

1. One day, week, or month after completing the activity sheet, have students check the temperatures of the cities they chose to see what changes have occurred. Students record their original answers and track changes. Ask students to predict whether the relationship between elevation and temperature will be more pronounced in the summer or in the winter.

2. Distribute copies of a United States map. Students color-code the temperature ranges (similar to the weather map in *U.S.A. Today*). Students compare their products with the *U.S.A. Today* map for the day.

3. Invite a weather forecaster to the school to discuss weather patterns.

Climb It!

Greetings, fair weather friends! Telnet to the Geographic Name Server (martini.eecs.umich.edu:3000) or another Internet site to find cities with the elevations listed on this page. Next, check out the current temperature and weather conditions in Weather Underground (telnet://madlab.sprl.umich.edu:3000). Chart the temperatures and elevations on a line chart. Is there a correlation between elevation and temperature? Try additional cities.

7. **Elevation > 3500:** City _____ Temperature _____

6. **Elevation > 2500 and < 3500:** City _____ Temperature _____

5. **Elevation > 1500 and < 2500:** City _____ Temperature _____

4. **Elevation > 1000 and < 1500:** City _____ Temperature _____

3. **Elevation > 500 and < 1000:** City _____ Temperature _____

2. **Elevation > 200 and < 500:** City _____ Temperature _____

1. **Elevation < 200:** City _____ Temperature _____

Learning About a Rain Forest

Objectives

To work cooperatively to research and present information about the importance of rain forests

To work cooperatively to research and present information about the animals that live in the Brazilian rain forest

Grade Levels: 4-8   **Final Product:** Class books

Internet Resources

Rain Forest Workshop Home Page (http://164.116.102.2/mms/ rainforest_home_page.html)

Rain Forest Action Network Home Page (http://www.ran.org/ran/index.html)

Procedure

1. Construct a class Knowledge Chart (containing columns for What We Already Know, What We Want to Know, and What We Found Out) about the animals, people, and importance of the rain forest. Brainstorm the first two components of the knowledge chart with your students and record their responses.

2. Divide the class into groups. Each group researches one of the following topics using the Internet and other media sources:

   Amphibians   Mammals   Birds   Plants   People   Importance of Rain Forest

3. Students create a bibliography of resources and note discrepancies in the data.

4. After gathering, evaluating, and synthesizing the information, student groups create a book with illustrations of their findings. Hole-punch the edges of the construction paper and lace with yarn to make books. Illustrations can be drawn or created with magazine pictures. Text can be written or word-processed and glued to the pages.

5. Each group creates a quiz (7 -10 questions) based on the information in their books.

6. Student groups exchange their books and complete each other's quizzes.

7. Conclude by filling in the column of the Knowledge Chart. (What We Found Out)

Learning About a Rain Forest (cont.)

Extension Activities

1. E-mail the Rain Forest Action Network to learn more or ask questions. (ran-info@econet.apc.org)

2. Students conduct additional research on endangered species and create a 12-month calendar depicting 12 different endangered species and facts about each. Information about endangered species can be found at the following Internet sites:

   Endangered Species Scratchpad (http://home.mem.net/%7Ewhisper/species.html)

   EarthWatch Endangered Species List (http://www.earthwatch.org/t/Tfieldsofstudy.html)

   Animal Information Data Base (http://www.bev.net/education/SeaWorld/infobook.html)

   Ecosystem news (http://www.reast.demon.co.uk//news.htm)

   Environmental Protection Agency WWW Server (http://www.epa.gov/)

   Students research endangered species in their state, find out what is being done to preserve them, and exchange this information with students in other states.

3. Study products of the rain forest. Student groups research various products of the rain forest and the political forces behind them. Which products are supported? Which products are being boycotted? Have students create posters calling for a ban of boycotted products and brochures that describe supported products. Information about rain forest products can be found at the following Internet sites:

   Ecosystem news (http://www.reast.demon.co.uk//news.htm)

   Kids' Action (http://www.ran.org/ran/kids_action/index.html)

   Endangered Species WWW Links (http://www.web.apc.org/save-species/wwwlinks.htm)

   Office of Protected Resources: Marine Species (http://kingfish.ssp.nmfs.gov/tmcintyr/prot_res.html)

What's Bugging You?

Objectives

To research and present information on a selected bug

To compare and evaluate information from a variety of resources

Grade Levels: 4-8   **Final Product:** Written reports and 3-D models

Internet Resources

The Yuckiest Site on the Internet (http://www.nj.com/yucky/index.html)

Iowa State's Department of Entomology (http://www.ent.iastate.edu/)

Ask Orkin (http://www.orkin.com/orkin.html)

Katerpillars & Mystery Bugs (http://www.uky.edu/Agriculture/Entomology/ythfacts/entyouth.htm)

Minibeast World of Insects and Spiders (http://www.tesser.com/minibeast)

Procedure

1. Construct a class Knowledge Chart (containing columns for What We Already Know, What We Want to Know, and What We Found Out) about bugs. For example, students may already know where certain bugs live, but they may want to know what certain bugs eat, how many offspring they have at one time, how long they live, who their predators are, and so on.

2. Brainstorm a list of different bugs and divide the class into groups. Each group researches a selected bug. Require students to use a variety of offline and online resources and to compare their findings among the sources and note any discrepancies. Students contact online experts with their questions.

3. After gathering, evaluating, and synthesizing the information, student groups create a written report of their findings. Reports should include a bibliography of the students' resources. Student groups also create a 3-D model of their selected bug and identify its components.

4. Student groups present their findings and models to the class.

From *The Internet and Instruction.* © 1998 Libraries Unlimited. (800) 237-6124.

What's Bugging You? (cont.)

Procedure (cont.)

5. Conclude by filling in the column of the Knowledge Chart (What We Found Out) and discussing what discrepancies (if any) students found in their research. Discuss the importance of gathering and comparing information from multiple sources.

Extension Activities

1. Student groups create a drawing of their bug in its environment and attach a short summary of facts related to their bug. Drawings and summaries are collected and reproduced for class calendars or calendar fund-raisers.

2. Student groups create a board or card game based on their bug. For example, *Cootie* is a game in which children gather and assemble the pieces to a plastic bug. Students may create a game based on this concept, or they may design their game to challenge a player's knowledge of their bug (like *Trivial Pursuit*).

3. Student groups create a storybook about their bug to present to younger students.

4. Student groups design a bug experiment and share the results with the class. For example, students may observe and chart the activities of ants in an ant farm or study the growth and activity of silk worms.

5. Student groups contact students in other states and countries and survey what they consider to be their most common bug problem. Students can exchange pictures of local bugs and learn about the role of bugs in other cultures. For example, some cultures may find certain bugs a delicacy, a religious symbol, and so on.

6. As a class, the students design a survey to e-mail to entomologists and ask them about how they became interested in Entomology, which bug they find the most fascinating, and so on. Students analyze, compare, and discuss the survey results.

Mathematics Resources and Activities

During the summer, Mr. Grizz and other teachers worked with community members to get Emily Dos Middle School connected to the Internet. Following the installation, Mr. Grizz helped the computer committee purchase filtering software and develop an acceptable use policy. In addition, several Internet workshops were developed and presented free of charge to Emily Dos Middle School teachers, parents, and community members.

The Internet was not new to Mr. Grizz; he had been exploring the Internet at home for the last two years and frequently used downloaded materials to enhance his lessons. Now it was time for the students to get involved.

The fall semester arrived quickly, and Mr. Grizz introduced his first Web-based unit: the abacus. The Internet added a new twist to the unit; it provided students with interactive, online abacus tutorials and access to experts, research, and other materials that were otherwise unavailable to his students. His students were intrigued to discover there are several types of abacuses and amazed that a skilled user of the abacus can solve addition and subtraction problems faster than a calculator! This inspired students to conduct their own in-class study.

Mr. Grizz knew he had opened many minds to the history of mathematics and early technologies. Ironically, he used today's technologies to bring those of the past to life. Mr. Grizz's next unit would use the Internet to help his students share and expand their mathematical knowledge and experiences with others.

The Internet provides students opportunities to learn and apply math skills in a variety of contexts. Students and teachers can contact and receive help from online experts; exchange math problems and solutions with other classes; collect and analyze data from all over the world; access online calculators, math simulations, and tutorials; download lesson plans and software; and much more.

This chapter features WWW sites that address several math topics and skills, including problem-solving, measurement and geometry, probability and statistics, decimals and fractions, algebra and calculus, and basic skills and vocabulary. For each topic the chapter provides one or two instructional ideas for two or more sites. These ideas and skills are not comprehensive; instead, they serve as starting points for exploration and activities. Following the highlighted sites is a list of other sites related to the topic; these sites are briefly described. The chapter ends with a list of general math sites and e-mail activities.

Note: Each site's current URL is given, but because the Internet is extremely dynamic, addresses and paths may change.

ALGEBRA AND CALCULUS

Students will be elated to know they are not alone in their pursuit of learning more about algebra and calculus. Several Web sites facilitate discussion of algebra and calculus and encourage students to exchange problems, solutions, and ideas.

Alvirne High School AP Calculus
http://www.seresc.k12.nh.us/www/alvirne.html

This Web site is maintained by the advanced placement (AP) calculus students at Alvirne High School. It provides resources and sample problems for the AP calculus exam.

Problem of the Week

Students download the guest problem of the week and Alvirne's problem of the week and send their solutions to Alvirne High School. Students can compare the difficulty of the questions, as well as their solutions for both of the problems. As a follow-up activity, students construct their own problem and submit it to the AP calculus students at Alvirne High School.

Information skills: Teach students how to locate information, read for significant details and concepts, evaluate data, and communicate results in a meaningful way.

Problem Portfolio

Students download and solve archived problems and create a portfolio of their work. Practice problems and their solutions can be downloaded from several archives on the main menu. Students categorize the problems and compare strategies and outcomes.

Information skills: Teach students how to locate information, read for significant details and concepts, analyze and categorize information, and record and communicate results in a meaningful way.

Virtual Algebra Problem
http://www.webcom.com/~vschool/problems/Mathproblems/algebra597.html

This site is part of the Virtual School (**http://www.webcom.com/~vschool/**). Lesson areas include mathematics, science, social studies, and language arts. Mathematics topics include problems of the week in algebra and geometry.

Weekly Problem

Students download the problem of the week, work it out, and submit their answer to their teacher and the Virtual School. Students share their answer and strategies with their classmates and then compare their results with the posted solution.

Information skills: Locate information; read for significant details and concepts; analyze information; communicate results in a meaningful way.

Additional Sites for Algebra and Calculus

Algebra Online
http://www.algebra-online.com/

Algebra Online provides personal online tutoring, a chat room, and an option to submit questions about algebra to its online experts.

Algebra Story Problems
http://www2.hawaii.edu/suremath/intro_algebra.html

Part of 21st Century Problem Solving (see page 120), this page provides algebraic word problems and demonstrates how they are solved.

AP Calculus on the Web
http://www.seresc.k12.nh.us/www/apsum.html

AP Calculus on the Web provides many resources for teaching calculus—links, materials, software, and more.

Computer Algebra Information Network (CAIN)
http://www.can.nl/

CAIN provides resources and links for teaching algebra, calculus, and other higher-level mathematics.

Girls to the Fourth Power Algebra Program
http://www-leland.stanford.edu/%7Emeehan/xyz/girls4.html

This Web site describes a tutoring program, provides a few algebra problems, and offers students the option of posting a message.

BASIC SKILLS AND VOCABULARY

Students and teachers will find many Web sites that focus on basic skills, mathematics vocabulary, and basic tools.

The Abacus
http://www.ee.ryerson.ca:8080/~elf/abacus/

The Abacus offers lessons for adding and subtracting on an abacus, information about the history of the abacus, interesting facts about the abacus, and an online interactive abacus written in Java. The Web site also provides links to related resources.

Abacus Research

Student groups create reports comparing different types of abacuses. Students investigate and compare the history of the abacuses, how to use them, what they look like, and so on. See the Compare and Further Investigation links on the main menu for additional information and links about the abacus. Students use multiple resources.

Information skills: Teach students how to locate, organize, and evaluate information on a specific topic from a variety of sources and how to effectively communicate findings.

Plus and Minus

Students learn to add and subtract on an abacus using the online tutorials and abacus. Students then predict which is faster: completing addition and subtraction problems on an abacus (not the virtual one) or on a calculator. Graph students' responses on a chart. Place students into groups of three (abacus, calculator, judge) and provide equations. Judges observe the fastest response for each equation and tally the most accurate. Student groups graph and discuss the results, including why they differ. Next, have students read "The Abacus vs. the Electric Calculator" (choose Contest from the main menu). Students compare their results to the findings in the article, explore what variables influence the results (that is, why results might differ), and discuss their reactions to what they have learned.

Information skills: Locate and apply mathematical tools on the Internet; analyze and compare data; create effective charts and graphs; communicate findings.

Mathematical Archives: Numbers
http://archives.math.utk.edu/subjects/numbers.html

This is one of many sites available from the Mathematical Archives Web site (**http://archives.math.utk.edu/**). This site provides links to many sites about numbers. Topics include pi, prime numbers, and number history.

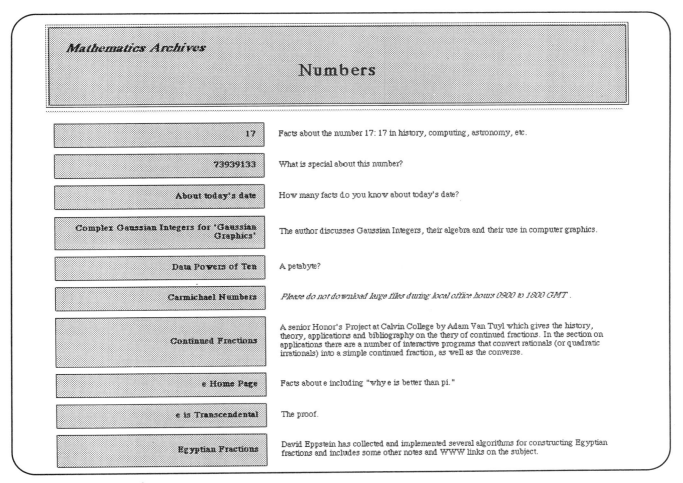

Mathematics Archives page.

Number News

Student groups create a newspaper about numbers. Students research and gather information from the various online and off-line resources to construct their newspapers. Newspapers are shared with the class and distributed in the school library. Students identify, compare, and evaluate each source of information. For follow-up, see the first activity of Using the Newspaper to Learn Math (**http://www.southam.com/calgaryherald/educa/Math1.html**).

Information skills: Teach students how to locate, organize, and evaluate information on a specific topic from a variety of sources and communicate findings in a newspaper format.

Numbers Talk

Students brainstorm a list of phrases, proverbs, titles, and so on that include numbers. For example, "It takes one to know one," "It takes two to tango," "Three's a crowd," and so on. Students brainstorm as many phrases as they can for as many numbers as they can, then create a bar graph to show how many phrases they thought of for each word. Students compare their lists with each other, then compare their lists to Numericon's "Numbers we've all heard of" list. (To access the list, first select Numericon from the Math Archives: Numbers main menu, then select Numbers We've All Heard Of. Or, enter **http://www.maths.uts.edu.au/number/common.html**.) Students keep a journal of number phrases. As a follow-up activity, students make phrase books that feature one of the numbers. For example, a student may write and illustrate a book with phrases that include the number three: Three Blind Mice, The Three Stooges, three-dimensional, and so on.

Information skills: Brainstorm; create effective graphs; analyze data; locate and evaluate information; communicate findings in a meaningful manner.

Additional Sites for Basic Skills and Vocabulary

Base Ten Count
http://www.edbydesign.com/btcount.html

Base Ten Count is a Java applet that helps students understand the concept of place value. This is sponsored by Education by Design. Additional activities are available at this site.

Baseball Math
http://www.gold-pages.com/math/

Baseball Math is an interactive game that requires students to use addition or multiplication skills to score hits and runs.

Flash Cards for Kids
http://www.wwinfo.com/edu/flash.html

Using interactive flash cards, students can practice addition, multiplication, division, and subtraction at various levels.

MonsterMath
http://www.lifelong.com/AcademicWorld/MonsterMath/

MonsterMath provides interactive math stories for younger students. The stories are presented in English or Spanish with both text and audio components. Students must solve a problem before continuing to the next part of a story.

Stanley Park Chase
http://schoolcentral.com/willoughby5/default.htm

Students use multiplication to help a dog locate buried gold.

Using the Newspaper to Learn Math
http://www.southam.com/calgaryherald/educa/Math1.html

This site represents one of the many newspaper activities sponsored by the *Calgary* (Alberta) *Herald*. Additional educational activities are available by clicking on the Education Online icon.

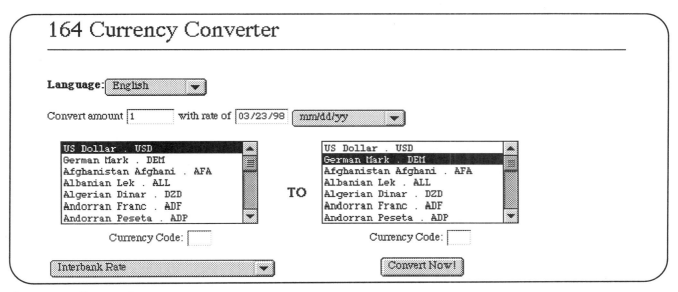

Currency Converter page.

DECIMALS AND FRACTIONS

Most sites that address fractions and decimals provide lesson plans, online tutorials, and software links. A Tour of Fractions (**http://forum.swarthmore.edu/paths/fractions/index.html**) is an excellent resource for links.

Currency Converter
http://www.oanda.com/cgi-bin/ncc

The Currency Converter converts more than 164 currencies. It provides both current and past exchange rates. Converting currency is a great way to teach real-world applications of decimals and fractions.

How Far Will My Dollar Go?

Students use the currency converter to determine the worth of one dollar in other locations. Students choose five of the available 164 options, note the value of the dollar (e.g., 1 U.S. dollar equals 1.8820 German Marks) and of the foreign currency (e.g., 1 German Mark equals 0.5313 U.S. dollars). Students chart and compare their results, ranking the amounts from highest to lowest; post their findings on the appropriate locations on a map; and share their findings with the class. Students construct a class chart showing everyone's findings. As a follow-up activity, students find and bring in pictures of foreign currencies, convert food menus to another currency, or determine the cost of selected items from a catalog using another currency. Older students may discuss the ramifications of fluctuations in currency values.

Information skills: Locate and use information tools on the Internet; analyze data and create effective charts; locate locations on a map; communicate findings in a meaningful manner.

Great World-Wide Pet Survey
http://www.webcom.com/hardy/cuis2/pets-kids.html

The Great World-Wide Pet Survey is one of the many activities available at the Cuisenaire Learning Place (**http://www.awl.com/www.cuisenaire.com/index2.html**). Students can participate in an online survey and compare their results with others. This is also a great site for conducting statistical analysis.

Double-Check That Data

Student groups review the data submitted to the Great World-Wide Pet Survey, noting duplicate entries and other invalid data. Students discuss their findings as a class and create a revised, accurate data list. The class constructs new charts and graphs to display the data and compares these to the charts online. Students discuss their findings in terms of fractions, percentages, and decimals. Students explain the importance of checking data and not taking given results for granted.

Information skills: Analyze and evaluate data; create effective charts and graphs; communicate findings.

Additional Sites for Decimals and Fractions

Decimals, Whole Numbers, and Exponents
http://www.mathleague.com/help/decwholeexp/decwholeexp.htm

This site provides information about decimals. Topics include adding and subtracting decimals, writing decimals in expanded form, and comparing decimals.

Egyptian Fractions
http://www.ics.uci.edu/~eppstein/numth/egypt/

This site provides information about Egyptian fractions and other math concepts, as well as links to related sites.

Elementary School Lessons & Materials for Teachers
http://forum.swarthmore.edu/paths/fractions/e.fraclessons.html

This site provides many links to fraction lesson plans and materials for elementary school teachers. Teachers may use this as their own resource or allow students to download lessons to teach their peers or younger students.

S.O.S. Mathematics: Algebra
http://www.math.utep.edu/sosmath/algebra/algebra.html

This site provides information about simple fractions, complex fractions, converting fractions, and more.

A Tour of Fractions
http://forum.swarthmore.edu/paths/fractions/index.html

This Web site contains many lesson plans and links for teaching fractions.

The Geometry Center
Center for the Computation and Visualization of Geometric Structures

A National Science Foundation Science and Technology Center at the University of Minnesota

WebEQ 2.2 is now available!

Geometry Center home page.

World Wide Math Tutorial
http://tqd.advanced.org/2949/

This Web sites features short tutorials about fractions and decimals.

MEASUREMENT AND GEOMETRY

The Internet provides many opportunities for students to apply their measuring skills and to learn more about geometry. In addition to online tutorials and lesson plans, the Internet offers access to many measurement and geometry tools, projects, and interactive activities.

Geometry Center
http://www.geom.umn.edu/

The Geometry Center features resources and information related to geometry. It is an excellent site for high school teachers and advanced geometry students.

The Art of Geometry

Students research, view, and critique various geometrical artworks and design their own pieces based on their findings. Graphics can be chosen by topic, author, or title. The teacher may want to assign specific graphics and compare students' responses. Student art can be based on a graphic found in the archive or on a particular concept. Students send their questions and comments to the Geometry Center. (To view the art, choose Geometry Reference Archives from the main menu, then choose Graphics Archive.)

Information skills: Select and apply information; seek information from professionals.

How Far Is It?
http://www.indo.com/distance/

This service uses the University of Michigan Geographic Name Server and a supplementary database of world cities to determine the latitude and longitude of two places, and then calculates the distance between them. It also provides a map showing the two places, using the Xerox PARC Map Server.

Chart a Course

Students chart a course between two U.S. cities on opposite coasts (i.e., east and west). Using the How Far Is It? Web site, students determine the distance between the two locations and chart the shortest course using a U.S. map. Next, using the driving directions option on How Far Is It?, students compare their course with the directions provided by MapQuest. Students highlight both courses in different colors on a map.

Information skills: Map skills; locate and apply information tools on the Internet; analyze and evaluate information.

Kali
http://www.geom.umn.edu/apps/kali/start.html

Kali is an interactive tool for creating Escher-like tilings, infinite knots, and other drawings. It creates patterns in all of the 17 planar symmetry groups.

Picture This

Students choose a symmetry group, notation, and pattern to create, and then print out a drawing using Kali. Students attempt to identify the symmetry group and notation of each other's drawings using various sources, including Kali.

Information skills: Locate and apply mathematical tools on the Internet; analyze and compare data.

Additional Sites for Measurement and Geometry

Aunt Annie's Craft Page: Geometric Playthings
http://www.auntannie.com/geomplay.html

Geometric Playthings provides instructions for making several paper projects that involve basic geometry. Most projects create 3-D objects.

Convert It!
http://microimg.com/science/

This Web site converts one unit of measure to another (e.g., centimeters to inches, inches to miles, feet to centimeters). Conversions are provided for units of length, area, mass, velocity, fluid, and more.

Countdown!
http://www.spiders.com/cgi-bin/countdown

This Web site calculates the seconds, minutes, days, and hours between two dates.

Geometry Problem of the Week
http://forum.swarthmore.edu/geopow/

This Web site features weekly geometry problems. Students can submit their answers and research problems previously submitted. Students can also try to solve the problem of the month.

Plane Math Activities
http://www.planemath.com/

Plane Math Activities features online, interactive math problems with student, group, and teacher activities corresponding to National Council of Teachers of Mathematics standards.

Storybook of Geometry
http://tqd.advanced.org/3654/

The Storybook of Geometry features a variety of interactive stories that require students to use their knowledge of geometry.

PROBABILITY AND STATISTICS

The Internet offers many ways students can collect data for statistical analysis and to study probability. In addition, online experts and databases, interactive tutorials, activities, and simulations are available.

Chance Database
http://www.geom.umn.edu/docs/snell/chance/

This Web site contains information, resources, and links to help educators teach introductory probability and statistics concepts. Topics include Chance News, Teaching Aids, and Other Related Internet Sources. Teaching aids include evaluation instruments, sample activities, computer resources, and information about probability and surveys. Chance is supported by the National Science Foundation and several other learning institutions.

In the News

Student groups read and discuss the statistics and probability concepts associated with the abstracts posted in Chance News. Based on the Chance News examples, students find newspaper and magazine articles that feature statistics and probability concepts. Students present their findings to the class, then submit abstracts of the articles to the Chance Database. Students may use online newspapers to conduct their research. To find links to online newspapers, choose Related Internet Resources from the Chance Database main menu.

Information skills: Read for significant details and concepts; locate, evaluate, and organize information for a specific topic; communicate information in a meaningful way.

Same Results

Student groups replicate an activity described in Activities (choose Teaching Aids from the main menu) and discuss and compare their findings.

Information skills: Teach students how to locate information, read for significant details, apply information, and communicate results.

EduStock
http://tqd.advanced.org/3088/

Edustock teaches students about the stock market. It includes tutorials about the stock market, company profiles, and a stock market simulation.

Company Profiles and Stocks

Student groups research an assigned company and chart the stock of the company over a given period of time. Student groups present a report about their company and its stock results to the class. Students compare the information posted on EduStock with information from other sources. (When assigning companies to students, select from the Company Profiles on EduStock's main menu.)

Information skills: Locate and organize information for a specific topic; create effective charts; analyze and evaluate data; communicate information in a meaningful way.

Stock Market Reports

Students learn about the stock market by using EduStock's online tutorial and other online and off-line resources. Students take notes, evaluate information, and synthesize their research into a final report. (Topics for student reports are based on the topics outlined in the tutorial.) Students submit 10 questions based on their research for use in a class Jeopardy game. Students play the game.

Information skills: Read for significant details and concepts; locate, organize, and evaluate information from a variety of sources; record, analyze, and synthesize data; communicate findings and demonstrate knowledge through a game format.

Global Grocery List Project
http://www.landmark-project.com/ggl.html

The Global Grocery List provides information about the price of groceries in various places around the world. The information is based on class submissions. The Global Grocery List provides instructions and a template for submitting prices.

Check It Out

Students follow the instructions given on the Global Grocery List to submit information about groceries. Students print out the given template and calculate the average prices of selected groceries. Students compare their findings to those already posted on the Global Grocery List.

Information skills: Locate and apply information; record and analyze data; communicate results.

Now and Then

Students examine current and past grocery price lists to determine the average cost of groceries and to compare the most expensive and least expensive grocery items. Students communicate their findings using tables, graphs, and charts.

Information skills: Analyze data; create effective tables, graphs, and charts.

Additional Sites for Probability and Statistics

DAU Stat Refresher
http://www.cne.gmu.edu/modules/dau/stat/

Stat Refresher is an interactive, online tutorial about statistics and probability.

K–12 Statistics
http://www.mste.uiuc.edu/stat/stat.html

K–12 Statistics provides links to lesson plans and data sets. Links are organized by the National Council of Teachers of Mathematics standards.

Statistics Every Writer Should Know
http://nilesonline.com/stats/

This is an introduction to basic statistics.

StatLib
http://lib.stat.cmu.edu/

This Web site is an extensive resource of statistics materials, including data sets, graphic models, software, and links.

Taking Chances: Online Probability
http://www.fi.edu/qa97/spotlight4/

This is a great site for teacher-tested probability lesson plans.

PROBLEM SOLVING

The Internet provides both formal and informal problem-solving opportunities across all areas of the curriculum. This section focuses on problem-solving situations involving mathematics and logic.

Ask Dr. Math
http://forum.swarthmore.edu/dr.math/index.html

Dr. Math answers questions from students at all levels. Archives of questions and answers are available. The site is divided into four levels; elementary school, middle school, high school, and college levels. Each level includes various topics: About Numbers, Division, Geometry, Math History, Puzzles, and so on.

A Passion for Puzzles

Student groups solve puzzles they download from Dr. Math. Students categorize the puzzles by type and level of difficulty, then organize them into a class puzzle book. To access puzzles, first select the appropriate grade level from the Ask Dr. Math main menu. Then select Puzzles. Answers are provided for each puzzle, so students can check their answers.

Information skills: Solve problems; categorize information.

Perplexing Puzzles

Student groups submit an unsolved puzzle to Dr. Math. Before submitting the puzzle, search the archives to be sure Dr. Math has not already solved it. Students may also submit puzzles and compare their answers to Dr. Math's answers, or students may search other puzzle sites and compare Dr. Math's solution to a puzzle solved by someone else.

Information skills: Seek information from professionals; locate and evaluate information from various sources.

MegaMath
http://www.c3.lanl.gov/mega-math/menu.html

MegaMath, sponsored by the Los Alamos National Laboratory, encourages creativity and an integrated approach to problem-solving activities. The site provides lesson plans that combine problem-solving with art, drama, language arts, and more.

Act It Out

Student groups perform the play "A Usual Day at Unusual School." (To access the script, select A Usual Day at Unusual School, then select Activities, and finally select Unusual School. The lesson plan is also available here.) After the performance, student groups create plays based on logic puzzles. For additional resources related to this activity, see Brain Teasers (**http://www.eduplace.com/math/brain/index.html**) and the Big List of Puzzle and Riddle Pages

This is MegaMathematics!

Welcome to MegaMath

Mathematical Topics

- The Most Colorful Math of All
- Games on Graphs
- Untangling the Mathematics of Knots
- Algorithms and Ice Cream for All
- Machines that Eat Your Words
- Welcome to the Hotel Infinity
- A Usual Day at Unusual School

MegaMath home page.

(http://huizen.dds.nl/~mahulsma/biglist.htm). Students send their comments, questions, and plays to MegaMath.

Information skills: Locate and apply information; seek information from professionals; assemble and communicate information in a creative manner.

University of Toronto Mathematics Network
http://www.math.toronto.edu/mathnet/mathnet.html

The Mathematics Network offers interactive problems and activities, problems and puzzles, resource materials, and a question-and-discussion area for high school students.

Classic Fallacies

Students record their responses while they attempt to discover the flaw in a false proof. The site provides immediate feedback to the student's response. Choose Interactive Projects and Activities, then Classic Fallacies. As a follow-up activity, students can research and report on various fallacies involving statistics, mathematical induction, and other topics.

Information skills: Read for significant details and concepts; record and analyze data.

Game Play

Students learn about the mathematics on which many games are based. Choose Interactive Projects and Activities, then Games with a Twist. Students record their findings in a journal and submit their questions to the Question and Answer Corner. Students research additional games, puzzles, and magic tricks based on mathematics, then add their findings to their journal.

Information skills: Read for significant details and concepts; record and analyze data; seek information from professionals.

Additional Sites for Problem Solving

21st Century Problem Solving
http://www2.hawaii.edu/suremath/home.html

This Web site is an excellent resource for learning more about problem-solving strategies, issues, curriculum integration, and so on.

Aims Puzzle Corner
http://www.aimsedu.org/Puzzle/PuzzleList.html

The Puzzle Corner provides monthly puzzles to engage students' imaginations and build their problem-solving skills. Past puzzles are available.

Brain Teasers
http://www.eduplace.com/math/brain/index.html

Sponsored by Houghton Mifflin, this Web site offers weekly brainteasers for students to solve. Students can submit their answers online and enter a contest. Archives of past brainteasers are available also. Hints and answers are included in the archives. Problems are categorized by grade levels: 3–4, 5–6, and 7–8.

Lemonade Stand
http://www.littlejason.com/lemonade

This is a Web version of the classic game Lemonade Stand, with additional options. For example, students have the option to advertise to try to attract more customers; in addition, they are automatically charged $.75 per day rent. The objective is to sell lemonade to make a profit. This interactive game combines weather, advertising, and other variables that affect the sale of lemonade. Kids can compete and win a place on the high scores list. This Web site provides links to other online games.

Magic Squares
http://forum.swarthmore.edu/alejandre/magic.square.html

This site features the history behind magic squares, examples, and explanations of how magic squares work.

Mathematics Problem Solving Task Centres
http://www.srl.rmit.edu.au/mav/PSTC/index.html

This Web site provides problem-solving activities and tips. Students are invited to submit their own problems. A discussion list is also available.

GENERAL MATHEMATICS RESOURCES ON THE WEB

Online Magazines and Newsletters

Mathematical Dictionary
http://www.mathpro.com/math/glossary/glossary.html

The Statistics Teacher Network
http://www.amstat.org/education/STN/

Zimaths
http://www.geocities.com/CapeCanaveral/Lab/3550/zimaths.htm

Other Sites

AIMS Education Foundation
http://www.aimsedu.org/

AIMS develops integrated math and science materials for K-9. The Web site contains activities, ideas, exchanges, puzzles, mathematics history, and more.

Appetizers for Math and Reason
http://www.cam.org/~aselby/lesson.html

This site provides a collection of material and problems to help students develop problem-solving and reasoning skills.

Big List of Puzzle and Riddle Pages
http://huizen.dds.nl/~mahulsma/biglist.htm

This Web site provides an extensive list of puzzle and riddle sites.

Blue Dog Can Count
http://kao.ini.cmu.edu:5550/bdf.html

Students create a simple arithmetic equation by filling in blanks on the screen. Blue Dog solves the equation, then barks to indicate the answer. (If the answer is 20, Blue Dog barks 20 times.)

Calculators On-Line
http://www-sci.lib.uci.edu/HSG/RefCalculators.html

Calculators On-Line provides links to more than 4,600 online calculators.

Cuisenaire Learning Place
http://www.awl.com/www.cuisenaire.com/index2.html

This site provides many online activities for students, a discussion area for teachers for their questions and comments about hands-on learning in science and mathematics, online lesson plans, and more.

Eisenhower National Clearinghouse
http://www.enc.org/

The Eisenhower National Clearinghouse provides miscellaneous resources for math and science teachers.

Encyberpedia: Math
http://www.encyberpedia.com/math.htm

This site provides an extensive list of math links.

The Explorer
http://explorer.scrtec.org/explorer/

The Explorer offers a collection of educational resources and lesson plans for mathematics and science.

Famous Curves Index
http://www-groups.dcs.st-and.ac.uk:80/~history/Curves/Curves.html

At this interactive site, users click on the name of a curve, then watch the computer draw it. Information about curves is also available.

Finity
http://www.finitycorp.com/tableof.htm

Finity features online activities to teach students about percentages and money. This site contains lots of teacher resources to print and download, and it includes interactive math games.

Fractal Galleries
http://www.glyphs.com/art/fractals/

This site contains information and pictures of fractals.

The Fractory
http://tqd.advanced.org/3288/

The Fractory provides an interactive tool for creating and exploring fractals.

Greek Mathematics
http://sunsite.unc.edu/expo/vatican.exhibit/exhibit/
d-mathematics/Greek_math.html

This site focuses on the history of Greek mathematics.

Helping Your Child Learn Math
http://www.ed.gov/pubs/parents/Math/

This Web site provides resources for parents (and teachers) helping kids learn math.

History of Mathematics

http://archives.math.utk.edu/topics/history.html

This site provides links to resources that focus on the history of mathematics.

History of Mathematics Archive

http://www-groups.dcs.st-and.ac.uk/~history/

This Web site contains biographies of mathematicians and other historical information about math.

The Hub

http://ra.terc.edu/HubHome.html

The Hub offers many resources for mathematics and science teachers.

Interactive Mathematics Miscellany and Puzzles

http://www.cut-the-knot.com/

This Web site provides information about many math topics and an enormous number of interesting activities and links.

Interactive Mathematics Online

http://tqd.advanced.org/2647/main.htm

This site addresses introductory topics in geometry, algebra, trigonometry, and chaos theory. Stereograms are also discussed.

It Figures

http://www.solutions.ibm.com/k12/teacher/fig1s.html

Sponsored by IBM, It Figures is an online math activity. To complete the activity, students must use information they find on other Web sites.

Kid's Web Math

http://www.npac.syr.edu/textbook/kidsweb/math.html

Part of Kid's Web, this site provides links to miscellaneous math sites.

The Math Archives

http://archives.math.utk.edu/

The Math Archives is a wonderful resource for math material, including lesson plans, resources, additional links, and software.

Math, Baseball, and the San Francisco Giants

http://www.kn.pacbell.com/wired/baseball/

This is an online math activity that requires students to use other Internet resources to complete the activity.

Math Central

http://MathCentral.uregina.ca/index.html

Math Central is a K–12 education math Web site that features online lesson plans, teacher forums, and an opportunity to submit questions.

Math Comics
http://www.csun.edu/~hcmth014/comics.html
Math Comics is a collection of math-related comics.

The Math Forum
http://forum.swarthmore.edu/
The Math Forum contains an enormous number of math lesson plans, links, and other resources. Users can search its database or browse by topic. This is an excellent starting place for finding desired mathematics topics and resources.

The Math League
http://www.mathleague.com/
The Math League provides math resources and helps with various math topics.

Mathematical Animation Gallery
http://mathserv.math.sfu.ca/Animations/animations.html
The Mathematical Animation Gallery contains QuickTime and MPEG movies of mathematical animations.

Mathematical Journey
http://nunic.nu.edu/~jchao/math/bc3000.html
Mathematical Journey contains many interesting topics related to the history of math, including numeral systems, mathematical games, magic squares, pi, and mathematicians.

Montessori Math Album Index
http://www.missouri.edu/~c575812/mts/math/_link.htm
This site offers Montessori lesson plans for a variety of math topics.

National Council of Teachers of Mathematics
http://www.nctm.org/
This is the official Web site of the National Council of Teachers of Mathematics (NCTM). It offers information about mathematics standards, upcoming events, NCTM products, and so on.

Pharaoh's Heart Resources
http://www.teleport.com/~ddonahue/phresour.html
This Web site provides links to information about Babylonian and Egyptian mathematics.

POPMathematics
http://archives.math.utk.edu/popmath.html
POPMathematics is another great site for locating miscellaneous math topics, finding activities, and accessing links to other math resources.

The Prime Page
http://www.utm.edu/research/primes/
The Prime Page provides information about prime numbers, including lists, factorizations, software programs, and frequently asked questions.

SAMI
http://www.learner.org/content/k12/sami/SAMI-home.shtml
Funded by the Annenberg/CPB Math and Science Project, this Web site provides many resources and links for science and math teachers.

SAT Skill Lessons
http://www.testprep.com/satmenu.html
This Web site provides online lessons and interactive quizzes for both math and verbal skills.

S.O.S. Mathematics
http://www.math.utep.edu/sosmath/
S.O.S. Mathematics helps students review math concepts in several areas, including algebra, trigonometry, and calculus.

Tessellation Tutorials
http://forum.swarthmore.edu/sum95/suzanne/tess.intro.html
This section of the Math Forum offers online templates, lesson plans, and information about tessellations.

ThinkQuest
http://tqd.advanced.org/
ThinkQuest provides many online mathematics activities. It also provides excellent activities for other subject areas.

Women Mathematicians
http://www.scottlan.edu/lriddle/women/alpha.htm
This site provides an index of biographies of women mathematicians.

E-MAIL EXCHANGES

Mathematics becomes more meaningful as students discover how it relates to everyday life, personal interests, and cultures. The following e-mail exchanges give students opportunities to apply mathematics and communicate mathematical ideas in real-world situations.

Comparative Shopping

Students communicate with other students in the United States and identify common brands of household items (for example, toothpaste, soap, detergent, food products). Students agree on a list of items to compare prices and visit three major grocery stores in their area. They analyze their own findings and compare them with their e-mail buddies. Students discuss why some prices are lower or higher in certain areas. Students create charts and graphs to display their findings and identify the locations of their e-mail buddies (along with a summary of their comparative findings) on a class map.

Mathemagic

Students exchange mathemagical math problems and challenge their e-mail buddies to explain how or why they work. Students may create a mathemagical Web site of their challenges and explanations.

Example:

Magician:	Think of a card.
Spectator:	Thinks of Jack of Hearts
Magician:	Multiply the value of your card by 2. An ace equals 1, a two equals 2, and so on. A jack equals 11, a queen equals 12, and a king equals 13.
Spectator:	11 x 2 = 22
Magician:	Add 1 to your total, then multiply that total by 5.
Spectator:	(22 + 1) x 5 = 115
Magician:	If your card is a club, add 6 to the total. If your card is a heart, add 7 to the total. If your card is a spade, add 8 to the total. If your card is a diamond, add 9 to the total.
Spectator:	115 + 7 = 122
Magician:	What is your total?
Spectator:	122.
Magician:	You picked the Jack of Hearts.
Solution:	The one's place represents the card's suit: Subtract 1 from the remaining digit(s) to figure out the value of the card. An ace = 1, a deuce = 2, etc. A jack = 11, a queen = 12, and a king = 13.

1 = club

2 = heart

3 = spade

4 = diamond

Total is 122; 12–1 = 11; 2 = hearts

Grade Levels	Road Trip	Research Level
4-8		Basic

Educational Goals

To access and apply the AutoPilot mapping system

To calculate and compare distance and time between two U.S. cities

Procedure

Using a large screen monitor or projection system, introduce students to the AutoPilot mapping system. Demonstrate several sample searches. Ask students how this tool may assist them or their parents. Provide students with an opportunity to explore the AutoPilot and practice real-world math skills by assigning the Road Trip activity. Students may work in pairs to complete the activity.

Resources

AutoPilot (http://www.freetrip.com/)

Extension Activities

1. Students write about which trip they would rather take and if they would choose the direct route or scenic route. Students explain their choices.

2. Students select their own cities to compare and answer the given questions.

3. Students select cities for other students to compare and create their own questions to accompany their cities.

4. Students compare the AutoPilot's data with data from other online and offline resources and report any differences among the sources' calculated miles and times. Students report on each source's options, also, and which resource they prefer and why. Additional online sources include:

   How Far Is It? (http://www.indo.com/distance/)

   Cybermaps (http://www.delorme.com/cybermaps/cyberrouter.htm)

   Maps on Us (http://www.mapsonus.com/)

Road Trip

Greetings, cross-country adventurers! Use AutoPilot (http://www.freetrip.com/) to calculate the distance and time between the following cities. Use the direct route, then choose the scenic route. Do not choose the hotel, restaurant, or points-of-interest options. Choose "No Preferences" for Tunnels/Ferries. Answer the questions that follow each set of cities.

Origination	Destination	Direct		Scenic	
		Miles	**Time**	**Miles**	**Time**
Anaheim, CA	Orlando, FL				

How many more miles is the scenic route than the direct route? _____ miles

What is the difference between the time it takes to drive the scenic route and the time it takes to drive the direct route? _____ hours _____ minutes

Using the direct route, how many days would it take you to reach Orlando if you drove for six hours a day? What if you took the scenic route?

Direct = _____ days   Scenic = _____ days

Origination	Destination	Direct		Scenic	
		Miles	**Time**	**Miles**	**Time**
Rock Hill, SC	Tempe, AZ				

How many more miles is the scenic route than the direct route? _____ miles

What is the difference between the time it takes to drive the scenic route and the time it takes to drive the direct route? _____ hours _____ minutes

Using the direct route, how many days would it take you to reach Orlando if you drove for six hours a day? What if you took the scenic route?

Direct = _____ days   Scenic = _____ days

Map one of the above trips and calculate how much you would need for gasoline if your car got 25 miles to the gallon and the average price of gasoline was $1.50.

Grade Levels	Making	Research Level
4-12	Allowance$	Original

Educational Goals

To chart and compare the average allowance among students in the United States

To analyze and evaluate averages related to real-world information

To determine the mode allowance and common chores among students in the United States

Procedure

Depending on the ability level of your students, divide them into small groups or conduct this activity as a whole class. Contact same grade-level students in other states (see chapter 3) and invite them to participate in a survey designed to gather information about students' allowances. Classes submit a list of students' allowances paired with the jobs required to earn the allowance. Your class calculates and compares the average allowance of classes throughout the U.S. Use the Making Allowance$ activity sheet as a follow-up to the students' research.

Resources

See chapter 3 for contacting other students and teachers.

Extension Activities

1. Students conduct the same survey with other classes throughout the U.S. and compare their results.

2. Students conduct the same survey with younger or older students and compare their results.

3. Student groups find and report on newspaper articles or other news sources related to equal pay for equal work, why certain items are more expensive in certain places, and so on.

4. Students write about how they manage the money they earn, e.g., what they spend it on, whether they have a savings account, if they have ever been in debt, and so on.

5. Student groups research, compare, and chart the salaries and requirements of different occupations.

6. Students perform additional statistical calculations with the data.

Making Allowance$

1. Place the average allowance of the contacted classes in the appropriate states.

2. Which state's class had the highest allowance? _____

3. Which state's class had the highest average allowance? _____

4. What are the most common chores that kids perform for their allowance? _____

   _____

5. What is the most common allowance? _____

6. Is the average allowance of the students in your classroom more or less than the average allowance of students in the classrooms in other states? Why? (Answer on the back of this sheet)

7. How could you determine what the average allowance is for students in the entire state of Texas? (Answer on the back of this sheet)

Bonus Activities

   • List what you consider to be a fair allowance for a given set of chores.

   • Do you think kids should earn an allowance? Why or why not?

Currency Exchange

Objectives

To recognize, compare, and become aware of currencies throughout the world

To work cooperatively to research, track, present, and compare currency exchange rates

Grade Levels: 4-8   **Final Product:** Journals and graphs

Internet Resources

Currency Converter (http://www.oanda.com/cgi-bin/ncc)

Foreign Exchange Rates (http://www.dna.lth.se/cgi-bin/kurt/rates)

Universal Currency Converter (http://www.xe.net/currency/)

Procedure

1. If possible, display a variety of currency for students to examine. Explain that many countries have unique currencies and some money is actually worth more than others. Have students brainstorm why this is so and how this relates to inflation and the country's economy.

2. Explain how currency rates are constantly changing. To explore this, student pairs track, record, and compare the values of several countries' currencies in relation to the U.S. dollar. Each pair should design a graph of currency values, with countries represented by a color code. Students record in a journal the daily values of each currency (average based on the variety of sources), discrepancies in the data from various sources, and comparisons among the countries.

3. Provide students with the Internet addresses listed in Internet Resources. Let students choose from the following countries (three countries per pair):

Argentina	Canada	ECU	Greece
Australia	Chile	Ecuador	Hong Kong
Austria	China	Egypt	Hungary
Belgium	Colombia	Finland	India
Brazil	Czech Republic	France	Indonesia
Britain	Denmark	Germany	Iran

Currency Exchange (cont.)

Procedure (cont.)

Ireland	Netherlands	Russia	Switzerland
Israel	New Zealand	Saudi Arabia	Taiwan
Italy	Norway	Singapore	Thailand
Japan	Pakistan	Slovak Republic	Turkey
Jordan	Peru	South Africa	U.A.E.
Lebanon	Philippines	South Korea	Uruguay
Malaysia	Poland	Spain	Venezuela
Mexico	Portugal	Sweden	

4. Ensure all of the countries are chosen. Students record and evaluate information each day for a month. At the end of the month, students discuss patterns they observed and other information about their countries' currencies.

5. As a class, construct a large graph to compare currencies from all of the countries. Students discuss their findings. Where would a U.S. dollar be worth the most? Where would the dollar be worth the least? Where did the most drastic changes occur? The least? Which, if any, types of currency appear to be getting stronger? Weaker? Why do they think these changes are occurring?

Extension Activities

1. Students research economic policies and current events of their countries.

2. Students investigate how and why communities within the U.S. are establishing their own currencies. See Local Currency Sites and Resources (http://www.prairienet.org/community/religion/idf/currency.html). Students contact these communities for sample bills or coins.

3. Students research the history of money from countries around the world. Students e-mail people to learn more or to receive samples of currency. (See chapter 3 for instructions about e-mail.)

4. Students compare the metals used to make coins from various countries.

5. Help students create a survey about yearly incomes, student allowances, and prices to distribute to students on e-mail in other countries. Collect the information and convert it to U.S. dollars based on current exchange rates.

Fast Food Facts and Figures

Objectives

To work cooperatively to research, chart, calculate, and compare nutritional information among fast food restaurants

To identify how mathematics can help students make healthy food choices

Grade Levels: 4-12   **Final Product:** Written report

Internet Resources

Wendy's Hamburgers (http://www.wendys.com/)

Jack in the Box (http://www.jackinthebox.com/)

McDonald's (http://www.mcdonalds.com/k_welcome)

Burger King (http://www.bk.com/)

Fast Food Calorie Counter (http://www.uiuc.edu/departments/mckinley/health-info/hlthpro/fastfood.html)

Procedure

1. As a class, list students' favorite fast food restaurants and food items. Ask what they consider to be healthy food choices and unhealthy food choices. Discuss reasons why people may make unhealthy food choices.

2. Ask how mathematics can help people make healthy food choices. See the Fast Food Calorie Counter (http://www.uiuc.edu/departments/mckinley/health-info/hlthpro/fastfood.html) and other health-related sites (see chapter 6 for more information).

3. Place students into cooperative groups to research and compare the nutritional information of fast food products served at Wendy's, Jack in the Box, McDonald's, Burger King, and other fast food restaurants of their choice. Student groups calculate and chart the calories, fat, salt, etc., of various food combinations for breakfast, lunch, and dinner and identify the most and least healthy combinations. Student groups organize their findings and charts into a written report. Students share their reports and make recommendations about eating at fast food restaurants based on their findings.

Fast Food Facts and Figures (cont.)

Extension Activities

1. Based on their Fast Food Facts and Figures research, students create word problems to share with other students. For example, "If Niles ate five Big Macs, how many calories did he consume?"

2. Students conduct research on the history of Wendy's, Burger King, Jack in the Box, or McDonald's and present their findings in a newsletter with math-related follow-up questions. For example, "How many years have passed since the first McDonald's restaurant opened?" Students read each other's newsletters and solve the newsletters' math questions.

3. Student groups research, chart, and compare the cost of purchasing different franchises (see the Franchise Handbook at http://www.franchise1.com/franchise.html). As a class, students develop a survey to e-mail to selected franchise companies and owners. Students analyze, compare, chart, and discuss the survey results.

4. Students conduct additional research on nutrition and physical fitness, emphasizing how the mathematics of nutrition and physical fitness can help people stay healthy. See the following resources:

    Food Safety and Nutrition Information (http://ificinfo.health.org/infofsn.htm)

    Food and Nutrition Information Center (http://www.nalusda.gov/fnic/)

    Healthfinder (http://www.healthfinder.gov/)

Language Arts Resources and Activities

Before the existence of the World Wide Web, Mrs. Schmitgall's class used e-mail to exchange stories, poetry, and book reviews with people in other states and countries. Her students seemed more conscientious about their writing when they knew that other people—peers, senior citizens, and persons in the armed forces—were going to review their work. Through e-mail exchanges, Mrs. Schmitgall's students learned more about their key pals' cultures, locations, likes, and dislikes.

Mrs. Schmitgall and her students already thought of the Internet as a window to the world, but now, with the ability to browse the Web, the window opened onto pictures and sounds as well as words. Mrs. Schmitgall's students continued their e-mail connections, but they also began to post their stories, poetry, and art to children's Web sites. Mrs. Schmitgall's students also read other students' writing, extended their e-mail connections, downloaded and examined versions of Aesop's fables and other stories, contacted children's authors, and used online library resources.

To Mrs. Schmitgall, the Internet was as natural a tool as pencil and paper were to other teachers. Mrs. Schmitgall cringed at the thought of not having Internet access. She compared the Internet to an endless library of information and resources. "Not having access to it would be like limiting yourself to one book," she said. "Why would anyone put a limit on knowledge?"

The Internet is an ideal medium for teaching students about the importance of communication, reading, and writing skills and for making learning personally relevant. Students can interact with stories, access and share information about their favorite books and authors, contact online experts, and share their work. The Internet provides many outlets and audiences for students' writing through e-mail exchanges and Web sites that post student writing.

In addition, the Internet provides access to many books, magazines, and other electronic texts (e-texts) that can be used to enhance writing and literature units. Besides bringing a world of resources into the classroom, e-texts can help students with specific difficulties, for example, text can be downloaded and enlarged with a word processor for visually impaired students or read by a speech synthesizer for students who have difficulty processing the written word. E-texts also provide access to reference works and other resources that may be unavailable in the school library media center.

This chapter features Web sites and pages that cover folktales, fables, and fairy tales; literary classics; children's authors and book characters; creative writing and poetry; readers theatre and drama; grammar and writing ideas; and writing and reference tools. For each topic, the chapter provides one or two instructional ideas for two or more sites. These ideas and skills are not comprehensive; instead, they serve as starting points for exploration and activities. Following the highlighted sites is a list of other sites related to the topic; these sites are briefly described. The chapter ends with a list of general language arts sites and e-mail activities.

Note: Each site's current URL is given, but, because the Internet is extremely dynamic, addresses and paths may change.

CHILDREN'S AUTHORS AND BOOK CHARACTERS

Children's books are gifts to and from the imagination. Their authors are wizards of words, captivators of the heart, and creators of unforgettable characters. The Internet can contribute to the joy and wonder of children's books by enabling students to learn more about authors and the characters they create. Many children's book publishers post biographies of authors, and many authors have their own Web pages. Students can research and interact with authors online, contact book publishers, and learn more about writing children's books.

Lewis Carroll Home Page
http://www.lewiscarroll.org/carroll.html

The Lewis Carroll Home Page provides useful information about Lewis Carroll, including links to reference materials, online texts, photographs and graphics, online experts, discussion boards, and more.

LEWIS CARROLL Home Page

Welcome to the Lewis Carroll home page. We hope to provide useful information for the Carroll enthusiast as well as the novice and all those in between. Cyberspace seems a suitable home for information regarding a man who didn't want his true identity linked to his best work.

What follows is a guide to Lewis Carroll resources and documents on-line and in print.

Life what is it but a dream?

1998 is the centenary of Carroll's death and what I'd like to see is a major web exhibition. I invite individuals and companies to contribute content to this extravaganza. Feel free to use Carroll as a vehicle to show off your talent, your fancy web tools, or just do it for good will. I have received some excellent items for the exhibit. Now what I need is a snappy entry page. Come on you Carrollian designers, come up with some whiz bang format. Otherwise it will just be another set of links. I know you're out there. Think Carrollian + 100!

Lewis Carroll home page.

Character Study

Student groups select a character from one of the many works of Lewis Carroll and investigate the character's history, illustrated art forms (e.g., Tenniel and Disney), influence on pop culture, trivia notes, and so on. Students use a variety of online and off-line sources, using the Lewis Carroll Home Page as a starting point for their research (see Graphics and Carroll in the Popular Culture). Students take notes, evaluate and compare their findings, and create a bibliography of their resources. In addition to a written report, student groups create a model or poster of their characters and present their findings to the class.

Information skills: Locate, organize, evaluate, and synthesize information from a variety of sources; read for significant details and concepts; compare and record information; and present findings through oral, visual, and written forms of communication.

Charles Lutwidge Dodgson

Student groups create a multimedia biography of the life and work of Lewis Carroll. Students use a variety of online and off-line sources, using the Lewis Carroll Home Page as a starting point for their research. Students take notes and create a bibliography of their resources. Students evaluate and compare information from various sources, and create outlines, flowcharts, and storyboards for their projects. Final projects are shared with the class. Questions can be submitted to online experts. (Choose Contacts on the main menu to contact experts.)

Information skills: Locate, organize, evaluate, and synthesize information for a specific topic from a variety of sources; record and analyze data; effectively organize information into flowcharts and storyboards; seek information from professionals; integrate text with images, videos, and sound clips in a meaningful manner.

Snoopy's Doghouse
http://www.unitedmedia.com/comics/peanuts/

Snoopy's Doghouse provides information about the Peanuts gang and Charles M. Shultz. It also provides information about galleries and museums hosting the Peanuts gang, television listings for Peanuts shows, and other topics related to this popular comic strip.

Character Analysis

Students use Snoopy's Doghouse and other online and off-line sources to research their favorite Peanuts character. They then create a book about the character. In addition to background information and the character's profile, books should include illustrations showing how the character's appearance has changed over time. Students should also explain why the character is their favorite. As a follow-up activity, students create a 3-D model of their character.

Information skills: Locate, organize, evaluate, and synthesize information from a variety of sources; compare and record information; present findings through visual and written forms of communication.

Yahoo: Children's Authors
http://www.yahoo.com/Arts/Humanities/Literature/Genres/Children_s/Authors/

Yahoo, one of the most popular Web guides on the Internet, provides an extensive list of links to children's authors. More information about literature can be accessed through Yahoo at **http://www.yahoo.com/Arts/Humanities/Literature**.

Who Wrote This?

Students select three authors of children's books and compare and contrast the authors' backgrounds, story themes and characters, writing tips, and other topics of interest. Students describe the similarities and differences among the writers and share their conclusions with the class. (Additional author information can be found on The Big Busy House, Penguin USA, and Read Along Express.

Information skills: Locate, organize, and evaluate information from a variety of sources; read for significant details and concepts; analyze, compare, synthesize, and record information; communicate findings.

Additional Sites for Children's Authors and Book Characters

The Big Busy House
http://www.harperchildrens.com/index.htm

Sponsored by HarperCollins, this site features information about HarperCollins children's authors and illustrators, how a book is made, and various word games.

Invite an Author to Your School
http://www.snowcrest.net/kidpower/authors.html

This Web site provides a list of children's authors who visit schools. Information about how to contact and invite an author to your school is also available. Links to biographical information are provided.

The Online Mystery Network
http://www.mysterynet.com

The Online Mystery Network provides information about the history of mysteries; mystery genres, authors, and characters; and more.

Penguin USA
http://www.butterfly.net/usa/

Sponsored by Penguin Books, this Web site provides information about Penguin books and authors. Online stories, a Winnie-the-Pooh page, and other resources are available.

Read Along Express
http://www.berkley.com/putnam/kids/index.html

Sponsored by Putnam Berkley Group, this Web site features Putnam book titles and biographies of Putnam authors. A "toy box" option features pictures to color, things to make, and other options. The Stories for all Season option categorizes Putnam stories by theme. Additional literature-related links are available also.

Seussville
http://www.randomhouse.com/seussville/

Seussville, sponsored by Random House (**http://www.randomhouse.com**), offers an assortment of online and off-line activities that feature the Cat in the Hat.

CREATIVE WRITING AND POETRY

Many Internet sites invite and display student writing; others offer feedback or allow students to join discussion rooms devoted to writing. In addition, several author pages provide tips and describe the author's personal experiences in writing.

American Verse Project
http://www.hti.umich.edu/english/amverse/

The American Verse Project is a collaborative project involving the University of Michigan Humanities Text Initiative (HTI) and the University of Michigan Press. It contains a searchable archive of American poetry prior to 1920. Students can perform a simple search (one word or phrase) or Boolean searches.

Favorite Poet

Using a variety of online and off-line resources, students present a biography and sample works of a selected American poet from the nineteenth century. Students take notes, evaluate and compare their findings, and create a bibliography of their resources. Final reports are presented to the class using a presentation tool such as Microsoft PowerPoint or Aldus Persuasion. From the main menu, choose The HTI's Bibliography to American Poetry to search for poets or Simple Search to locate more information about a particular poet.

Information skills: Learn techniques for using electronic media to locate, organize, evaluate, and synthesize information from a variety of sources; record and analyze data; and assemble and communicate information using a presentation tool.

Winter Poems

Students examine and compare poems about winter. Using the Simple Search option, students enter the keyword *winter* to start the search. Students work in teams to view or download several poems. Students examine and compare the poems' tone, mood, and theme, then summarize and share their findings. As a follow-up activity, students write poems about winter and explain why they chose a particular tone, mood, or theme. Students submit their poems to Positively Poetry (see page 143). This activity can be done with other seasons.

Information skills: Conduct searches using the Internet; read for significant details and concepts; compare, analyze, and summarize information.

The Young Writers Club
http://www.cs.bilkent.edu.tr/~david/derya/ywc.html

The Young Writers Club accepts student stories, poems, story starters, and articles for publication. It also posts student book reviews, movie reviews, research projects, suggested activities, and ongoing stories (called storybooks). The site features a word of the week, an online magazine, key pal connections, many writing topics and activities, and links to related resources. Many kids communicate here.

Seven Line Poem

Students follow the guidelines in "For all poetry buffs..." and submit their own poem. (To access the guidelines, select Activities from the main menu.) Students read and critique some of the posted poems and share their poems with the class.

Information skills: Select and apply information; read for significant details.

Young Writers Clubhouse page.

Story Outcomes

Students contribute to a storybook of their choice biweekly for two weeks. Students keep track of the storybook's progress, recording the number of entries before and after each of their own entries. Students print and create an ending for the storybook. Students put the story into book format, including illustrations and author credits. Students discuss the development of the storybook, what they dislike and like about it, and what they would have done differently. (Select Storybooks from the main menu.)

Information skills: Read for significant details and concepts; record and analyze information; assemble information in a meaningful manner.

Young Writer's Clubhouse
http://www.realkids.com/club.htm

The Young Writer's Clubhouse features information about famous "young authors," keys to writing success, frequently asked questions, an opportunity to e-mail questions to and chat with a children's book author, an online critique group, teacher resources and links, a story room, writer's links, and more.

Story Critique

Students participate in the Story Critique Group by submitting their own stories and by commenting about other writers' stories. Before beginning this activity, be sure students read and agree to abide by the Critique Group Member Agreement.

Information skills: Select and apply information and effectively communicate information.

Submitting a Manuscript

Students learn about the publishing process by following the guidelines presented in Keys to Writing Success (choose the key icon or enter **http://www.realkids.com/keys.htm**). Students contact a publisher (see Children's Publishers on the Internet at **http://www.ucalgary.ca/~dkbrown/ publish.html**), obtain writer's guidelines, and learn about and write a query letter based on a story they have written or plan to write. In addition, students create a final report that includes writing tips and the steps for submitting a story. Students use a variety of online and off-line resources for their final report and include a bibliography.

Information skills: Select and apply information, read for significant details and concepts, seek information from professionals, locate information from a variety of sources, and communicate information in a meaningful manner.

Additional Sites for Creative Writing and Poetry

Creative Writing for Kids
http://childrenwriting.miningco.com/

One of the many links sponsored by the Mining Company (**http://www.miningco.com/**), Creative Writing for Kids features a variety of writing links. Sites are frequently updated. Previously featured sites are archived.

A Handbook of Terms for Discussing Poetry
http://www.cc.emory.edu/ENGLISH/classes/Handbook/Handbook.html

A Handbook of Terms for Discussing Poetry offers information about figurative language, language and meaning, genres, rhythm and meter, and stanzas and verse forms.

Inkspot
http://www.inkspot.com/

Inkspot offers a variety of writing resources for teachers and students. Topics include genres, authors, basic information about writing, discussion forums and chat rooms, and information and links for young writers. It also provides links to sources that solicit stories, articles, poetry, and other types of writing from students.

KidNews
http://www.vsa.cape.com/~powens/Kidnews3.html

> KidNews publishes work by children, including stories, poetry, sports news, and school newspapers. It features writing forums for just about every topic. In addition, it posts students' book reviews and key pal requests, provides a forum for teachers and parents, and provides links to additional resources.

Kidpub
http://www.kidpub.org/

> Kidpub publishes stories by young people from all over the world. In addition, Kidpub provides reader statistics, key pals, and interesting writing activities. KidStuff (**http://www.KidStuff.org/index.html**) publishes students' stories and poems also.

Positively Poetry
http://advicom.net/~e-media/kv/poetry1.html

> Positively Poetry publishes poetry by children from all over the world. Also see Poetry Pals (**http://www.geocities.com/EnchantedForest/5165/**).

FOLKTALES, FABLES, AND FAIRY TALES

> The Internet can retrieve folktales, fables, and fairy tales from all over the world. Students can read traditional tales or read the work of other students. Students can also submit their own stories for publication on the Web.

Aesop & Me
http://i-site.on.ca/Isite/Education/Aesop/

> Aesop & Me is one of several activities available on the I-Site on Canada Web site. I-Site on Canada is based on the premise that it takes three—the contributor, the publisher (I-Site), and the reader—to make the Internet work. It hosts a variety of activities that encourage student participation and contribution. For example, at Book Nook, students can read other students' book reviews and post their own; Jaunts encourages students to submit a picture of and a paragraph about hometown welcome signs; and Aesop & Me requests that students submit original fables. The site also discusses several international projects, including KidoPedia, which allows students to create an international encyclopedia. To access these options, click on the Home Page button on the Aesop & Me page.

Aesop's Fables

Students compare various versions of Aesop's fables by downloading versions from Aesop & Me and Wiretap (**http://wiretap.area.com/**) and by locating print versions, retold versions, illustrated editions, and video and audio adaptations in the library media center and the public library. Students create a Venn diagram to compare the Paperless Edition (from Wiretap, choose Books online) and the fables available on Aesop & Me, Townsend translation. Students may note that the Townsend translation is more difficult to read and interpret than the

Paperless Edition. Students create additional Venn diagrams to compare other versions of Aesop's fables to the Paperless Edition or the Townsend translation. Students identify the moral of each fable. As a follow-up activity, students write their own fables (based on the version they most prefer, Paperless or Townsend) and submit them to Aesop & Me.

Information skills: Locate, organize, and compare information from a variety of sources; read for significant details and concepts; organize information using a Venn diagram; make inferences; communicate information.

A Man Called Aesop

Students research and write a report about Aesop using a variety of online and off-line sources. Students take notes, evaluate and compare their findings, and create a bibliography of their resources. Information about Aesop is available from the Aesop & Me main menu. Additional Aesop Web sites include Aesop's Reader's Book Guide (**http://www.mmit.com/bookguide/aesop.html**) and Aesop's Fables on the Fly (**http://www.pacific.net/%7Ejohnr/aesop/**).

Information skills: Locate, organize, and evaluate information from a variety of sources; analyze, synthesize, and record information; assemble information in a meaningful manner.

Faerie Lore and Literature
http://faeryland.tamu-commerce.edu/~earendil/faerie/faerie.html

This site features fairy stories, poems, and anecdotes from all over the world. It categorizes the stories by events or other defining characteristics (e.g., changelings, music, dancing, magic). It also includes many articles relating to the origins of and beliefs in fairies, as well as links to legends, myths, and fairy tales.

Changelings

Students compare and contrast three changeling stories from different cultures (e.g., Ireland, Germany, and Scotland) and share their findings. See also Wonder: Folk and Fairy Tales From Around the World (**http://darsie.ucdavis.edu/tales/**). As a follow-up, students write changeling stories for a class book. Changeling stories are available from the main menu; choose Fairy Stories and Anecdotes From All Over the World.

Information skills: Locate and compare information; read for significant details and concepts; communicate information in a meaningful manner.

Fairy Origins

Students research various sources to discover the origins of fairies in different cultures. Findings are described in a fairy book with illustrations and text. Students investigate the folklore and other related sources on the Faerie Lore and Literature home page, as well as examine additional online (see Fairy Tale Origin and Evolution at **http://easyweb.easynet.co.uk/~cdaae/fairy/**) and off-line sources. Students keep notes and create a bibliography of their sources.

thekids home page.

Information skills: Locate, organize, evaluate, and synthesize information from a variety of sources; record and analyze data; present findings through visual and written forms of communication.

thekids.com
http://www.thekids.com

This Web site offers illustrated stories from around the world, discussion rooms, and information for parents. Coloring pages for the stories are also available, and students can submit their own stories for others to read.

My Own Tale

Students read and discuss fables and submit their own fable for publication. Online fables can be accessed by choosing Tales to Tell from the main menu, and then selecting Fables & Animal Stories. Choose Kids' Stuff from the main menu, followed by Sound Off! to submit a story.

Information skills: Locate and evaluate information; read for significant details and concepts; present information for Web publication.

Stories from Everywhere

Students read stories from various cultures and regions to compare characters, settings, problems, and outcomes. Students mark the locations of the cultures and regions on a class map and create a class chart that categorizes the stories by common themes or elements. (To access the stories, choose Tales to Tell from the main menu, then choose Stories From Everywhere.)

Also see Tales of Wonder: Folk and Fairy Tales From Around the World (**http://darsie.ucdavis.edu/tales/**) and Faerie Lore and Literature (**http://tamu-commerce.edu/~earendil/faerie/faerie.html**).

Information skills: Locate, compare, analyze, and categorize information; read for significant details and concepts; find locations on a map.

Additional Sites for Folktales, Fables, and Fairy Tales

Fairy Tale Origin and Evolution
http://easyweb.easynet.co.uk/~cdaae/fairy/

This is an excellent site for learning more about the origins and meaning of fairy tales, as well as their authors and various versions.

Links to Fairy Tales, Stories, Myths and Legends
http://www.ifi.uio.no/~reierp/bat/stories.html

This Web site provides many links to fairy tales, storytelling, and other related resources.

Realistic Wonder Society
http://www.wondersociety.com

The Realistic Wonder Society features online fables and fairy tales, and it provides opportunities for readers to share their thoughts about the stories.

Story Sources on the Internet: Folktales and Myths
http://users.aol.com/storypage/sources.htm

This is a large collection of links to stories and other resources related to folktales and myths.

Tales of Wonder: Folk and Fairy Tales From Around the World
http://darsie.ucdavis.edu/tales/

This Web site contains a large collection of stories from many parts of the world, including Africa, India, China, Ireland, Scandinavia, Russia, and Siberia. Additional links to other fairy tale resources are provided.

GRAMMAR AND MORE WRITING IDEAS

The Internet provides students with many writing opportunities. In addition to traditional e-mail, many Web sites provide interactive story starters, grammar instruction, and other writing opportunities.

The Grammar Lady
http://www.grammarlady.com/

The Grammar Lady provides English grammar instruction, answers to frequently asked questions, and an online expert who provides answers to students' questions.

Spelling Rules

Students brainstorm spelling rules (plurals, prefixes and suffixes, double final consonants, and other rules) and compare them with the spelling rules presented by The Grammar Lady and other sources. Students e-mail questions to The Grammar Lady. Students compile their research into a spelling handbook and devise methods to help them remember the rules. (Choose English Grammar from the main menu, then select Spelling Rules.)

Informational skills: Brainstorm and specify required information for a particular topic; seek information from professionals; compare and evaluate information; assemble information in a meaningful format.

Pitsco's Ask an Expert
http://www.askanexpert.com/askanexpert/

Pitsco's Ask an Expert is a directory of links to people who have volunteered their time to answer questions. It features links to more than 300 Web sites of experts, and it can be used across the curriculum. Experts are divided into 12 categories, including Science/Technology, Career/Industry, Health, Internet/Computers, Recreation/Entertainment, Education/Personal Development, International/Cultural, Resources, Money/Business, Fine Arts, Law, and Religion. Pitsco's Ask an Expert offers students the opportunity to organize their questions and write to online experts about specific careers and other topics for research reports. Choose Categories from the main menu or use the Web site's search engine to locate experts.

Similarities and Differences

Students select five online experts from different fields and submit an interest survey designed by the class. The survey may ask: How much schooling have you had? Do you work for yourself? Do you believe science can make the world a better place to live? Why did you choose your profession? Each student contacts different experts. Students analyze their results, looking for similarities and differences among the responses. Students create a chart and write a report that explains their findings. Students make a class chart of all of their findings and discuss the results in terms of similarities and differences in interests of people in the same field, different fields, and as a whole group. Before gathering the data, students may be asked to list what they think are the interests of people in a particular field. For example, they may guess that people in the writing field prefer cats, like to read, and enjoy gourmet meals. Students can explain their guesses, then compare their predictions or stereotypical views with the survey results.

Information skills: Seek information from professionals; develop and administer a survey; interpret survey results; record, analyze, and compare data; assemble and communicate information in a meaningful manner.

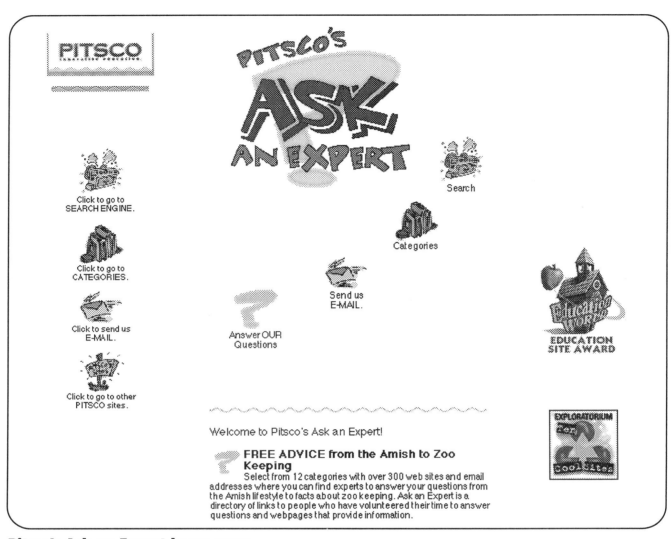

Pitsco's Ask an Expert home page.

Wacky Web Tales
http://www.hmco.com/school/tales/

Sponsored by the Houghton Mifflin Company, Wacky Web Tales provides many online tales that require students' input. Students choose a tale and fill in a form that requests various words and parts of speech (e.g., friend's name, noun). Students receive a personalized story or anecdote. Students may submit their own wacky tale.

A Tale of My Own

Students write a wacky tale and submit it to Wacky Web Tales. Students create a wacky tale by writing a brief story with blanks in place of keywords (like the main character's name) with descriptions of what kind of word goes in the blank (e.g., friend's name or plural noun). Find the submission procedures by selecting Instructions under Choose one of YOUR tales.

Information skills: Locate and apply information; read for significant details and concepts; publish information on the Web.

Additional Sites for Grammar and More Writing Ideas

Care Quest
http://www.worldkids.net/CareQuest/careqst.htm

Care Quest provides several ongoing writing projects for children, including writing letters to children in hospitals and to the elderly.

Diary Project
http://www.well.com/user/diary/

The Diary Project allows middle and high school students to share their personal thoughts and feelings, ask questions, and find answers about growing up.

An Elementary Grammar
http://wwebl.hiway.co.uk/ei/intro.html

This Web site provides information about English grammar. It includes more than 20 topics, such as Nouns, Comparisons of Adjectives, and the Past Continuous Tense.

Grammar Safari
http://deil.lang.uiuc.edu/web.pages/grammarsafari.html

This Web site provides grammar activities that can be printed out or completed online.

Online English Grammar
http://www.edunet.com/english/grammar/index.html

This Web site provides English grammar instruction, answers to frequently asked questions, and online experts who answer students' grammar questions. In addition, it provides English-language practice pages, an audio alphabet, and links to other resources. This is an excellent source for English as a Second Language (ESL).

Online Writing Lab
http://owl.english.purdue.edu/

Sponsored by Purdue University, this site provides many links for writers and writing teachers.

LITERATURE CLASSICS

Literature sites on the Internet provide online books and other e-texts, discussion groups, author information, and related links.

The Complete Works of William Shakespeare
http://the-tech.mit.edu/Shakespeare/works.html

The Complete Works of William Shakespeare features full-text versions of Shakespeare's plays, a discussion area, links to additional Shakespeare resources, and more. The list of plays can be viewed chronologically, by category, or in alphabetical order. Hypertext links provide definitions of unfamiliar words.

Tragedy for Two

Students download, read, and compare two of Shakespeare's tragedies and discuss the symbolism, characterization, conflicts, and universal applications. Students use the discussion area to submit their conclusions and to survey other people's thoughts about the plays. They then compare their own conclusions to the survey results. Students present their findings to the class.

Information skills: Locate and compare information; read for significant details and concepts; seek information from others; communicate information in a meaningful manner.

Who Was This Man, William Shakespeare?

Students use the Complete Works of William Shakespeare and other online and off-line resources to research the life and work of William Shakespeare. Students can submit questions to the discussion area and to the author of the Web site. Students take notes, evaluate and compare their findings, and create a bibliography of resources. Students submit findings in a written or multimedia format. Links to additional Shakespeare Web sites are available on the main menu.

Information skills: Locate, organize, and evaluate information from a variety of sources; analyze, synthesize, and record information; seek information from professionals; assemble information in a meaningful manner.

Perspectives in American Literature (PAL): A Research and Reference Guide
http://www.csustan.edu/english/reuben/pal/table.html

Perspectives in American Literature is an outstanding resource for learning more about American literature and authors. Developed by Dr. Paul P. Reuben at California State University at Stanislaus, PAL is an ongoing project that offers information about various time periods, authors, stories, and so on. It also includes ideas for writing assignments, study questions, and research topics.

Two Real

Students compare and contrast the works of two authors from the late nineteenth-century Realism period. Students use a variety of online and off-line resources, take notes, evaluate and compare their findings, and create a bibli-

The Complete Works of William Shakespeare

Welcome to the Web's first edition of the Complete Works of William Shakespeare.

The original electronic source for this server is the Complete Moby(tm) Shakespeare, which is freely available online. There may be differences between a copy of a play that you happen to be familiar with and the one of this server. Don't worry, this is a very common phenomenon.

Contents

- Shakespeare discussion area
- Search the complete works
- Shakespeare resources on the Internet
- What's new on this sever
- A chronological listing of plays, and an alphabetical listing
- Frequently asked questions about this server
- Bartlett's familiar Shakespearean quotations
- About the glossary

Comedy	History	Tragedy	Poetry
All's Well That Ends Well	Henry IV, part 1	Anthony and Cleopatra	The Sonnets
As You Like It	Henry IV, part 2	Coriolanus	A Lover's Complaint
The Comedy of Errors	Henry V	Hamlet	The Rape of Lucrece
Cymbeline	Henry VI, part 1	Julius Caesar	Venus and Adonis
Love's Labours Lost	Henry VI, part 2	King Lear	
Measure for Measure	Henry VI, part 3	Macbeth	Funeral Elegy by W.S.
The Merry Wives of Windsor	Henry VIII	Othello	
The Merchant of Venice	King John	Romeo and Juliet	
A Midsummer Night's Dream	Richard II	Timon of Athens	
Much Ado About Nothing	Richard III	Titus Andronicus	
Pericles, Prince of Tyre			
Taming of the Shrew			
The Tempest			
Troilus and Cressida			
Twelfth Night			
Two Gentlemen of Verona			
Winter's Tale			

version of this page without the table

About the categories

Shakespeare's plays are often arranged in three categories: tragedy, comedy, or history. I've included that arrangement here (along with a fourth column for poetry), based on the arrangement of the electronic Moby edition, but it is important to realize that the categories are not Shakespeare's.

The Complete Works of William Shakespeare home page.

ography of their resources. The PAL Web site provides information and links for several authors of the late nineteenth-century Realism period.

Information skills: Locate, organize, and evaluate information from a variety of sources; analyze, compare, synthesize, and record information; assemble information in a meaningful manner.

Women Writers

Using PAL and its links to related sites, as well as off-line resources, students research the works and backgrounds of women authors from the Romantic to the Modern periods. Students compare and contrast styles, themes, authors' backgrounds, and so on. Students share and discuss their findings with the class. The class creates a time line of U.S. women's authorship from the Romantic to the Modern periods. Students record, evaluate, and compare their off-line and online resources.

Information skills: Locate, organize, and evaluate information from a variety of sources; read for significant details and concepts; analyze, compare, synthesize, and record information; assemble information in a meaningful manner.

The Sherlockian Holmepage
http://watserv1.uwaterloo.ca/~credmond/sh.html

The Sherlockian Holmepage provides an extensive list of resources for learning more about Sir Arthur Conan Doyle and the Sherlock Holmes stories. The Web site is maintained by Chris Redmond, University of Waterloo, author of several books about Sherlockiana. The Web site includes links to the full text of original Sherlock Holmes stories, information about Sir Arthur Conan Doyle and Sherlock Holmes societies, Sherlock Holmes parodies, and links to sites for mystery fans.

Sherlock Holmes

Students choose two different Sherlock Holmes stories from the Sherlock Holmes Stories on Web link, and use a Venn diagram to depict similarities and differences between the stories. Students summarize each story and share their diagrams and opinions of the stories with the class. Student summaries and opinions of stories are added to a Sherlock Holmes class database. Students may wish to e-mail the author of the home page regarding their questions or interest in Sherlock Holmes.

Information skills: Locate, compare, and summarize information; read for significant details and concepts; organize information using a Venn diagram; construct a database; seek information from professionals.

Sherlock Holmes Times

Beginning with the Sherlockian Holmepage and its related links, student groups use online and off-line resources to research Sherlock Holmes. Students present their findings in newspaper format. Students evaluate and compare information from different resources, take notes, and create a bibliography.

Information skills: Locate, organize, and evaluate information for a specific topic from a variety of sources; analyze, synthesize, and record information; present information in an established format.

Additional Sites for Literature Classics

The English Server Fiction Collection
http://english-www.hss.cmu.edu/fiction

This site offers works of and about fiction (novels and short stories), poetry, and drama, including the full text of works in the public domain, and links to other sites.

The Life and Works of Herman Melville
http://www.melville.org/

This Web site provides information about Melville and his writing, including links to related resources.

The Wiretap Electronic Text Archive
http://wiretap.area.com/

Wiretap provides the full text of more than 200 books (choose Books online), an extensive library of poetry and other articles (choose The Wiretap Online Library), and links to government and civics archives. Authors include Aesop, Benjamin Franklin, Sir Arthur Conan Doyle, Dickens, Shakespeare, and Poe. All of the documents can be read on screen or sent to your e-mail address.

The www.americanliterature.com
http://www.americanliterature.com/MAIN.HTML

This Web site features many online books, including *The Red Badge of Courage*, *The Wizard of Oz*, *Moby Dick*, and *The Last of the Mohicans*. It also features a Chapter a Day activity that includes a discussion forum, a young readers library, and an author index with links to pages about American authors.

Yoxely Old Place: Sherlock Holmes on the Web
http://www.geocities.com/Athens/Forum/7846/

In addition to information about Sherlock Holmes, this Web site provides more than 900 links to related sites. Choose Commonplace Book from the main menu.

READERS THEATRE, STORYTELLING, AND DRAMA

Readers theatre, storytelling, and other dramatic activities enhance students' reading, speaking, and listening skills. The Internet provides access to resources for these activities and to experts in readers theatre and storytelling.

Author Online! Aaron Shepard's Home Page
http://www.aaronshep.com/

This Web site features stories told and retold by Aaron Shepard, scripts and other resources for readers theatre and storytelling, resources for use by children's writers, and tips and tools for teachers, parents, and students.

RT Performances

Student groups learn about readers theatre and choose a script to present to the class. Following group performances, students compare and contrast readers theatre with other types of performances. Students e-mail Aaron their questions about readers theatre and their selected scripts. Information about readers theatre is accessed by choosing What is RT? and scripts are available by choosing Reader's Theater Editions (from the main menu, scroll down to Resources and select Aaron's RT Page or enter **http://www.aaronshep.com/rt/index.html**).

Information skills: Select and apply information; read for significant details and concepts; seek information from professionals; compare and analyze information.

Storytellers

Students research the art of storytelling and present a story to younger students (e.g., high school students may perform for elementary students). Choose Aaron's Storytelling Page from the main menu (or enter **http://www.aaron-shep.com/storytelling/index.html**). Choose Tell a Story! to learn more about storytelling. Additional information can be accessed by choosing The Inside Story and Other Resources. Stories are available by choosing Gifts of Story, A Storyteller's Bookshelf, and Other Resources. Students rehearse their stories in small groups. Final reports include students' self-evaluations, their research, and a bibliography of their resources.

Information skills: Locate information from a variety of sources and select, apply, record, analyze, and evaluate information.

Stage Hand Puppets
http://fox.nstn.ca/~puppets/activity.html

This Web site features a variety of puppet activities, including creating puppets, designing a puppet show, writing scripts, and more. In addition, students can e-mail a puppet expert, submit their own puppet scripts, read puppet scripts from other students, and learn about ventriloquism.

Playwrite

Students write a play and submit it to Stage Hand Puppets. (To submit, choose On-Line Puppet Theatre from the main menu.) Students review posted plays for ideas and play formats.

Information skills: Locate, evaluate, and apply information; write for publication on the Web.

Puppet Performance

Student groups contact The Professor, an online puppet expert (select Tips on the main menu), about staging their own puppet show. Students conduct additional research on performing with puppets and put together a puppet performance handbook based on their research. Students use a variety of online and off-line resources and include a bibliography in their book. Students apply what they have learned by performing a puppet show.

Information skills: Locate, organize, evaluate, and synthesize information from a variety of sources; seek information from professionals; record and analyze data; apply information; assemble information in a meaningful manner.

Additional Sites for Readers Theatre, Storytelling, and Drama
The Art of Story Telling
http://www.seanet.com/~eldrbarry/roos/art.htm

The Art of Story Telling provides information about storytelling, reviews of books about storytelling, frequently asked questions, and links to stories, story-tellers, and other storytelling sites.

The Puppetry Home Page
http://www.sagecraft.com/puppetry/

> Puppet resources available here include online experts, puppetry definitions, information about creating puppet shows, and information about puppetry traditions around the world. Students can learn about puppet performers and follow links to related sites.

The Storyteller Home Page
http://members.aol.com/storypage/index.htm

> Sponsored by the Tejas Storytelling Association, the Storyteller Home Page provides information about storytelling and many links to storytelling resources. It also includes links to puppetry.

Storytelling, Drama, Creative Dramatics & Readers Theater for Children & Young Adults
http://falcon.jmu.edu/~ramseyil/drama.htm

> This Web site provides a list of links to storytelling, drama, readers theatre, and puppetry Web sites.

WRITING AND REFERENCE TOOLS

Whether students are writing reflections about how they solved a math problem or a research paper for a science class, writing and reference tools can help to build students' research and writing skills.

The Internet provides search engines, online libraries and databases, and virtual reference desks that can help students locate information about a topic. In addition, many Web sites provide how-to guides for citing online sources, materials about writing skills, searchable dictionaries and thesauruses, and information about plagiarism and copyright.

My Virtual Reference Desk
http://www.refdesk.com/index.html

> My Virtual Reference Desk is an exemplary Web site. It categorizes and provides links to an enormous amount of resources, including a variety of online dictionaries (rhyming, foreign languages, spelling, grammar, acronyms, quotations, etc.); encyclopedias; links to specific subjects; and much, much more. My Virtual Reference Desk is an excellent resource for research and writing activities across the curriculum.

Crosswords

Students enhance their vocabulary skills by using the Crossword Dictionary (**http://192.239.148.29/cgi/getdict.bat?C%3F%3F**) or Crossword Solver (**http://www.ojohaven.com/fun/crossword.html**) to help them complete crossword puzzles. Both of these links are accessible from My Virtual Reference Desk by selecting My Facts Page, then Dictionaries. Crossword puzzles may be created by the teacher, downloaded from the Web (select Crosswords from My Virtual Reference Desk's main menu), or selected from local newspapers.

Students keep track of the words they needed help with and compare and list the results of the two crossword sites.

Information skills: Locate, compare, record, and apply information; read for significant details and concepts; communicate information in a meaningful manner.

Playing with Palindromes

Students create an illustrated palindrome book. Students start by using the Dictionary and Language Resources to learn more about palindromes. Students select several palindromes to research and create at least one palindrome of their own to include in their book. Students may choose a particular theme for their book or simply include their favorite palindromes. Books should contain the definition of a palindrome and other interesting facts about palindromes (e.g., the longest palindrome, number palindromes). Students share their books with each other and make them available in the school library. As a follow-up activity, students post e-mail messages inviting other students to send palindromes to the class. Students compile a class book documenting the most common, the most original, the longest, and the funniest palindromes received. (To access palindrome links, choose My Facts Page from the main menu. Next, choose Dictionaries. Scroll down and choose the Palindromes link.)

Information skills: Locate and compare information; read for significant details and concepts; assemble information in a meaningful manner.

Word Play
http://homepage.interaccess.com/%7Ewolinsky/word.htm

Word Play offers a lengthy list of links to sites that feature fun with words. There are links to homonym, ambigram, anagram, antagonym, and oxymoron lists, a mnemonics page, lists of clichés, interactive word games, and more.

Anagrams

Download examples of anagrams from the Anagram Hall of Fame and share them with students. Explain that anagrams are the result of rearranging letters in other words or phrases. Provide students with words or a phrase from the Anagram Hall of Fame and see how their answers compare to the anagram on the Anagram Hall of Fame. Next, ask students to create an anagram from their name (first, middle, and last name). Students submit their name to the Anagram Genius main menu and compare the Genius anagram to their own. Students choose one of the anagrams from their name as a story starter or title.

Information skills: Locate, compare, and apply information; read for significant details and concepts; communicate information in a meaningful manner.

Mnemonics

Download mnemonics from the Mnemonics directory at Amanda's Mnemonics Page (choose Amanda's Mnemonics Page from the main menu) and challenge students to decipher them. Ask students if they know variations of the mnemonics (e.g., Every Green Banana Draws Flies is the same as Every Good Boy Does Fine, representing the line notes for treble clef). Students collect mnemonic strategies from other classes, online peers, relatives, and members of the community. Students combine their findings into a class chart and determine the subject area in which people use mnemonics the most, how mnemonic devices differ, how mnemonic devices are alike, which mnemonics are the most common, and so on. As a follow-up activity, students create their own mnemonic device for remembering how to spell a word or remembering a word's definition.

Information skills: Learn about memory aids; locate, gather, and analyze information from a variety of sources; read for significant details and concepts; assemble information in a meaningful manner.

Additional Sites for Writing and Reference Tools

Connected Classroom Conference: Citing Internet Addresses
http://www.classroom.net/classroom/CitingNetResources.html

A how-to guide for referencing online sources in student bibliographies.

Elements of Style
http://www.columbia.edu/acis/bartleby/strunk/

This is the online version of the classic guide to usage and style by William Strunk, Jr., and E. B. White.

The Natural Language Playground
http://bobo.link.cs.cmu.edu/dougb/playground.html

The Natural Language Playground provides links to interactive language tools.

Online Resources for Writers
http://www.ume.maine.edu/~wcenter/resource.html

Sponsored by the University of Maine, this Web site provides links to many online writing resources. Links provide access to materials on writing skills, online dictionaries and thesauruses (including foreign language dictionaries), information about citation formats, and more.

Plagiarism
http://www.indiana.edu/~wts/wts/plagiarism.html

This site provides examples of plagiarism and instructs students on how to avoid it.

Resources for Writers and Writing Instructors
http://www.english.upenn.edu/~jlynch/writing.html

This site contains many links to writing instruction, resources, and tools.

GENERAL LANGUAGE ARTS RESOURCES ON THE WEB

Online Magazines and Newsletters

Bits and Pieces
http://www.ryzome.com/toc.htm

The Children's Bookwatch
http://www.execpc.com/~mbr/bookwatch/cbw/

Children's Literature: A Newsletter for Adults
http://www.parentsplace.com/readroom/childnew/index.html

Connect-time
http://www.connect-time.com

CyberKids
http://www.cyberkids.com/index.html
or
http://www.mtlake.com/cyberkids/index.html

Little Planet Times
http://www.littleplanet.com/

The Looking Glass Gazette
http://www.cowboy.net/~mharper/LGG.html

MidLink
http://longwood.cs.ucf.edu:80/~MidLink/

The Palindromist Magazine
http://www.realchange.org/pal/

Stone Soup
http://www.stonesoup.com/

Young Author's Magazine
http://www.yam.regulus.com/

Weekly Reader's Galaxy
http://www.weeklyreader.com/

Other Sites

ACEKids
http://www.acekids.com/kidshome.html
ACEKids publishes students' stories, offers online homework help, provides additional links for kids, and posts a round-robin story created by students. It also offers many other activities.

Carol Hurst's Children's Literature Site
http://www.carolhurst.com/

Carol Hurst provides reviews of children's books and ways to use the books in the classroom. The site also provides links for professional resources.

The Case
http://www.thecase.com

The Case provides online mysteries for students to read and solve. Mysteries can be e-mailed to students or teachers weekly.

Children's Literature Web Guide
http://www.ucalgary.ca/~dkbrown/index.html

The Children's Literature Web Guide is an invaluable Web site for educators. It features book reviews and discussion boards; information about children's book awards and best-sellers; teaching ideas for children's books; many links to authors and stories on the Web; recommended book lists; resources for teachers, parents, storytellers, writers, and illustrators; children's publishers; and more.

Children's Storybooks Online
http://www.magickeys.com/books/

This Web site provides links to illustrated stories. Some include animations, sounds, and follow-up questions.

Early Childhood.com
http://www.earlychildhood.com/

This Web site provides access to online experts, articles and resources, arts and crafts, and additional links related to early childhood education. Users can also post questions and inquiries.

Early Childhood Education and Activity Resources
http://www.intex.net/~dlester/pam/preschool/preschoolpage.html

This Web site provides information about a variety of topics, with many links. It offers information for teachers and parents of young students, crafts, projects and games, songs, and other activities for young students.

Enchanted Learning Software
http://www.EnchantedLearning.com/

Sponsored by Enchanted Learning Software, a children's software company, this site provides many online activities and links for young students, including rebus rhymes, short stories, and math activities.

Froggy Tales
http://frog.simplenet.com/froggy/tales.shtml

Part of the Froggy Page Web site (http://frog.simplenet.com/), this page list links to frog stories on the Internet.

Giraffic: The Multimedia Book Company
http://www.megabrands.com/alice/doalice.html

This Web site provides multimedia stories. For optimal viewing, you will need Netscape Navigator 3.0 with JavaScript enabled. Stories include "Alice in Wonderland," "Little Bo Peep," and "Ikintar the Giraffe." Many interactive options are available in the stories.

Indigenous People's Literature
http://www.indians.org/welker/natlit01.htm

This is an e-text archive of indigenous literature.

KidLit
http://mgfx.com/Kidlit/

KidLit provides students the opportunity to read other students' stories, submit their own stories and art, and read book reviews. Kidlit also provides links to additional literature sources.

Kids' Space Connection
http://www.KS-connection.com/

Kids' Space Connection is dedicated to young children. Students can read other students' stories and submit their own stories. Kids' Space provides pictures to write about and incorporate into stories. Hop Pop Town helps children learn about music. E-mail options are available.

Kids Window Library
http://jw.stanford.edu/KIDS/LIBRARY/

This site provides links to audio stories in English and Japanese.

Kidscom
http://www.kidscom.com/index1.html

Students can publish their own stories, access a variety of games and crafts, learn about various topics, and link to other sites for kids.

Kidworld
http://www.bconnex.net/~kidworld/

Kidworld provides an assortment of activities for children and young people under 16. Students can connect with key pals and publish stories on Kidworld.

Language Arts Resources—Elementary
http://falcon.jmu.edu/~ramseyil/childlit.htm

This Web site contains an extensive list of links to elementary language arts resources.

LifeLong Universe Literature Links
http://www.lifelong.com/EditorsChoice/EChoiceLiterature.html

This Web site provides links to literature projects, online books, and other literature resources.

Links to Talking Sites
http://www.mvpsolutions.com/PlugInSite/Talker.html@otherlinks
This site provides links to Web sites that incorporate audio.

Mike Rofone: The Roving Reporter
http://www.indigo.ie/local/mikero/
This Web site features online stories featuring Mike Rofone. It also includes lots of links for kids.

Nikolai's Web Site
http://www.nikolai.com/
Students can read other students' stories, submit their own stories, and interact with online adventures.

Postcards
http://postcards.www.media.mit.edu/Postcards
At Postcards, students pick a card, write a message, and send it off. The recipient is notified by e-mail that a card has been sent. Cards are claimed at the Web site's Pick-up Window.

Reading Project Watch
http://www.hmco.com/hmco/school/projects/rdgproj.html
Sponsored by the Houghton Mifflin Company, this site lists links to language arts projects.

The Reading Room
http://www.inform.umd.edu/EdRes/ReadingRoom
The Reading Room features links to online books, poetry, journals, book reviews, and more.

Starnet Holiday Cards
http://www.azstarnet.com/public/holiday/holiday.html
Similar to Postcards, students can send an electronic holiday card to someone on the Internet. Recipients of holiday cards get a message alerting them that a card has been sent. Cards are claimed at the Web site.

Story Creations
http://www.searsportrait.com/storybook/index.html
This Web site creates personalized stories from a student's word list.

Story Resources Available on the Web
http://www.cyberenet.net/~sjohnson/stories/
This Web site contains many links to story resources, including storytelling, audio stories, stories by children, familiar tales, and interactive stories.

Theodore Tugboat Online Activity Center
http://www.cochran.com/theodore/
The Theodore Tugboat Online Activity Center provides many resources and materials for teachers and students. One activity is an interactive story that

allows young children to make choices for Theodore Tugboat and manipulate the story's outcome. Coloring activities, sounds and movies, and character information are other Theodore Tugboat options. This Web site also features Berit's Best Sites for Children, an outstanding resource for locating additional links for children.

Web Topics Preschoolers
http://www.dimensional.com/~janf/wtpreschool.html
This Web site provides miscellaneous links for preschoolers.

E-MAIL EXCHANGES

E-mail activities establish communication links with students around the world, providing students with a variety of audiences and real-world learning experiences. E-mail activities stress the importance of communication skills and collaboration. The following activities provide students with opportunities to share information, work collaboratively, and learn more about themselves and others.

Favorite Books

After establishing a common format for writing book reports, students write, exchange, collect, and compare reports about favorite books with students from other schools. Students create an electronic database to track the author, number of pages, title of the book, summary, and the reviewer's name and state. Students can also compare required reading lists for various countries and locations. For example, in Russia, books by Jack London are considered essential reading, but they are not always included in reading lists in the United States. Students discuss why such differences might exist, then e-mail experts (such as educational associations, teachers, scholars in literature from various countries) to ask them why. Students compare their predictions to the experts' responses.

Playing Around

Following a discussion about descriptive writing, have students describe the playground and e-mail the description to another class. The other class sends its playground descriptions to your class. Students in both classes draw the other class's playground based on the written descriptions. Exchange the drawings using fax or mail so students can see how their descriptions were interpreted. Finally, exchange photographs of the playgrounds. Discuss the results, including what it was like to draw based on another person's description and the importance of descriptive words.

Tele-Field Trips

Ask students in a remote location to ask questions about tourist attractions and historical sites in your area. Students answer those questions with accurate and interesting information.

Grade Levels	The House of Poe	Research Level
6-12		Basic

Educational Goals

To introduce students to the works of Edgar Allan Poe and to electronic searching using Data Resource Associates

To infer meaning and make connections from story abstracts to story titles

Procedure

Distribute the House of Poe activity sheet. Students work in groups of two or three to match the story summaries to the titles. Chart each group's decisions, and assign groups to use Data Resource Associates (telnet://dra.com) to check their work. Groups compare their findings with their original decisions. Students complete the additional writing and reading activity on their own. Students share their stories and discuss Poe's stories.

Answers

1. The Cask of Amontillado
2. The Purloined Letter
3. The Fall of the House of Usher
4. The Tell-Tale Heart
5. The Pit and the Pendulum
6. The Gold Bug

Extension Activities

1. Students use the Internet to contact other students who have read a story by Poe. Create a database of stories read, story reviews, and where in the world the stories were read.

2. Students use Data Resource Associates to find the subject category for each story listed on the activity sheet The House of Poe. Which stories are classified as Horror? Mystery? Crime? Into which classification do most of the stories fall? Based on these classifications, students describe Poe as a writer.

3. Students read a biography of Edgar Allan Poe. How does his writing style reflect his life? Students discuss what they find most interesting about Poe and why. How might Poe's writing and popularity differ if he lived today? Why?

4. Students use Data Resource Associates to list five other authors and their book titles in each of the following categories: Horror, Mystery, Crime. Students choose one category and one book from that category. Students read the chosen book and a story by Poe in the same category, then compare and contrast the authors' writing styles.

THE HOUSE OF POE

In the following rooms are brief descriptions of stories written by Edgar Allan Poe. Read the description of each story and see if you can guess its title. Using Data Resource Associates (telnet://dra.com), find the story title and read its abstract to check your work. Which story sounds the most interesting? Why? Write your own short story based on a selected summary. Compare your story to Poe's. Poe's short stories can be found at The Wiretap Electronic Text Archive (http://wiretap.area.com/) and The English Server Fiction Collection (http://english-www.hss.cmu.edu/fiction).

Titles

• The Pit and the Pendulum

• The Gold Bug

• The Tell-Tale Heart

• The Purloined Letter

• The Cask of Amontillado

• The Fall of the House of Usher

1. After enduring many injuries of the noble Fortunato, Montresor executes the perfect revenge.

Title Guess:_____

Actual Title:_____

2. The brilliant Duplin uses psychological reasoning to deduce the hiding place of a stolen object.

Title Guess:_____

Actual Title:_____

3. A visitor to a gloomy mansion finds a childhood friend dying under the spell of a family curse.

Title Guess:_____

Actual Title:_____

4. The murder of an old man is revealed by the beating of his heart.

Title Guess:_____

Actual Title:_____

5. Judged guilty by the Inquisition, a condemned man is slowly tortured.

Title Guess:_____

Actual Title:_____

6. A coded message on a shoreline sends William Legrand and his friends on a treasure hunt.

Title Guess:_____

Actual Title:_____

Grade Levels	Cinderella,	Research Level
4-8	Cinderella	Advanced

Educational Goals

To compare and contrast versions of *Cinderella*, identifying story elements and writing styles

To introduce Venn diagrams

Procedure

Many students identify the story of Cinderella with Walt Disney. The Cinderella Project (http://www-dept.usm.edu/~engdept/cinderella/cinderella.html) posts several versions of *Cinderella*, including poems. Stories and poems can be differentiated by author and the date they were written. To begin, download two stories from the Cinderella Project (select *archive inventory*). Have students work in pairs to read and compare the two stories. Using the Cinderella, Cinderella Venn diagram activity sheet, students write how the two stories are different and how they are alike. Students explain why they like one version better than the other and how the stories compare to the Disney version.

Resource

The Cinderella Project (http://www-dept.usm.edu/~engdept/cinderella/cinderella.html)

Extension Activities

1. Assign students to research Cinderella stories from various cultures and compare and contrast them to the stories discussed in class.

2. Have students create plays or illustrate books based on various Cinderella stories.

3. Have students create dioramas that display a scene or circumstance that varies among the Cinderella stories.

4. Assign students to research multiple versions of other fairy tales and present them in class.

5. Contact students in other countries to learn more about cultural variations of the Cinderella story. Obtain Cinderella stories from various cultures and look for similarities and differences among the stories.

Cinderella, Cinderella

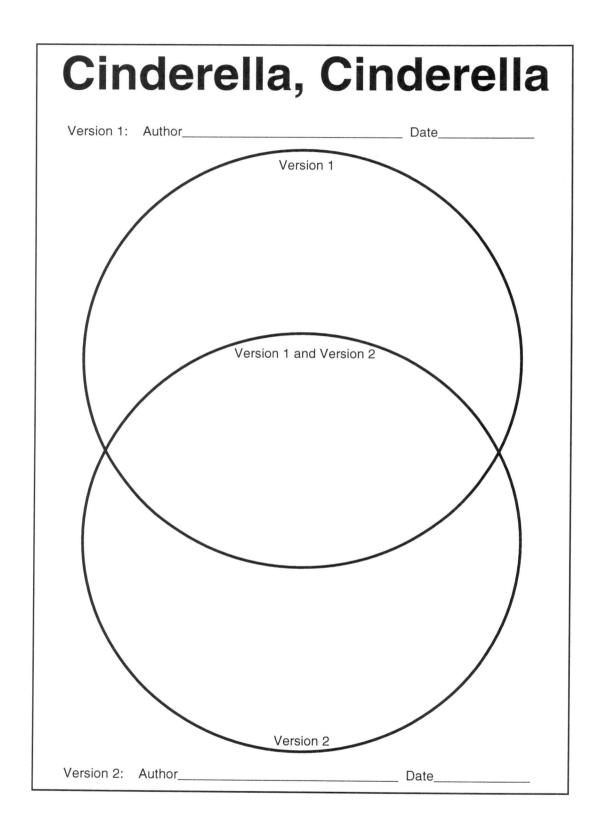

Version 1: Author_____ Date_____

Version 1

Version 1 and Version 2

Version 2

Version 2: Author_____ Date_____

Tales from Around the World

Objectives

To cooperatively research, gather, analyze, and compare fairy tales from different countries

To learn more about different cultures

To illustrate a selected fairy tale

Grade Levels: 6-12   **Final Product:** Class presentations and illustrated books

Internet Resources

Tales of Wonder (http://itpubs.ucdavis.edu/richard/tales/)

Fairy Tale Origin and Evolution (http://easyweb.easynet.co.uk/~cdaae/fairy/)

Links to Fairytales, Stories, Myths, and Legends (http://www.ifi.uio.no/~reierp/bat/stories.html)

Faerie Lore and Literature (http://faeryland.etsu.edu/~earendil/faerie/index.html)

Procedure

1. Ask students to list and discuss their favorite fairy tales. Ask how fairy tales do and do not relate to real life. Inquire why some fairy tales may be more popular than others, if students are aware of multiple versions of fairy tales, and if students know any fairy tales from other countries.

2. Assign student groups to research and analyze fairy tales from various countries (see Tales of Wonder at http://itpubs.ucdavis.edu/richard/tales/). Each group is assigned to a particular country. Students use a variety of offline and online resources and keep a bibliography of their research.

3. Student groups contact students from their assigned country to learn more about the meaning and origins of the fairy tales and how they relate to the students' culture (see chapter 3 for more information about contacting students and teachers).

4. Groups select and illustrate their favorite fairy tale from their assigned country and share their illustrated storybook with the class. Student groups present their findings to the class.

Tales from Around the World (cont.)

Procedure (cont.)

5. Students compare and categorize the fairy tales and findings from the different countries. Students examine and compare the characters, settings, plots, and so on. In addition, students look for similarities and differences among the fairy tales and people's cultures.

Extension Activities

1. Students write their own fairy tale and post it on the WWW.

2. Student groups research the origins and variations of *Little Red Riding Hood*, *Cinderella*, and other fairy tales (see Fairy Tale Origin and Evolution at http://easyweb.easynet.co.uk/~cdaae/fairy/).

3. Students write parodies of fairy tales and make books to share with younger students. Display the books in the school library.

4. Students select a fairy tale from another country and perform it for the school.

5. Students create puppet shows based on fairy tales from other countries and perform them for younger students.

6. Using a variety of online and offline resources, student groups research and write a report on their selected country.

All the Write Stuff

Objectives

To work cooperatively to research information from a variety of sources

To integrate the use of technology into research methods

To employ descriptive, analytical, and creative writing skills

Grade Levels: 4-8   **Final Product:** Animal newspaper

Internet Resources

NetVet (http://netvet.wustl.edu/)

Birmingham Zoo (http://www.birminghamzoo.com/)

Animal Information Database (http://www.bev.net/education/SeaWorld/homepage.html)

Froggy Page (http://frog.simplenet.com/froggy/)

Care for Pets (http://www.avma.org/care4pets/)

Wiretap Electronic Text Archive (http://wiretap.area.com/)

International Lyrics Server (http://www.lyrics.ch/)

Procedure

1. Ask the students to name their favorite animal. Chart responses. Ask why they chose the animal and what they know about it.

2. Next, place students in teams of two and assign them one of the following animals:

dog	cat	frog	horse	pig
cow	ferret	whale	dolphin	rabbit
turtle	gorilla	mouse	guinea pig	hamster

All the Write Stuff (cont.)

Procedure (cont.)

3. Have students create an idea web of things they may already know about the animal, using the following topics:

    Characteristics (description, habitat, diet, life span, domestic or wild, etc.)
    Stories, fables, or myths
    Famous animals (fictional or true)
    Songs
    Interesting facts
    Places the animal is found

4. Students research to verify what they know as well as what they don't know about the animal. Students write their findings in a newspaper format with each article about a different topic from the preceding list. Students create a name for their newspaper and include graphics. In addition, students write an original poem (any form) about the animal.

5. Provide students with the Internet addresses listed in Internet Resources. The International Lyrics Server can be used to search for songs about animals, and Wiretap can be used as a source for animal stories and fables. The other sites provide background information about various animals, animal health tips, and other interesting animal facts. Students create a bibliography of their sources and note discrepancies in data.

6. When the newspapers are completed, students present their findings to the class and exchange newspapers. Make enough copies of the newspapers for all students. Display the students' newspapers in the classroom or in the school library.

7. Students create another idea web with the same topics as the first, then compare and discuss what they learned.

Extension Activities

1. Create paper sculptures, puppets, pictures, or dioramas to accompany the students' newspapers.

2. Read and discuss the similarities and differences among the three versions of *The Frog Prince* (Russian, Scandinavian, and Grimm Brothers). These stories can be found on the Froggy Page. Compare and contrast other animal stories.

3. Students put themselves in an animal's place and write a story. Students can share their stories with other students using e-mail.

Social Studies and Geography Resources and Activities

David signed up for sixth-period social studies with Mr. Sisko because he had heard that Mr. Sisko used the Internet in his classes. David had also heard that Mr. Sisko assigned lots of homework, but students enjoyed his class. The teacher David had last year for social studies was nicknamed Mr. Snooze because he turned social studies into monotonous bookwork, daily multiple-choice quizzes, and hand-cramping writing exercises that including copying the Declaration of Independence. David enjoyed learning about people; to him, social studies meant learning about as well as interacting with people, not just remembering important dates.

Mr. Sisko challenged his students to think beyond what they thought they already knew. He did this by engaging his students in group projects that required them to rethink their own thinking, make compromises, and see things from different points of view. In addition, students actively participated in the construction of new knowledge by investigating topics from a variety of perspectives. The Internet was a wonderful tool for this. In addition to off-line sources, student groups were required to investigate specific Web sites, contact online experts, and e-mail questions to people related to their topic of study. The Internet provided the students access to current real-world information, personal accounts, and the opportunity to efficiently analyze and evaluate information from a variety of resources. "This," David thought, "is social studies."

The Internet is used by millions of people in countries all over the world. This global presence makes it an ideal medium for studying social studies and geography. There are many opportunities to learn about cultures and places in the world using e-mail, telnet, and Web pages. Through e-mail, students can obtain firsthand information and personal responses to news events; telnet provides students with access to specific research tools; and Web pages offer students access to international newspapers, online experts, virtual libraries and museums, government resources, and other information.

This chapter features Web sites related to social studies and geography, including ancient civilizations, U.S. government, U.S. history, world history, and multicultural education. For each topic, the chapter provides one or two instructional ideas for two or more sites. These ideas and skills are not comprehensive; instead, they serve as starting points for exploration and activities. Following the highlighted sites is a list of other sites related to the topic; these sites are briefly described. The chapter ends with a list of general geography and social studies sites and e-mail activities.

Note: Each site's current URL is given, but, because the Internet is extremely dynamic, addresses and paths may change.

ANCIENT CIVILIZATIONS

Many Web sites help students learn more about ancient cultures by providing access to online experts, time lines, images, ancient maps, teaching materials, and related documents.

Exploring Ancient World Cultures
http://eawc.evansville.edu/index.htm

Exploring Ancient World Cultures features a search engine that is limited to ancient and medieval topics on the Internet. The result is many links to predefined or specified topics on ancient and medieval history. Students can limit the search to sites, text, images, or essays. Chronological lists of events are also available.

Chronological Comparisons

Student groups create a class time line that summarizes and compares events taking place among different civilizations. Choose Internet Index from the main menu. A search menu will appear. Search by chronology and global. Students compare their findings with other sources.

Information skills: Conduct searches; locate, compare, evaluate, and organize information.

The Seven Wonders of the Ancient World

The Seven Wonders of the Ancient World home page.

Roman Empire

Using a variety of online and off-line resources, students write a report about the Roman Empire. Students take notes, evaluate and compare their findings, assess the validity of their sources, and create a bibliography. Choose the Roman Empire link from the text on the main menu or select Search Argos from the main menu and enter Roman Empire.

Information skills: Use search techniques for electronic media; locate, organize, evaluate, and synthesize information; record and analyze data; assemble information in a meaningful manner.

The Seven Wonders of the Ancient World
http://pharos.bu.edu/Egypt/Wonders/Home.html

The Seven Wonders of the Ancient World provides pictures, maps, answers to frequently asked questions, and links to related resources.

Other Wonders

Students compare ancient, modern, and natural wonders. Students report why the wonders are considered wonders, research the wonders' history, and identify the wonders' locations on a map. Students use online and off-line resources and create a bibliography. Students share their reports with the class. Choose Other Wonders from the main menu. As a follow-up activity, students research and discuss what else they might consider to be a modern or natural wonder. Students submit their proposals and questions to the editors of the Seven Wonders of the Ancient World.

Information skills: Locate, organize, and evaluate information from a variety of sources; analyze, compare, record, and synthesize information; identify locations on a map; communicate findings.

Seven Wonders

Student groups research one of the seven wonders of the ancient world using a variety of online and off-line resources. They present their findings and a three-dimensional sculpture or drawing of their wonder to the class. Students take notes, evaluate and compare their findings, and create a bibliography to accompany their report. Choose The Canonical List from the main menu.

Information skills: Locate, organize, evaluate, and synthesize information from a variety of sources; record and analyze data; display findings using a two- or three-dimensional format; and work collaboratively to assemble and present information.

Tour Egypt
http://interoz.com/egypt/

Tour Egypt offers a tremendous amount of information about Egypt through a variety of interesting links. Through Tour Egypt, students can learn about Egyptian tourism, research Egyptian history, send messages and chat, learn about the animals of Egypt, and much more. Little Horus and Rosetta Stone are excellent sites for elementary students.

Egyptian Mythology

Student groups read about Egyptian mythology and create a poster and a biography of one of the characters. Student groups share their biographies and posters with the class. As a follow-up activity, students write a story based on one or more of the class's characters. Students use a variety of resources, evaluate and compare their findings, and create a bibliography of their resources. Information about Egyptian mythology can be located on Tour Egypt by selecting Egyptian Antiquities from the main menu, then Egyptian Mythology.

Information skills: Locate, organize, and evaluate information; read for significant details and concepts; record and analyze data; and communicate through oral presentations, writing, and drawings.

History of Egypt

Student groups research different time periods of Egyptian history using Tour Egypt and other sources. Students take notes, evaluate and compare their findings, and create a bibliography of their resources. Students combine their research to create a class time line of Egyptian events. (Choose Egyptian Antiquities from the main menu, then choose History of Egypt to access different time periods of Egyptian history.) As a follow-up activity, student groups can compare ancient Egypt with Egypt today.

Information skills: Locate, compare, evaluate, synthesize, and organize information.

Additional Sites for Ancient Civilizations

Ancient Russia

http://www.interknowledge.com/russia/rushis02.htm

This is the official site of the Russian National Tourist Office. It includes a clickable time line of Russian history and information about Russian art and architecture, cities, and history.

Ancient World Web

http://atlantic.evsc.virginia.edu/julia/AncientWorld.html

This Web site provides an index of sites about the ancient world.

Egyptian Hieroglyphs

http://www.torstar.com/rom/egypt

Sponsored by the Royal Ontario Museum, this Web site contains information about Egyptian hieroglyphics, an online hieroglyphics translator, and an option to e-mail hieroglyphic messages.

Little Horus

http://www.horus.ics.org.eg/

Little Horus helps elementary students learn about Egypt. Topics include Egypt Today, History, and Entertainment. Students can e-mail their questions about Egypt, take online tours, and learn about Egyptian attractions.

Rosetta Stone

http://www.clemusart.com/archive/pharaoh/rosetta/

Sponsored by the Cleveland (Ohio) Museum of Art, Rosetta Stone allows elementary students to learn more about pharaohs, e-mail questions to experts, take an online quiz, download Egyptian coloring pages, and much more.

Science Museum of Minnesota: Mayan Adventure

http://www.sci.mus.mn.us/sln/ma/map.html

Mayan Adventure, sponsored by the Science Museum of Minnesota, provides information about ancient and modern Mayan culture. The site includes pictures and online experiments.

MULTICULTURAL EDUCATION

The Internet serves as a meeting place for people from all over the world. In addition to learning about people and places through firsthand accounts, students can access Web sites designed to help the people of the world learn more about each other.

 Introduction:

The American Immigration Home Page was started as a part of a school project for a 10th grade American History Class. The project was meant to give information as to how immigrants not only were treated, but also why they decided to come to America. Feel free to explore the rest of the site.

The American Immigration home page.

The American Immigration Home Page
http://www.bergen.org/AAST/Projects/Immigration/

The American Immigration Home Page allows students to investigate immigration topics by time period. Topics include: Reasons for Immigration, Who Were/Are the Immigrants of the U.S., Peaks/Waves of Immigration, Methods of Transportation and Ports of Arrival, Process of Entering the U.S., and Destination/Places Where They Settled. The site also provides information about Ellis Island, quotes about immigration, and links to newsgroups and other resources.

Immigration Over Time

Student groups research a selected immigration topic and report on the differences, similarities, and trends over time. Student groups create time lines showing the development or important events related to their topic and discuss their findings with the class. Students use online and off-line resources to research their topic and compare and evaluate the sources. Students create a bibliography of their sources. As a follow-up activity, student groups research current events related to their topic and submit their questions to immigration newsgroups, publications, and departments (see Links and Newsgroups).

Information skills: Locate, organize, evaluate, and synthesize information about a specific topic; assemble information in a time line; communicate findings.

Quote Interpretations

Students access Quotes About Immigration from the main menu. They explain what each of the quotes means, whether they agree with it, and the extent to which the quotes represent or do not represent the perspectives of the Federation for American Immigration Reform (see Links and Newsgroups) or other organizations. Students share and discuss their responses with the class.

Information skills: Locate and evaluate information; read for significant details and concepts; examine information from a variety of perspectives; communicate, compare, and analyze interpretations.

Multicultural Pavilion
http://curry.edschool.Virginia.EDU/go/multicultural/

Sponsored by the University of Virginia, the Multicultural Pavilion provides an extensive list of resources related to multicultural education. Information and links are organized by category, including Teacher's Corner, Research and Inquiry, Multicultural Awareness Archives, Multiculturalism on the Internet, and more. The site also features an online discussion board, listservs, and a search engine.

Culture Study

Using a variety of online and off-line sources, student groups research a particular culture and present their findings to the class. They take notes, compare and evaluate their resources, and create a bibliography of their sources. Students can access online information about particular cultures by choosing Research and Inquiry from the main menu (see Online Libraries and Information Archives, Online Statistical Databases and Archives, etc.). Students may also want to join discussion groups or e-mail the creator of the Multicultural Pavilion.

Information skills: Locate, organize, evaluate, and synthesize information from a variety of sources; record and analyze data; effectively communicate findings.

Words of Wisdom

Students analyze two speeches (by different people) from the Historical Speeches Archives (see Teacher's Corner). Students create a Venn diagram to help them identify similarities and differences between the two speeches. Students research the events leading up to each speech. Students share their findings with the class and note how each speech defines the importance of freedom or equality. (Choose Teacher's Corner from the main menu, then select Historical Speeches Archives.)

Information skills: Locate, analyze, evaluate, and compare information; organize information using a Venn diagram; communicate findings.

The Web of Culture
http://www.worldculture.com/

The Web of Culture provides links and a wealth of information about many multicultural topics. Topics include Cuisine, Currency, Experts, Gestures, Religions, Resources, and many more. A bulletin board and e-mail options are also available.

Meaningful Gestures

Student groups research the meaning of gestures in various cultures. Student groups compare the meanings of gestures among the cultures and present their findings to the class. Students use online and off-line resources to compare and evaluate their findings. Students create a bibliography of their sources. As a class, students discuss how body gestures have different meanings, depending on the country in which they are expressed, and why it is important to be aware of such differences. As a follow-up activity, students e-mail students from other countries regarding "proper body etiquette."

Information skills: Locate, organize, evaluate, and synthesize information from a variety of sources; communicate information in a meaningful manner.

Personal Perspective

Using a variety of online and off-line resources, students research a selected country. They take notes, compare and evaluate resources, and create a bibliography. Students can choose Sites, Servers, and other links from the main menu to locate information about their particular country. In addition, students choose Contact from the main menu to contact people living in the selected country. As a class, students design a survey to administer to the contact persons. Students include information about their contact persons in their reports and present their reports to the class. A class chart is created to compare and contrast the countries.

Information skills: Locate, organize, evaluate, and synthesize information from a variety of sources; record and analyze data; develop and administer a survey; interpret survey results; assemble and communicate information.

Additional Sites for Multicultural Education

African Americana
http://www.lib.lsu.edu/hum/african.html

Sponsored by the Louisiana State University Libraries, African Americana provides a wealth of information about African Americans and links to related sites.

Centre for Immigration and Multicultural Studies
http://coombs.anu.edu.au/SpecialProj/CIMS/CIMSHomePage.html

Sponsored by the Australian National University, this site provides many links to multicultural resources, including Web and gopher servers, mailing lists, and online publications.

Intercultural E-Mail Classroom Connections
http://ww.stolaf.edu/network/iecc/

This is a free service to help teachers and classes link with partners in other countries and cultures for classroom key pal and project exchanges.

Kid's Window Homepage
http://www.jwindow.net/KIDS/

This interactive site offers students the opportunity to learn about Japanese culture, stories, student artwork, and more.

LatinoLink
http://www.latinolink.com/

This informative site provides current news, discussion forums, chat rooms, and many links to sites related to Latino culture.

Multicultural Home Page
http://pasture.ecn.purdue.edu/~agenhtml/agenmc/index.html

Maintained by Purdue University, this site provides information about various countries. The site includes graphics, audio clips, and additional links.

U.S. GOVERNMENT

Using the Internet, students have immediate access to current government information, press releases, and data. Students can e-mail their representatives, senators, the vice-president, and the president. They can access census information, the CIA *World Fact Book*, and other government databases.

In addition to the many Web sites sponsored by U.S. government agencies, there are many Web sites about government issues sponsored by other individuals and organizations. Students can evaluate and compare information published by the U.S. government and sources and discuss various organizations' perspectives on various issues.

U.S. Census Bureau
http://www.census.gov/

In addition to providing statistical information, the U.S. Census Bureau Web site offers news and links to related sites. Menu options include census news and information, a search option, a subject index, and activities.

State Comparisons

Students compare census information about two states. Students create Venn diagrams, charts, and graphs to display their results. Findings are shared with the class. Choose Just For Fun from the main menu. Next, choose Map Stats. Students select two states to compare, clicking on the desired states. As a follow-up activity, students compare information published by the U.S. Census Bureau with the same information published by each state. Students look for discrepancies between the data and e-mail their findings and questions to the state governments.

Information skills: Locate and compare information; create effective charts and graphs; organize information using a Venn diagram; communicate findings.

State to State

Student groups compare past and predicted census information about age among three states. Students chart and graph their results; share the results with the class; and discuss the impact of age on the economy, health issues, and so on. Choose Subjects A-Z from the main menu. Next, select Age, then State Level. For past information, choose Censuses, Lookup, STF3A, and the desired state (then press Submit). Choose the table option (press Submit), then select category P13 (age) and press Submit. Next, choose the HTML format and press Submit again. For predictions, choose Projections instead of Censuses after selecting State Level. Next, choose "by age and sex."

There are many categories of information to choose and compare. As a follow-up activity, students can choose their own area of interest and write a report of their findings. Students can also compare their findings to international data.

Information skills: Locate, compare, and contrast information; analyze and evaluate data; synthesize information; create effective charts and graphs; communicate findings.

The U.S. Treasury Homepage
http://www.ustreas.gov/

The U.S. Treasury Homepage provides information about Treasury offices, officials, and news events. The site also provides answers to frequently asked questions, e-mail options, events in U.S. Treasury history, and a kid's page.

Money Matters

Student groups select a research topic from the list of frequently asked questions. Students report their findings in the form of a newsletter. Newsletters are shared with the class. Students write a final report explaining what they found most interesting, what facts they were unaware of, and what questions they still have about each topic. Students then e-mail their remaining questions to the U.S. Treasury department. (To send e-mail, select Correspondence from the main menu. An e-mail option appears at the bottom of the Correspondence page.)

Information skills: Locate and organize information about a specific topic; seek information from professionals; organize findings into an established format; evaluate and respond to information.

Money Mysteries

Student groups use a variety of online and off-line resources to research topics such as the following: types of counterfeit money, protecting yourself against counterfeit money, the history of U.S. money, and features of U.S. money.

Student groups present their findings to the class by writing and performing a skit about their topic. For example, students researching counterfeit money may write a skit that includes the character of Sherlock Holmes investigating types of counterfeit money. Students take notes and create a bibliography of their resources. Information about money can be located on the U.S. Treasury Homepage by selecting Kids Page, then Know Your Money.

Information skills: Locate, organize, and evaluate information from a variety of sources and present information to others using a nontraditional approach.

The White House
http://www.whitehouse.gov

The White House Web site allows students to e-mail the president, the vice-president, and the First Lady; take a virtual tour of the White House and learn about its history; view White House documents and photographs; listen to speeches; link to other federal Web sites; and much more. Students may visit another White House Web site designed for younger students, The White House for Kids (**http://www.whitehouse.gov/WH/kids/html/home.html**).

Press Releases

Student groups search the White House Press Releases, Radio Addresses, Photos, and Web Pages for a particular topic (e.g., the ozone layer, AIDS, education, technology, violence). The search option provides students with materials from various resources. For example, a search on the ozone layer may yield a list of more than 40 documents related to environmental administration, the Environmental Protection Agency, the president's remarks during an Earth Day speech, and executive orders governing ozone depletion. Students study the topics and compare the information from the search with information from groups that represent differing viewpoints. Do the information sources agree about what is happening and what should happen? Students compile the findings with other resources to create a written or hypermedia class report, which they present to the class. Note: Students may limit their searches to specific dates. (Choose The Virtual Library from the main menu. Next, choose All White House Web Features Combined.)

Information skills: Conduct searches; locate, organize, and evaluate information about a specific topic from a variety of sources; consider facts from a variety of perspectives; synthesize information; communicate findings.

Social Statistics

Student groups research, analyze, and chart statistical data on topics such as the following: crime, demographics, education, and health. Students gather newspaper articles relevant to their topic and present their findings to the class. Students share their concerns about these issues; identify problems and possible solutions; and submit their questions to the president, vice-president, or First Lady. From the main menu, choose The Briefing Room. Next, scroll down

The White House home page.

and select Social Statistics Briefing Room (SSBR). E-mail addresses can be accessed from the main menu by choosing The President & Vice President.

Information skills: Locate, analyze, compare, and organize information; create effective charts; evaluate and respond to information; seek information from professionals; effectively communicate findings.

Additional Sites for U.S. Government

Central Intelligence Agency
http://www.odci.gov/cia/

The Central Intelligence Agency (CIA) site provides access to CIA publications, information about the CIA, the agency's public affairs office, and links to sites related to the CIA and the intelligence community. The CIA *World Fact Book* (choose CIA Publications) is an excellent resource for country reports.

FedWorld Information Network
http://www.fedworld.gov

The FedWorld Information Network provides links to and search options for many federal Web sites.

House of Representatives
http://www.house.gov/

This is the official Web site of the House of Representatives. Students can get information about their representative, including how to write to him or her; they can also get information about the various House committees and read about House organizations, commissions, and task forces.

Thomas
http://thomas.loc.gov/

This site, from the Library of Congress, provides links to several U.S. government resources. Students can read committee reports, obtain information about current bills, and view historical documents. They can also learn how laws are made. There are many more resources at this site.

The United States Senate
http://www.senate.gov/

This is the official Web site of the United States Senate. Students can read about legislative activities, committees, and Senate history. Students can also e-mail their senators from this site.

U.S. Postal Service
http://www.usps.gov/kids/welcome.htm

This site is designed for kids. It includes interactive games and information to help students learn more about the post office, stamps, mail delivery, and more. Links lead to unforgettable letters and stories, e-mail opportunities, and additional information about the postal service.

U.S. HISTORY

The Internet allows students to investigate U.S. history from a variety of perspectives, analyze and evaluate data, contact online experts, and obtain materials that might otherwise be unavailable to them. Many lesson plans and other activities on the Web help educators prepare units about U.S. history.

Great American History
http://www.cais.com/greatamericanhistory/

In addition to other topics, the Great American History Web site provides free educational material and information about the Civil War. The Civil War Library section features outlines, quizzes, games, and additional links.

Kid Info: American Revolution home page.

Topic of Interest

Students choose a topic of interest related to the Civil War (e.g., women of the Civil War, food and cooking, music, African Americans in the Civil War, famous battles). Topics can be selected from the Outline of the Civil War from Great American History. Students use online and off-line resources, e-mail the editors of the Great American History Web site regarding discrepancies in or questions about their findings, take notes, compare and evaluate information, and create a bibliography of their sources. Students share their reports with the class and create a diorama, sketch, disk, tape, skit, etc., to accompany their report.

Information skills: Specify a topic of interest; locate, select, and evaluate information from a variety of sources; contact online experts; organize findings in an established format; communicate findings in a meaningful manner.

Kid Info: American Revolution
http://www.kidinfo.com/American_History/American_Revolution.html

This is one of many sites sponsored by Kid Info (**http://www.kidinfo.com**). The site contains links to glossaries and time lines, information about the colonies, historical events related to the American Revolution, and much more. The site also includes links to homework helpers and searchable encyclopedias.

Causes of the American Revolution

Student groups examine and compare Web sites that discuss the causes of the American Revolution (see Causes of American Revolution) with information from their textbooks or other off-line sources. Students discuss the perspectives represented on the Web sites, then contact students in Great Britain and ask them to share their perspective on causes of the American Revolution. Students compare and discuss their findings. (See chapter 4 for more information on contacting other classes.)

Information skills: Conduct searches; locate, compare, evaluate, and organize information; read for significant details and concepts.

Historical Documents

Student groups research, print out, and explain the significance of historical documents related to the American Revolution. Each group shares the content and background of a different document. As a follow-up activity, the class charts the similarities, differences, and relationships among the documents.

Information skills: Teach students how to locate and organize information about a specific topic and to communicate this information in a meaningful way.

New Perspectives on the West
http://www.pbs.org/weta/thewest/

Sponsored by Public Broadcasting Service and General Motors Corporation, this Web site features many topics related to the American West. It is divided into five main sections: Tour the West, Events in the West, Places in the West, People in the West, and Archives of the West. The site also provides interactive quizzes, historical documents (including journal entries), photographs, maps, e-mail opportunities, search options, and links to other sites.

Lewis and Clark

Student groups create a multimedia project based on their research about Lewis and Clark. They use a variety of off-line and online resources, compare and evaluate their resources, and create a bibliography. Lewis and Clark information and links can be accessed by choosing Search Site (scroll down the right bottom frame) and entering Lewis and Clark (click on Search). Students house their projects in the school's media center or make them available on the Internet for other schools. Additional project topics include Native Americans, the Oregon Trail, the California Gold Rush, and the Multicultural West. Links to these topics can be found under Links to the West from the main menu.

Information skills: Search electronic media; locate, organize, and evaluate information; analyze, synthesize, and record information; organize and present findings using a multimedia tool.

Perceptions of the California Gold Rush

Student groups research, analyze, reflect upon, and evaluate comments made by people during the California Gold Rush. Before their investigations, students write down their own comments or thoughts about how they think people felt, what they think people experienced, and why they think people went to California during the Gold Rush. In conducting their research, students search for letters, diaries, memoirs, official documents, and other materials that contain quotes from men, women, and children who took part in the California Gold Rush. Following their research, students compare their own comments with their findings. Students discuss life during the California Gold Rush and compare it to life today. Choose Search Site (scroll down the right bottom frame) and enter "California and Gold and Rush" (click on Search). Significant links include Luzena Stanley Wilson's Memoirs of the Gold Rush, Archives of THE WEST—1848 to 1856, and William Swain Letter.

Information skills: Conduct searches; locate, compare, evaluate, and organize information; read for significant details and concepts; communicate information in a meaningful way.

Additional Sites for U.S. History

American History Archive Project
http://www.ilt.columbia.edu/k12/history/aha.html

This Web site is an ongoing project designed to encourage classroom collaboration, student publication and research, and other opportunities related to the study of American history. In addition to photo, video, and document archives, this Web site includes information about the American Revolution, Native Americans, and Gettysburg.

American Memory
http://lcweb2.loc.gov/ammem/amhome.html

American Memory is an outstanding resource of historical collections maintained by the Library of Congress. Links include photos and prints, documents, motion pictures, and sound recordings. Students can search or browse the site.

Archiving Early America
http://earlyamerica.com/

This site features discussion groups, maps, writings, famous documents (e.g., Bill of Rights, U.S. Constitution), photographs, an online journal, and other information related to early America.

Civil War Project
http://www.rochester.k12.mn.us/john-marshall/overton/cwproj/main/civilframe.html

The Civil War Project is a collection of student work about the Civil War. Students can evaluate the work and submit their own reports. Assignment directions and a grading rubric are included.

From Revolution to Reconstruction
http://grid.let.rug.nl/~welling/usa/usa.html

This site features a hypertext version of American history.

Lesson Plan: The Civil War
http://www.smplanet.com/civilwar/civilwar.html

This Web site provides information and links useful in developing a unit on the Civil War. In addition to an online unit, this Web site provides a list of recommended books, integration and enrichment ideas, links to relevant resources, and links to additional sites about the Civil War.

WORLD HISTORY

Web sites devoted to world history allow students to e-mail people involved in historical events or read their personal accounts of the events. (Some people involved in historical events are war veterans and survivors of the Holocaust.) Students can contact historians from various countries to learn about world history from their perspectives.

History of the World
http://www.hyperhistory.com/

The History of the World Web site hosts the HyperHistory Online project. HyperHistory Online provides an enormous number of links and information relating to almost 3,000 years of world history. Information can be viewed synchronoptically, meaning users can choose a time period and view events occurring in various parts of the world during that time. Topics include people, events, history, and maps. People and events are color coded according to various categories: Science, Technology, Economy, and Discovery; Culture, Philosophy, Art, Music, and Poetry; Religion and Theology; Politics and Statecraft; and War.

Concurrent Events

Student groups investigate and report on events that took place during a selected year between 1941 and 1945. In addition to HyperHistory Online, students use online and off-line resources for their research. Students compare and evaluate resources, take notes, and create a bibliography of the sources. Students present their findings in a videotaped newscast format. (Choose HyperHistory Online from the home page, then choose Events, then select 1939–1945.)

Information skills: Locate, organize, and evaluate information from a variety of sources; analyze, synthesize, and record information; identify locations on a map; communicate findings using a video format.

Famous Contributions

Student groups research and report the contributions of different people between 1850 and 1950. Groups are responsible for different types of contributions based on the color-codes of HyperHistory Online (e.g., science, politics,

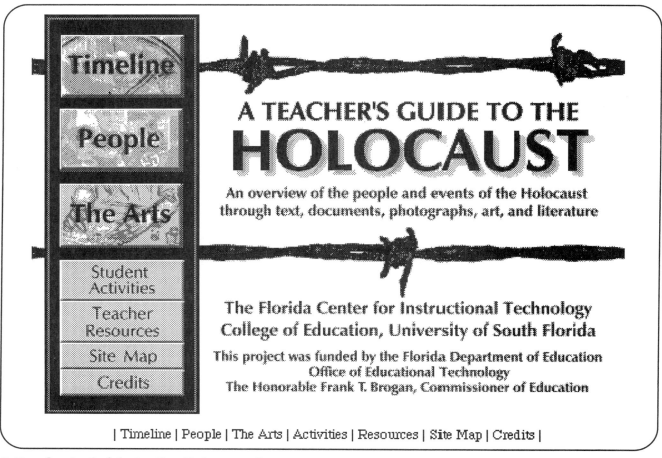

A Teacher's Guide to the Holocaust home page.

theology, etc.). In addition to HyperHistory Online, students use a variety of online and off-line resources for their research. Students compare and evaluate resources, take notes, and create a bibliography. Student groups share their findings with the class. Students comment on the different contributions from around the world and post their findings on a class world map. Choose HyperHistory Online from the home page. Next, choose People, then select 1500–1996 for the time period. Scroll between 1800 and 1996.

Information skills: Locate, organize, and evaluate information from a variety of sources; analyze, synthesize, and record information; identify locations on a map; communicate findings.

A Teacher's Guide to the Holocaust
http://fcit.coedu.usf.edu/holocaust

This site is sponsored by the Florida Center of Instructional Technology at the University of Florida. Funded by the Florida Department of Education, A Teacher's Guide to the Holocaust offers student activities, teacher resources, a time line of events, and information about people related to the Holocaust.

People of the Holocaust

Students reflect upon and share what they know or believe about the people of the Holocaust. Next, student groups are randomly assigned a group of people to research: victims, perpetrators, bystanders, resisters, rescuers, liberators, and survivors. Students use a variety of resources for their research, take notes, compare and evaluate resources, and create a bibliography of their sources. Final reports are shared with the class. Students discuss how their research changed or confirmed their beliefs about people of the Holocaust. (Choose People from the main menu. Additional links are available within each topic.) Also consult the US Holocaust Memorial Museum (**http://www.ushmm.org**), the I*EARN Holocaust/Genocide Project (**http://www.peg.apc.org/~iearn/hgpproject.html**), and the Anne Frank House (**http://www.channels.nl/ annefran.html**).

Information skills: Locate, organize, evaluate, and synthesize information about a specific topic from a variety of sources; record and analyze data; assemble information in a meaningful manner.

WW1: Trenches on the Web
http://www.worldwar1.com/index.html

This Web site contains a wealth of information about the events, people, places, crafts, and artillery of World War I. The Reference Library categorizes information by who, what, when, and where. There are maps, photos, a search engine, miscellaneous bits of information, discussion forums, audio files, additional links, and much more.

MM WWI

After browsing through Trenches on the Web, student groups choose a topic of interest to research. Findings are presented through a multimedia project. Students use online and off-line resources (including the Trenches on the Web Discussion Forum), compare and evaluate their resources, and create a bibliography. Final reports are linked to a class menu of World War I topics. The final project can be distributed through the Web or the school media center.

Information skills: Locate and specify a topic of interest; find, organize, evaluate, and synthesize information from a variety of sources; integrate text with images, videos, and sound clips in a meaningful manner.

WWI Poetry

Students discuss what they think soldiers in World War I may have thought about and wrote about. Following this discussion, students read and interpret poems written by the soldiers. Students share their thoughts and talk about how the poems changed or confirmed what they believed about World War I soldiers. Choose Search Facility from the home page text, or enter **http://www.worldwar1.com/tsearch.htm**. Enter *poetry* as the search word and click on Search. From the results, select Trenches on the Web—Special: German War Poetry (Translated) and Trenches on the Web—Special: Italian War Poetry. Students may research poetry from resources as well.

Information skills: Conduct searches; locate, compare, evaluate, and organize information; read for significant details and concepts; communicate information in a meaningful way.

Additional Sites for World History

Cybrary of the Holocaust
http://remember.org

> The Cybrary of the Holocaust provides information, resources, personal accounts, and links related to the Holocaust.

NM's Creative Impulse
http://history.evansville.net/index.html

> NM's Creative Impulse focuses on the artist's view of world history and Western civilization. Emphasis is on art, music, drama, and literature.

Women in World History Curriculum
http://home.earthlink.net/%7Ewomenwhist/

> This sites provides many resources and links to information about women in history.

World History Archives
http://www.hartford-hwp.com/archives/index.html

> This site provides an enormous collection of resources for the study of world history, including topics such as World Historiography, the Americas, the World, Africa, Asia, and Europe. Each topic is divided into specific categories that link users to additional Web pages that contain links to specific areas of study related to the chosen category. The site also includes a link to Images from History.

World History Links Page
http://we.got.net/docent/scwriter.htm

> The World History Links Page provides links to countries and regions of the world, world newspapers, world poetry, and much more.

World War II: The World Remembers
http://192.253.114.31/D-Day/Table_of_contents.html

> Created by students and faculty at Patch American High School and Patch Elementary School (Europe), this site provides many links to World War II resources from a variety of perspectives.

GENERAL SOCIAL STUDIES AND GEOGRAPHY RESOURCES ON THE WEB

Online Magazines and Newsletters

American Journalism NewsLink
http://www.newslink.org/news.html

CNN Interactive
http://www.cnn.com/

Editor and Publisher Online Newspapers
http://www.mediainfo.com/ephome/npaper/nphtm/online.htm

Mungo Park
http://www.mungopark.com

National Geographic
http://www.nationalgeographic.com/contents/

Pleasant Company
http://www.americangirl.com/

Other Social Studies Sites

Amazon Adventure
http://vif27.icair.iac.org.nz/
At this Web site, students can learn about the people, places, animals, and history of Amazonia.

Black History Month
http://www.kn.pacbell.com/wired/BHM/AfroAm.html
This Web site features information, links, and activities related to Black history and African American issues.

Britannica Birthday Calendar
http://www.eb.com/calendar/calendar.html
Students can find out which famous people share their birthday.

Create Your Own Newspaper
http://crayon.net/
This site allows students to create their own online newspaper. News articles are the result of students' interests.

Flints and Stones: Real Life in Prehistory
http://www.ncl.ac.uk/~nantiq/menu.html
Flints and Stones provides information about the people and the environment during the Stone Age. The site includes photographs, an online quiz, and information on common misconceptions about prehistory.

Foreign Languages for Travelers

http://www.travlang.com/languages/index.html

Foreign Languages for Travelers is an outstanding resource that automatically translates words from one language to another, provides text and sound files, and offers links to other language sources on the Web.

Geonet Game

http://www.hmco.com/school/geo/indexhi.html

Geonet Game is an online geography game based on the National Geography Standards.

Girltech

http://www.girltech.com

Girltech offers more than 200 pages of fun, educational content. It features games, an advice column, a weekly diary, women role models, science projects, inventions, sports, and a boys' area designed to encourage and increase communication and understanding between girls and boys.

Global Online Adventure Learning

http://goals.com/

This site provides opportunities for students to explore the world with real-world travelers. Students have the opportunity to read about real-life adventures, interact with explorers, and take virtual field trips. Also see GlobaLearn (**http://www.globalearn.org/**) and High Points of the Americas (**http://www.23peaks.com/**).

GORP: Great Outdoor Recreation Page

http://www.gorp.com

This Web site offers information related to outdoor recreation and travel. GORP provides information about travel locations around the world, interactive forums, trip tales, outdoor recreation options, and more. Students have the opportunity to learn about geography activities.

Historic Audio Archives

http://www.webcorp.com/civilrights/mlk.htm

This site features audio clips, including Adolf Hitler, Winston Churchill, Malcolm X, Richard Nixon, Ronald Reagan, George Bush, and Bill Clinton.

Historical Archaeology

http://spirit.lib.uconn.edu/ArchNet/Topical/Historic/Historic.html

This site provides links to archaeological sites and tours on the Web.

Historical Text Archive

http://www.msstate.edu/Archives/History/index.html

Housed at Mississippi State University, the Historical Text Archive is an outstanding resource for locating information and resources about various topics. Learn about the history of Africa, Asia, Canada, Europe, and more. U.S.

resources include links to Native American history, U.S. historical documents, the colonial period, U.S. wars, U.S. presidents, and much more. The Web site also provides links to miscellaneous e-mail addresses (historians, military, colleges, etc.), databases, and other social studies and history links.

The History Net
http://www.thehistorynet.com/

Sponsored by the National History Society, this Web site features information and links related to world history, American history, eyewitness accounts, personality profiles, famous battles, interviews, and much more.

History/Social Studies Web Site for K–12 Teachers
http://www.execpc.com/~dboals/boals.html

This Web site provides an extensive list of links to history and social studies sites.

Holidays on the Net
http://www.holidays.net

Holidays on the Net provides information about various holidays. The site also includes holiday activities and additional links.

Ingenius
http://www.ingenius.com

Ingenius provides teacher and student resources. It also features Ask A.N.D.I.E., software that gathers and delivers the news from 20 different news wires around the world.

Internet Public Library
http://ipl.sils.umich.edu/

The Internet Public Library provides links to reference materials, online texts and magazines, librarian information, and more. It also provides links for kids and links to sites with resources for learning about various languages.

Invention Dimension
http://web.mit.edu/invent/

The Invention Dimension provides information about inventions and inventors from around the world.

Journey North
http://www.learner.org/content/k12/jnorth/

Journey North invites students to participate in the observation of wildlife migration.

Lesson Plans and Resources for Social Studies Teachers
http://www.csun.edu/~hcedu013/index.html

This site provides many links to resources for social studies teachers, including lesson plans, online activities, educational standards, other social studies resources, and more.

MapQuest
http://www.mapquest.com/

MapQuest is an interactive resource for locating destinations, calculating distances, planning routes, and making custom maps. It is an outstanding resource that can be integrated in all areas of the curriculum.

Martin Luther King, Jr.
http://www.seattletimes.com/mlk/

Sponsored by the *Seattle Times*, this Web site provides information about Martin Luther King Jr. Also see the Martin Luther King Jr. Home Page (**http://www.emich.edu/public/nasa/martin.htm**) and Martin Luther King Jr. (**http://www.netgaincc.com/sddemocrats/mlk.html**).

Medieval World
http://history.evansville.net/medieval.html

Medieval World offers links and information about the people, places, events, and art of medieval times. Its extensive list of resources is categorized by people, places, events, resources, art and architecture, literature and drama, music and dance, and daily life and culture. A search option is also available.

Murry Bergtraum High School Social Studies References
http://mbhs.bergtraum.k12.ny.us/referenc.html

This site offers an extensive list of links to many social studies Web sites.

My Hero
http://myhero.com/home.asp

My Hero is all about heroes from all walks of life. Students can submit essays they have written about their own heroes.

Online Resources
http://socialstudies.com/online.html

Online Resources provides a list of links to social studies topics arranged in the following categories: world, United States, and general history.

ParkNet
http://www.nps.gov/

ParkNet, from the U.S. National Park Service, is an outstanding resource for learning about national parks, their resources, history, locations, historic places, and more. The site includes many online resources and links, including tools for teachers.

Research It!
http://www.iTools.com/research-it/research-it.html

This site offers a currency converter, language translator, and search tools and links for many categories.

Social Studies Bag O' Tricks

http://www.vkool.com/grapeshot/socials/homepage.htm

Social Studies Bag O' Tricks provides links to miscellaneous social studies sites and lesson plans, including mock trials, advertising analysis, and history links.

Travel by City.Net

http://www.city.net/

This Web site offers a wealth of information about cities all over the world. In addition to interactive maps, City.Net provides tourist information, search options, weather reports, discussion areas, and additional links.

UNICEF

http://www.unicef.org/

This site offers information about UNICEF, child rights, and other child-related issues. It contains a links to Voices of Youth (a forum where children can share their thoughts), a learning place with games and activities, and resources for teachers.

USA CityLink

http://usacitylink.com/

USA CityLink is a comprehensive listing of Web pages featuring states and cities. Students can learn more about each city by clicking on its name or state. Also see CitySearch (**http://www.citysearch.com/**).

Visitor's Guide to Taiwan

http://peacock.tnjc.edu.tw:80/ADD/TOUR/main.html

This site provides information about Taiwan, including regions, outdoor activities, culture and cuisine, festivals and holidays, and more.

World Surfari

http://www.supersurf.com/

World Surfari offers students the opportunity to to learn about the history and culture of people from around the world. E-mail, quizzes, activities, and additional links are also available.

World Wide Web Virtual Library: Anthropology

http://www.usc.edu/dept/v-lib/anthropology.html

This Web site provides links to information about archeology, evolution, Asian studies, paleontology, ethnology, and critical theory.

World Wide Web Virtual Library: History

http://history.cc.ukans.edu/history/WWW_history_main.html

This site categorizes resources alphabetically and by era, region, and subject. By investigating resources organized by era, students can make and compare time lines for various countries. Time periods are Prehistory and Archaeology;

Ancient: ca. 4000 BC–AD 500; Medieval: 500–1500; and Modern: 1500–present. Students can also research history servers by subject. Subjects include National Cultures, International Cultures, Asian Studies, Buddhist Studies, Latin American Studies, and American Studies.

Xerox PARC Map Viewer

http://pubweb.parc.xerox.com/mapdocs/mapviewer.html

The Xerox PARC Map Viewer accepts requests for a world or USA map and returns an image of the requested map. Each map image is created on demand from a geographic database.

E-MAIL EXCHANGES

E-mail exchanges can help students learn about societies and geographical locations. It is an excellent tool for contacting people. E-mail allows people to communicate without biases related to color, race, age, or disability. It allows students to focus on what they have in common and to respect their various differences.

Real-World Accounts

Ask people in other states or countries for firsthand accounts of current events. Assess how their reactions or statements reflect or differ from what is reported. This activity provides students with a human perspective of current events.

School Around the World

Contact students in other countries and exchange and discuss class schedules and other school-related topics. Compare which subjects are covered, how many minutes are allotted for each subject, length of the school day, recess and lunch periods, emphasis on physical education and music, requirements to be a teacher, and so on.

Senior Exchange

Arrange for the residents of a retirement home to exchange e-mail messages with your students. Students may inquire about what the world was like when the senior was their age, what seniors did for fun when they were young, how much things cost several years ago, what the seniors enjoy doing now, and so forth. The senior citizens may help students with their homework, give advice, and listen to problems. The school's parent-teacher organization might support the endeavor by providing the retirement home with a computer, a modem, and training.

Grade Levels	Illinois Jones and	Research Level
4-12	the Last Lemonade	Basic

Educational Goals

To access and use the Geographic Name Server

To cooperatively use problem-solving skills to identify a secret number

To access and locate a specific book using its ISBN number at the Library of Congress via the Internet

Procedure

This activity provides a fun introduction to the Geographic Name Server. Students work in teams of two or three. Introduce the Geographic Name Server as a resource of information about cities around the world, and how this server may be used for research. Describe Illinois Jones and the Last Lemonade as a game to learn more about the server. Distribute the activity sheet to teams.

Answers

Clue 1: **08952**. Marfrance's zip code is 25981. Less 1, this equals 25980. Reverse the numbers to read: 08952. (Apple Valley appears 5 times in the U.S.)

Clue 2: **9**. Karen's zip code is 48339. Ann's zip code is 29067. The only number these have in common is 9.

Clue 3: **626**. The area code of Timbuktu is 503. 503 + 123 = 626.

Clue 4: **8**. Transylvania's zip code is 71286. The first two digits, 7 and 1, add up to 8.

The ISBN number is **0895296268**. If you search the Library of Congress for this ISBN number, you'll discover this book is the *Lemon Tree Very Healthy Cookbook*.

Extension Activities

1. Students create their own Geographic Name Server problem-solving adventure to share with their classmates or other students via telecommunications.

2. Students substitute the clues on the Illinois Jones and the Last Lemonade activity sheet with other clues that will provide the same answer.

3. If possible, obtain the *Lemon Tree Very Healthy Cookbook* and prepare selected recipes. Students exchange and prepare their favorite lemonade recipes.

From *The Internet and Instruction.* © 1998 Libraries Unlimited. (800) 237-6124.

Illinois Jones and the Last Lemonade

Greetings, Jones. We are relying on your geographic expertise to save us from another dilemon – I mean dilemma. As you may be aware, the secret recipe for the world's greatest-tasting lemonade is hidden in some unknown book. The only clues we have are those that may identify the book's ISBN number. Sort these out using the Geographic Name Server. Once you have determined the ISBN number, go to the Library of Congress and find the book that holds the secret recipe! Good luck!

To access the Geographic Name Server, use

telnet://martini.eecs.umich.edu:3000

Enter a city or a zip code at the "." prompt. Type **exit** to log out.

To access the Library of Congress, use

http://marvel.loc.gov

CLUE 1

To find the first five digits of the ISBN number, find the zip code of Marfrance, West Virginia, and subtract 1. Write the zip code backward (include all five digits).

Tip: The fourth digit of the ISBN number is the number of cities called Apple Valley in the U.S.

CLUE 2

The sixth digit is the common digit between the following two cities' County FIPS codes:

Karen, Texas
Ann, Missouri

CLUE 3

The seventh, eighth, and ninth digits can be represented by the area code of Timbuktu, plus 123.

CLUE 4

The last digit is the sum of the first two digits of the zip code of Transylvania.

Grade Levels	What Do You	Research Level
4-12	Think?	Original

Educational Goals

To make students more aware of biases or preconceived ideas they may have toward a group

To learn more about another group of people

Procedure

At the beginning of a semester, invite students to participate in a survey of how they perceive people in another state. Distribute the What Do You Think? rating scale activity sheet and have students agree or disagree with statements made about people in a particular state (e.g., California). Next, pair students with students in the selected state and have them exchange messages about whatever they like. Brainstorm with students to get started. During the semester, hold class discussions about the effects of preconceived ideas about groups of people and how these biases can be changed. Students keep a daily journal of their experiences or observations of bias and stereotyping.   At the end of the semester, administer the What Do You Think? survey to students. Students compare their responses to the initial survey with their responses on the last survey and comment on things they learned.

Resources

See chapter 3 for contacting students and teachers.

Extension Activities

1.   Use the same activity for communicating with students in another country.

2.   Students bring in news articles about current events concerning stereotypes and biases.

3.   Students write a research report on the effects of bias and stereotypes.

4.   Students research and discuss issues in American history concerning bias and stereotypes.

What Do You Think?

Mark an X in the box that best describes your impression of people in _____.
***

	Strongly agree	Agree more than disagree	Disagree more than agree	Strongly disagree
People in *** work mostly on farms.				
People in *** are mostly rich.				
People in *** prefer country music.				
People in *** work mostly in the city.				
People in *** are unusual.				
People in *** think I'm unusual.				
People in *** watch a lot of TV.				
People in *** are friendly.				
People in *** are very health conscious.				
People in *** don't have gang problems.				
People in *** enjoy cold weather.				
People in *** are a lot like me.				
People in *** are always in a hurry.				

Remembering the Holocaust

Objectives

To work cooperatively to research and present findings about different topics related to the Holocaust

To discuss the impact of discrimination, prejudice, and hatred in today's society

Grade Levels: 9-12   **Final Product:** Written or multimedia reports

Internet Resources

Cybrary of the Holocaust (http://remember.org/)

Holocaust Pictures Exhibition (http://modb.oce.ulg.ac.be/schmitz/holocaust.html)

Shamash (http://shamash.org/holocaust)

United States Holocaust Memorial Museum (http://www.ushmm.org/education/ed.html)

Teacher's Guide to the Holocaust (http://fcit.coedu.usf.edu/holocaust)

Procedure

1. Students in groups of four discuss what they know about the effects of discrimination, prejudice, and hatred throughout history. A group member records their responses. After a few minutes, groups share their responses with the whole class.

2. Explain that the Holocaust is a historical event and that governments made choices that not only legalized discrimination but allowed prejudice, hatred, and mass murder to occur. (Download *A Guide to Teaching the Holocaust* at the United States Holocaust Memorial Museum [http://www.ushmm.org/education/ed.html].) It is an excellent resource designed to assist educators who are preparing to teach Holocaust studies and related subjects.) Discuss how peer pressure, conformity, indifference, and obedience may cause people to overlook or remain silent about oppression of another person.

3. Students in groups research and report various events of the Holocaust. Assign topics or let groups pick their own topic. The following topics can be researched using the Internet and other media sources. (Note: E-mail addresses are also available. See Cybrary of the Holocaust [http://remember.org].)

Remembering the Holocaust (cont.)

Procedure (cont.)

A Brief History of the Holocaust   Children of the Holocaust
Individual Accounts of the Holocaust   Images of the Holocaust
Conspiracy and Denial Issues   Perpetrators

4. Students create a bibliography of their resources and note any discrepancies in data.

5. After gathering, evaluating, and synthesizing information, students create a 5-to-10 page written report, including a bibliography. The report should be illustrated with images downloaded from one of the Holocaust sites. Students print the images and write a summary for each one.

6. Each group presents its findings. Encourage the use of visuals for the presentations.

7. Following the presentations and any further discussion, students write what they learned about the Holocaust and how they think this information is relevant today. Students discuss solutions to discrimination and prejudice as well as peer pressure, conformity, indifference, and other relevant issues.

Extension Activities

1. Students explore and discuss poetry, art, and music of the Holocaust and create their own poem or image about the Holocaust. Students share these poems and images with others on the Internet.

2. Instead of a written report, students with the topic Individual Accounts of the Holocaust dramatize and record a personal account found on the Internet. (One source is the Cybrary of the Holocaust. Choose Survivors under Witnesses.)

3. Download and present the appropriate topics listed under the Holocaust and Genocide Curriculum.

4. Students research and write a report about one of the many death camps or other specific topics (e.g., Adolf Hitler, Jews, etc.) that stand out in the history of the Holocaust. Students accompany their reports with a diorama, sculpture, or painting illustrating their topic.

Women in History

Objectives

To research and present information on the contributions of women in history

To create a class timeline that reflects the contributions of women throughout history

Grade Levels: 4-12   **Final Product:** Multimedia or written report and class timeline

Internet Resources

Women in World History Curriculum (http://home.earthlink.net/%7Ewomenwhist/)

Great American History (http://www.cais.com/greatamericanhistory/)

The White House (http://www.whitehouse.gov)

Girltech (http://www.girltech.com)

Perspectives in American Literature (PAL): A Research and Reference Guide (http://www.csustan.edu/english/reuben/pal/table.html)

Women Mathematicians (http://www.scottlan.edu/lriddle/women/alpha.htm)

Procedure

1. Ask students to list the names and contributions of women in American and world history. Arrange the list by categories, e.g., science, literature, mathematics, and so on.

2. Assign student pairs to research additional names and contributions of women to add to the class list. Use both online (see Internet Resources) and offline resources.

3. After the class has generated at least 50 names, assign students to create a multimedia or written biography of a selected woman. Each student researches the life and contributions of a different woman. Students use both online and offline resources for their research, create a bibliography of their sources, and note any discrepancies among their resources of information.

4. Students create a short summary of their person's accomplishments to place on a class timeline.

Women in History (cont.)

Procedure (cont.)

5. Final reports are shared with the class.

Extension Activities

1. Students create a painting, drawing, or sculpture of their person to accompany their biography.

2. Students locate their person's place of birth and death on a class map. Students create a chart to compare the women's origins.

3. Students contact women online experts (see Pitsco's Ask an Expert at http://www.askanexpert.com/askanexpert/) and local community members and ask them about their career choices.

4. Student groups write and perform a play that tells about famous women in history.

5. Using a variety of online and offline resources, student groups research and write about women suffrage, stereotypes, inequalities, and other topics.

6. Students contact students in other countries (see chapter 3) and survey and compare the role of women among the different countries.

Art, Music, and Theater Resources and Activities

Dina's favorite style of music was ragtime. Her grandmother had introduced her to the music and told her about some of the famous ragtime composers of the early 1900s. Now Dina had the opportunity to share her love of ragtime with her classmates. Ms. Norton, Dina's teacher, assigned the class to create a multimedia project that focused on the history of a particular style of music. Most students fought over rock and roll; Dina quickly chose ragtime.

In addition to her grandmother's recollections, Dina used the Internet to research her topic. She summarized information from several Web sites to include. Fortunately, there were several sites to choose from, and most had links to additional sources. The Ragtime Home Page was especially helpful. She also located several commercial music sites and downloaded sample ragtime music clips and learned about current ragtime composers. Dina was thrilled to discover that her love for ragtime was not limited to her and her grandmother!

Dina's final project included graphics, music clips, and information about the history and composers of ragtime. She used a variety of off-line and online sources; however, Dina noted in her bibliography that off-line sources for ragtime (other than her grandmother!) were difficult to find and very limited. The

Internet helped her to locate additional ragtime resources, to integrate the required media elements, and to finish her report.

The Internet provides a treasure trove of audio and video clips, photographs, song lyrics, movie and television scripts, lesson plans, and much more. The Web offers students the opportunity to tour virtual museums, hear music online, view movies on their computers, share their musical compositions and artwork, contact online experts, and access hundreds of databases related to the arts. It provides a library of media resources that students might not otherwise have.

This chapter features art, music, and theater Web sites. Topics include animation, music, the cinema, art and music history, theater, and performers and music of the early 1900s. For each topic, the chapter provides one or two instructional ideas for two or more sites. These ideas and skills are not comprehensive; instead, they serve as starting points for exploration and activities. Following the highlighted sites is a list of other sites related to the topic; these sites are briefly described. The chapter ends with a list of general art, music, and theater sites and e-mail activities.

Note: Each site's current URL is given, but, because the Internet is extremely dynamic, addresses and paths may change.

ANIMATION

Children's fascination with animation begins when they watch their first cartoon. As they grow older, they learn that the cartoon characters are not real but created by artists. For many students, however, the process of animation is puzzling. Resources on the Internet help to demystify animation by providing animation studios, animation sequences, online experts, and other resources.

Animation World Network
http://www.awn.com/

The Animation World Network features an animation gallery, an online magazine, links to animators, a searchable database, discussion forums, and additional links and topics related to animation. The animation gallery features current and past exhibits of artists' work. The online database can be searched by category, audience, genre, technique, country, or original language of the film. The Animation World Network also features downloadable shareware, freeware, and video clips.

Animation Experts

As a class, students brainstorm and submit questions to animation experts. Results are recorded, analyzed, and compared among the different animators. Select Animators (under the Animation Village) from the main menu.

Information skills: Brainstorm questions for a specific topic, seek information from professionals, and categorize and compare information.

Animation World Network home page.

Critiques

Students view, compare, and critique video clips located in the Downloadable Files Archive. (Choose The Vault on the main menu.) Students discuss the animators' techniques and analyze the clip by stepping through each frame. Students learn more about each animator by searching The Vault database. Students share and compare their critiques with the class. As a follow-up activity, students submit their own animated clips to the Animation World Network. (For younger students, the video clips can be used to generate story ideas.)

Information skills: Conduct searches; locate, compare, analyze, and evaluate information.

Ron Kurer's Toon Tracker Home Page
http://ftp.wi.net/%7Erkurer/index.htm

This site features background information about classic animations, including *The Gumby Show, The Dick Tracy Show, Wink Dink and You, Calvin and the Colonel, Beany and Cecil, Mr. Magoo,* and more. The site provides music themes, graphic resources, and an extensive list of animation links.

Cartoons of Today and Yesterday

Students compare a classic cartoon with a similar cartoon of today (e.g., clay animation is compared with clay animation, a detective-themed cartoon is compared with a detective-themed cartoon, and so on). Students create a Venn diagram to display their findings. In addition to the information found on Toon Tracker Home Page, students may go to their local library or video store for copies of animated classics. Students can compare settings, characters, animation, and so on.

Information skills: Locate, analyze, evaluate, and compare information; organize information using a Venn diagram; communicate findings.

Favorite Classics

Students design a hypermedia project that provides information about five of their favorite classic cartoon characters. In addition to background information and pictures of the characters, students include why they like the character. Projects should also include audio and other information related to the characters. Student share their projects with the class.

Information skills: Teach students how to locate and organize information for a specific topic from a variety of sources and to integrate text with images, videos, and sound clips in a meaningful manner.

Warner Brothers' Animation
http://www.wbanimation.com/cmp/ani_01hm.htm

Warner Brothers' Animation features a variety of links, including Warner Brothers' Animation 101, What's Happening, and Favorite Places. Warner Brothers' Animation 101 provides a step-by-step approach for creating animated cartoons; students learn about the importance of writers, storyboards, layout and background artists, and more. What's Happening features current news about Warner Brothers' cartoons, employees, and upcoming events. Favorite Places includes links to other cartoon and comic sites.

Animation 101

Using Warner Brothers' Animation 101 and other online and off-line resources, student groups research the process of creating animated cartoons. Student groups apply what they have learned by creating their own animation design teams to create a two-minute animation using a computer or video camera. Findings and cartoons are shared with the class. Choose Animation 101 from the main menu.

Information skills: Locate and compare information; read for significant details and concepts; apply information in a meaningful manner.

Superhero Villains

Student groups research the history of Batman and compare and contrast the villains in Batman: The Animated Series (choose Favorite Places from the main menu, then Batman: The Animated Series). Student groups create a time line depicting the introduction of each character, along with a short biography of each character. The groups share their findings as a class and discuss characteristics of villains. Students apply what they have learned by creating their own villain to star in a Batman cartoon. Students write a character biography, create a picture of the villain, and write a script that introduces their character to Batman. As a follow-up activity, students compare and contrast villains in Batman to other animated villains in Disney, Superman, and other cartoons. Student groups may also create a cartoon parody of Batman and the villains, or create their own superhero cartoon.

Information skills: Locate, organize, and evaluate information; create a time line; effectively communicate and apply findings.

Additional Sites for Animation

Animation Companies & Animators
http://www.pb.com.au/pb/cat/14.htm

This site provides an alphabetized list of links to information about animation companies and animators.

Animation, USA
http://www.animationusa.com/

This site provides information about various characters, art, and animators.

CartoonGallery.com
http://www.cartoonarts.com/

This commercial site provides information about collecting animation cels. Students can learn about different types of cels, collecting art, limited editions, and so on. Also see The Cartoon Factory (**http://www.cartoon-factory.com/ home.html**).

Hovis.com
http://www.bendnet.com/users/brianhovis/

This site features online tutorials about GIF animation and links to GIF software and files.

Kids' Cool Animation
http://www.kaleidoscapes.com/kc_intro.html

Kids' Cool Animation features online tutorials that teach students about animation on the Internet, 3-D art, and animation. The site also provides students with the opportunity to create their own animated Web page, to participate in discussion groups, and to link to other animation resources.

Women in the Realm of Computer Visual Arts, Effects, and Animation
http://www.animation.org/women/

This site features interviews with women in computer visual arts, effects, and animations. Information about a mentorship program is also available.

ART AND MUSIC HISTORY

Art and music history resources are not always easy to come by in the school. Fortunately, the Web offers many resources about the history of music and art. In addition to online experts, the Web provides virtual museum tours, interactive tutorials, artist biographies, and access to multimedia components related to the history of music and art.

Comic Art & Graffix Gallery Virtual Museum and Encyclopedia

This site features the history of comic art, including a pictorial history of sequential art, a chronological history of comic art in America, and much more. Students can also access artist biographies, information about collecting comic art, and additional comic-related links.

The History of Comic Art

Using a variety of online and off-line resources, student groups research the history of comic art. Students take notes, evaluate and compare their findings, and create a bibliography of their resources. Student groups report their findings by creating a comic strip time line. Each panel of the comic strip time line includes illustrations and information related to the comic characters and artists during a specified time period. Students share their time lines with the class. (Choose The History of Comic Art from the main menu.)

Information skills: Locate, organize, evaluate, and synthesize information about a specific topic from a variety of sources; record and analyze data; effectively organize information into a time line.

Music History 102
http://www.ipl.org/exhibit/mushist/index.html

Music History 102 is a permanent exhibit of the Internet Public Library (**http://www.ipl.org/**). Music History 102 surveys Western classical music, focusing on the stylistic trends in music from the Middle Ages to the present. In addition to excerpts from famous musical works, the site presents information about styles and composers of music. Topics include the Middle Ages, the Renaissance, the Baroque Age, the Classical Period, and the Romantic Era.

Famous Composers

Students research the life and music of a selected composer of Western classical music. They create a multimedia project to display their findings. Projects should include a biographical summary, a picture of the composer, and sample music clips. Projects are connected through a class menu and are shared with the class. Students create review questions to test each other's knowledge of their composer. As a follow-up activity, student groups can participate in a Jeopardy game related to the students' research.

Information skills: Locate, organize, and evaluate information; record and analyze data; integrate text with images, video, and sound clips in a meaningful manner; develop comprehension questions.

the Internet Public Library

Music History 102

a Guide to Western Composers and their Music
from the Middle Ages to the Present

The sound files that form a part of Music History 102 are encoded using RealAudio. To be able to access and play these files, you will need to download a copy of RealAudio Player software on your computer. This software is available free of charge via the RealAudio Web Page. Just follow the instructions on the page to download. You will need to provide your name and email address, and will need to know your operating system platform, processor type, and connection speed.

CONTENTS of *Music History 102:*

As is usual with information on the history of Western music,
this site has been organized according to the eras of history:

- The Middle Ages
- The Renaissance
- The Baroque Age
- The Classical Period
- The Romantic Era
- The Twentieth Century

The Middle Ages

Around 500 A.D., western civilization began to emerge from the period known as "The Dark Ages," the time when invading hordes of Vandals, Huns, and Visigoths overran Europe and brought an end to the Roman Empire. For the next ten centuries, the newly emerging Christian Church would dominate Europe, administering justice, instigating "Holy" Crusades against the East, establishing Universities, and generally dictating the destiny of music, art and literature. During this time, Pope Gregory I is generally believed to have collected and codified the music known as Gregorian Chant, which was the approved music of the Church. Much later, the University at Notre Dame in Paris saw the creation of a new kind of music called organum. Secular music was sung all over Europe by the troubadours and trouvères of France. And it was during the Middle Ages that western culture saw the arrival of the first great name in music, Guillaume de Machaut.

Music History 102 home page.

Style Comparisons

Students compare two styles of Western classical music. Comparisons include information about the styles' history, composers, and musical elements. Students create Venn diagrams and other charts to display their findings in their reports. In addition to Music History 102, students use other resources to research their styles. Students take notes and create a bibliography of their resources.

Information skills: Locate, organize, and evaluate information about a specific topic from a variety of sources; record and analyze data; organize information using a Venn diagram and other charts.

WebMuseum
http://sunsite.unc.edu/louvre/

The WebMuseum features art exhibits, famous paintings, and biographies of artists. Students can research paintings and artists by themes, access an index of artists, and learn more about painting styles from an online glossary. Pictures of paintings can be viewed and enlarged on screen. Each picture is accompanied by descriptive text. The WebMuseum also features an online auditorium where students can hear classical music and link to additional multimedia resources.

Famous Painters

Students write a biography of a famous painter and re-create one of the subject's famous works. Using a variety of online and off-line sources, students take notes, evaluate and compare findings, and create a bibliography. Students present their findings and artwork to the class. Choose Famous Painters from the main menu.

Information skills: Locate, organize, evaluate, and synthesize information; record and analyze data; assemble information in a meaningful manner; present findings through visual and written media.

Painting Styles

Using a variety of online and off-line resources, student groups create a multimedia report on a selected painting style, for example, Baroque, Cubism, Impressionism, and so on. In addition to the history of the selected style, reports should include information about artists, graphics, and other information related to the chosen style. Students take notes, evaluate and compare their findings, and create a bibliography of their resources. Projects are linked to a class menu, shared with the class, and placed in the school library. Choose Famous Paintings from the main menu.

Information skills: Locate, organize, and evaluate information for a specific topic from a variety of sources; record and analyze data; integrate text with images, videos, and sound clips in a meaningful manner.

Additional Sites for Art and Music History

Exploring Leonardo
http://www.mos.org/sln/Leonardo/LeoHomePage.html

Sponsored by the Museum of Science (Boston), this site helps teachers and students learn more about the work and life of Leonardo da Vinci.

History Happens
http://www.ushistory.com/cool.htm

This site provides songs and lyrics related to American history. RealAudio is required.

Minneapolis Institute of Arts
http://www.artsMIA.org/index.html#index

The Minneapolis Institute of Arts provides curriculum and information for teachers, online quizzes, and information about the museum's current and permanent exhibits.

Rock and Roll Hall of Fame and Museum
http://www.rockhall.com

The Rock and Roll Hall of Fame and Museum provides information about songs and artists, online lesson plans and resources, forums, and music trivia.

Southern Music Network
http://www.southernmusic.net/

This site provides information about southern music in the twentieth century. By clicking on a specific year, students can obtain information about the music, composers, and other related topics for that year. Additional links include News, Education, City Links, Chat, and Instruments. (Also see The Blue Highway at http://thebluehighway.com/.)

World Wide Web Virtual Library: Classical Music
http://www.gprep.org/classical/index1.html

This site is one of the largest and most comprehensive indexes of music-related information and resources on the Internet. Topics are organized by categories. Students can follow links to biographical information about composers and artists, online periodicals, computer software, discussion forums, and reference sites.

THE CINEMA

The history of the cinema and its reflection of society continues to be an interesting area of research. People from all over the world have constructed sites dedicated to their love of the cinema.

Alfred Hitchcock: The Master of Suspense
http://nextdch.mty.itesm.mx:80/~plopezg/Kaplan/Hitchcock.html

This site, dedicated to the life and work of Alfred J. Hitchcock, features a biography, answers to frequently asked questions, information and trivia about Mr. Hitchcock's films, and other interesting information related to Mr. Hitchcock.

Essays

Students analyze and critique one of the essays available on the site, based on their own interpretation of the film. (Choose Essays from the main menu.) Students write a comparative essay, citing information with which they agree or disagree. Students share their comparative essays with the class for class discussion.

Information skills: Teach students how to locate and evaluate information, to read for significant details and concepts, and to communicate information in a meaningful manner.

A Game of Thought

In addition to the Alfred Hitchcock: The Master of Suspense Web site, student groups use off-line and online resources to create a filmography book of Mr. Hitchcock's movies. The book should include the films' plots, genre, trivia, and so on, as well as a bibliography of sources. Next, student groups design a board game based on their research. This may be modeled after Trivia Pursuit, Jeopardy, or another knowledge-based game. Students can also exchange questions about Mr. Hitchcock's movies with other classes through e-mail. Classes try to stump each other. As a follow-up activity, student groups create their own

version 3.0 revision #3456

I N D E X

BASICS:

Frequently Asked Questions
A Hitchcock guide to the novice, and a follow-up to your emails.

Alfred Hitchcock

Biography
A small summary of his life work, and personal milestones.

the mystery, the madness, the suspense all wrapped up in a neat little box.

Alfred Hitchcock: The Master of Suspense home page.

movie in the Hitchcock style. Movies can be exchanged with e-mail partners through the mail.

Information skills: Locate, organize, and evaluate information about a specific topic from a variety of sources; analyze, synthesize, and record information; inform others of their findings using a nontraditional approach.

Hollywood Online
http://www.hollywood.com/

Hollywood Online features many movie-related databases, guides, and news items. Topics include MoviePeople, MovieTunes, Multimedia, Hollywood News, and more. The site also features reviews of current movies, interviews, and a Hollywood Almanac.

Hollywood Today

Student groups script and videotape their own Hollywood news show based on the top stories, current events, almanac information, and other facts available on Hollywood Online. Student groups brainstorm and research topics for their show, assign production and acting roles, and present their videotape to the class. Student groups can critique each other's communication skills, presentation, news relevance, and so on.

Information skills: Brainstorm and specify required information on a particular topic; locate, select, evaluate, and synthesize information; organize and present findings in a nontraditional format.

Multimedia Movie Review

Students create a multimedia movie review of their favorite film. (Media elements and information for various films can be accessed by choosing Multimedia from the main menu.) In addition to the students' reviews, projects may include information about the film's plot, actors and actresses, director(s), soundtrack, interesting facts, and information about the book that the movie is based on (if applicable). Additional movie information can be accessed by choosing MoviePeople from the main menu. Search for information about the movie by its title.

Information skills: Teach students how to locate, organize, and evaluate information for a specific topic from a variety of sources and to integrate text with images, videos, and sound clips in a meaningful manner.

Movies at Home
http://ecreations.com/movies/frame.html

Movies at Home features movie reviews, actor biographies, discussion forums, movie quotes, music files, current events, links to other movie sites, and much more. Students have the opportunity to submit their own movie reviews, e-mail reviewers, take an online survey, and access information about past and current movies.

Movie Review

Students write reviews of their favorite movies and submit them to Movies at Home. Students compare their reviews with others. Students share their reviews with the class and comment on others' reviews. Select Write a New Review from the main menu. To access other reviews, choose Reader Submissions from the main menu. Additional links are available from the main menu. (To access the links, choose Links, then Movie Sites.) See also Reviews in Rhyme (**http://www.datasync.com/~booda/rir.html**). Students can read and submit reviews.

Information skills: Locate and compare information and assemble it in a requested format for Web publication.

Multimedia Movies

Student groups create a multimedia stack that focuses on a selected movie soundtrack (choose MIDI Files from the main menu). For example, student groups may incorporate the music from *Evita* into a stack that discusses the story, characters, and so on of the movie *Evita*. Students use a variety of online and off-line resources for their projects. Stacks are linked to a class menu and shared with the class. As a follow-up activity, after watching the selected movie, students compare the book (if available) to the movie.

Information skills: Teach students how to locate and specify a topic of interest; to find, organize, evaluate, and synthesize information from a variety of sources; and to integrate text with images, videos, and sound clips in a meaningful manner.

Additional Sites for the Cinema

AFI Online Cinema
http://ptd15.afionline.org/cinema/

AFI OnLine Cinema offers real-time, online, classic Hollywood movies. Requires VDOLive Player (available from site; see Instructions).

Buttered Popcorn
http://web-star.com/buttered/popcorn.html

This site features easy-to-read movie reviews. The reviews include links to the movies' sites.

Channel One
http://www.channelone.com/index.html

Channel One invites students to answer surveys related to television shows and policies, read and add their own movie and music reviews, and access current entertainment news.

Cyber Film School
http://www.cyberfilmschool.com/

This site contains an assortment of movie-related links, including articles about filmmaking, news and reviews, digital downloads, online magazines, and more.

Film 100
http://www.film100.com/

This site contains information about the 100 most influential people in the history of cinema.

MUSIC

RealAudio is a plug-in that enables Web browsers to play "real-time" audio files without waiting for the entire file to transfer. It is one way students can hear and evaluate music using the Web. In addition to audio clips, the Web provides access to lyrics, scores, students' compositions, and online experts. Many lesson plans and other activities focus on integrating music across the curriculum.

Children's Music Web
http://www.childrensmusic.org/

The Children's Music Page features a comprehensive index of children's music sites, a database of music events for children, e-mail opportunities, music activ-

Welcome to the

Children's Music Web

We are a non-profit organization dedicated to music for kids

Children's Music Web home page.

ities, sound clips, and information about music organizations for children. It also features songs written by other students, ideas for creating songs, music reviews, and a newsletter for music teachers. (See Fun Music Ideas on the Pipsqueaks page.) The Children's Music Page offers RealAudio and other sound files.

Sing a Song

As a class, students learn and evaluate songs written by children from other schools. Choose Pipsqueaks from the main menu, then select Sing Along (under Sing) to see and hear music written by other students. Students illustrate their favorite songs. The songs are then tallied and compared on a class bar chart.

Information skills: Evaluate and respond to information and to construct charts.

A Song of My Own

Working individually, in small groups, or as a class, students create and submit a song to the Children's Music Page. (For instructions, select How to Write Your Own Song on the Sing Along page.) Choose Pipsqueaks from the main menu, then select Sing Along (under Sing).

Information skills: Read for significant details and concepts; assemble information in a requested format for Web publication.

Young Composers
http://www.youngcomposers.com/

> Young Composers features original work by students. Students can listen to compositions, e-mail the composers, join online chat rooms and discussion boards, and submit their own musical compositions to the site.

> #### Composer of Choice

> Following a class discussion about differentiating between personal preference and good work, students review and evaluate a variety of compositions and choose their favorite young composer. Students design a list of interview questions to e-mail to their favorite young composer and share the composer's music and responses with the class. (Select Earlier Works and New Releases from the main menu.)

> *Information skills:* Locate and evaluate another's work; develop and administer interview questions; assemble and communicate information in a meaningful manner.

Additional Sites for Music

All-Music Guide
http://205.186.189.2/root/amg/music_root.html

> All-Music Guide is a searchable database for locating information about musicians, albums, songs, music styles, and more. Also see the International Lyric Server (**http://www.lyrics.ch/**).

DanMan's Music Library and Creativity Club
http://www.DanmansMusic.com/

> DanMan's Music Library allows students the opportunity to view popular song lyrics and classical scores. Music Study provides information about music topics. The Creativity Club invites students to submit original work and view other submissions.

Kathy Schrock's Guide for Educators: Music
http://www.capecod.net/schrockguide/enter/music.htm

> This site contains an extensive list of music sites on the Web.

On-air.com
http://www.on-air.com/

> This site features music from the 1950s, '60s, '70s, '80s, and '90s. It also includes dance tunes. RealAudio is required, and can be downloaded from the site.

SchoolHouse Rock
http://genxtvland.simplenet.com/SchoolHouseRock/

> This site contains song lyrics, audio files, and other information related to the SchoolHouse Rock series.

Tots2Teens Music and Arts Links
http://www.jasper1.com/kidz/art.html

This site includes links to lyrics to Muppet songs (**http://www.cs.unc.edu/~arthur/ muppet-songs.html**), Disney songs (**http://zeus.informatik.uni-frankfurt.de/ %7Efp/Disney/Lyrics/**), and other songs.

PERFORMERS AND MUSIC OF THE EARLY 1900s

The early 1900s was an exciting time for theater, movie, and other performing arts. The Web offers many sites dedicated to these early pioneers of comedy, drama, and showmanship. This section is an eclectic collection of sites related to the performers and music of the early 1900s.

Flapper Station
http://www.sns.com/%7Erbotti/index.html

The Flapper Station is dedicated to the 1920s and early 1930s, providing information about music, fashions, movies, motor vehicles, radio, and movies. Many links are available for further research.

1920s Performers

Student groups create a multimedia project focusing on a selected performer of the 1920s. Students use a variety of online and off-line resources, take notes, evaluate and compare their findings, and create a bibliography. Projects should include photographs and other media related to the performer. Select Boarding for the Silver Screen from the main menu. See also Autographs: Hollywood Legends (**http://www.autographics.com/legends.html**).

Information skills: Locate, organize, and evaluate information; record and synthesize data; integrate text with images, videos, and sound clips in a meaningful manner.

Roaring '20s Variety Page

Student groups research the performers, shows, and other highlights of the 1920s, then create a 1920s newspaper. Students write as though they were writing during the 1920s; each group chooses a different year. Students use a variety of off-line and online resources and evaluate and compare their findings. Student groups share their newspapers with the class and create comprehension questions for their classmates to answer. Newspapers and questions can be exchanged with other classes via the Internet. Classes can exchange newspapers that focus on events that took place in their state during the 1920s.

Information skills: Collaboratively define topics and identify specific information needs; locate, organize, evaluate, and record information; develop comprehension questions; communicate findings in a meaningful format.

The Houdini Museum
http://www.microserve.net/%7Emagicusa/houdini.html

This site features information about the Houdini Museum in Scranton, Pennsylvania. (Houdini was a magician and escape artist.) The site includes an abundance of Houdini-related information, including a biography, trivia, information about his brother, and so on. Students and teachers are encouraged to use the site as an up-to-date and reliable source of information about Houdini.

Houdini

Students use a variety of off-line and online resources to create a biography of Houdini. In addition, students create a short presentation of what they find most interesting about Houdini and share it with the class. Students take notes, evaluate and compare their resources, and create a bibliography of their sources. An assortment of information about Houdini can be accessed from the main menu.

Information skills: Locate, organize, and evaluate information about a specific topic from a variety of sources; analyze, synthesize, and record information; assemble information in a meaningful manner.

Ragtime Home Page
http://www.ragtimers.org/

Ragtime Home Page features links to audio clips of ragtime music (sound files are in MIDI format), information about ragtime and its composers, and links to related sites. It also features a Terra Verde Corner, where students can learn about this style of music. Information about ragtime books, recordings, and events is also available.

History of Ragtime

Using a variety of online and off-line resources, student groups create multimedia projects that detail the history of ragtime. Projects should include audio clips, information about composers, the definition of ragtime, and other interesting facts. Students take notes, evaluate and compare their sources, and create a bibliography. Projects are shared and evaluated by the students as well as the teacher. Files in the MIDI format, composer information, frequently asked questions, and additional ragtime links can be accessed from the main menu.

Information skills: Locate, organize, and evaluate information; record and synthesize data; integrate text with images, videos, and sound clips in a meaningful manner.

Why I Like Ragtime

In small groups, students discuss why they like or dislike ragtime. Students share their comments with the class. They create a chart that lists reasons for liking and disliking ragtime. Next, students read "Why I Like Ragtime" essays

Ragtime home page.

available on the Ragtime Home Page. Students analyze and compare the essays with their own opinions and add their findings to the class chart. Students can contact some of the authors about their essays. Ask the students what they might learn from the essays (e.g., favorite ragtime themes, when the authors realized they liked ragtime, if more females or males appear to like ragtime, and so on). As a follow-up activity, students who like ragtime submit their own essays to the site.

Information skills: Locate, analyze, and compare information; read for significant details; communicate information in a meaningful manner.

Additional Sites for Performers and Music of the Early 1900s

American Variety Stage: Vaudeville and Popular Entertainment
http://lcweb2.loc.gov/ammem/vshtml/vshome.html

This Library of Congress site is a multimedia anthology of popular entertainment during the period 1870–1920. The site features information about Houdini, sound recordings (RealAudio and WAV versions), playscripts, motion picture recordings, and information about motion pictures.

Autographs: Hollywood Legends
http://www.autographics.com/legends.html

This is a searchable database of biographies of Hollywood Legends and Web pages devoted to them.

The Marx Brothers
http://members.aol.com/marxbroths/index.htm

> This site provides biographical information about the Marx Brothers, their performances, and links to additional Marx Brothers pages.

Ragtime Vaudeville Show
http://bestwebs.com/vaudeville/index.html

> The Ragtime Vaudeville Show features RealAudio recordings of famous vaudeville performers, performer biographies, and a brief history of vaudeville.

Vaudeville Home Page
http://www.microserve.net/~magicusa/vaudeville.html

> The Vaudeville Home Page contains links to resources about vaudeville performers, including Laurel and Hardy, Charlie Chaplin, Abbott and Costello, Al Jolson, and many others. It also contains links to ragtime songs and vaudeville sites.

THEATER

> The Internet provides educators with additional resources to teach students about the theater, including opera and Broadway productions. It exposes students to a world they might not otherwise experience.

OperaWeb
http://www.opera.it/English/OperaWeb.html

> OperaWeb is an outstanding resource for learning more about opera stories, singers, and history. OperaWeb includes files in the MIDI format of famous arias, information about singing, an interactive quiz, and links to other opera sites.

Opera History

Using a variety of online and off-line resources, students research the history of opera. Students evaluate and compare resources, take notes, and create a bibliography of their resources. Students create a written report and time line of their findings. (Choose The Crazy Opera History from the main menu.) Questions can be e-mailed to OperaWeb's online experts.

Information skills: Locate, organize, and evaluate information about a specific topic from a variety of sources; analyze, synthesize, and record information; assemble information in a meaningful manner.

Opera Story

Student groups research an opera and create a multimedia report about its story, history, and so on. Groups present their reports to the class, and reports can be linked by a class menu, then posted on the school's Web site. As a follow-up activity, students can participate in the OperaWeb's online quiz and record their results. (Choose Opera from the main menu.)

Information skills: Locate and organize information about a specific topic; integrate text with images, videos, and sound clips in a meaningful manner.

Theatre Central
http://www.theatre-central.com/

Theatre Central features an extensive list of resources related to the theater. In addition to current events, students can access information about shows playing around the world. Students can join discussion groups, access online experts and multimedia links, and take online quizzes to test their knowledge of theater. The main menu remains in a frame on the screen during searches.

Broadway Shows

Student pairs research a selected Broadway show and present their findings to the class in a 15-minute videotaped presentation highlighting the show. Choose Broadway (under Listings) from the main menu. Students create review questions to test each other's knowledge of their shows.

Information skills: Locate and organize information, develop comprehension questions, and present findings using a nontraditional format.

Occupation of Interest

Students brainstorm careers in the theater, then form groups based on a career that interests them. Each group develops a survey to send to people in that occupation (e.g., composers, dancers, choreographers). The groups analyze and chart their results and share their findings with the class. (Choose Theatre Central from the main menu, then choose Connections from the main page. A search option will appear. Scroll down to an occupation of choice and click on Search.)

Information skills: Conduct searches; develop and administer a survey; interpret and chart survey results; assemble and communicate information in a meaningful manner.

The World of Mime Theatre
http://www.geocities.com/Broadway/5222/

The World of Mime Theatre provides information about mime performances, artists, and history, as well as other interesting facts. Students can contact mime performers, access mime sites, and read about or see pictures of specific performances.

History of Mime

Using a variety of online and off-line resources, students research the history of mime. They take notes, evaluate and compare resources, and create a bibliography. Choose Library from the main menu. Students may also access additional mime sites by choosing Information & Resources from the main menu, then Websites.

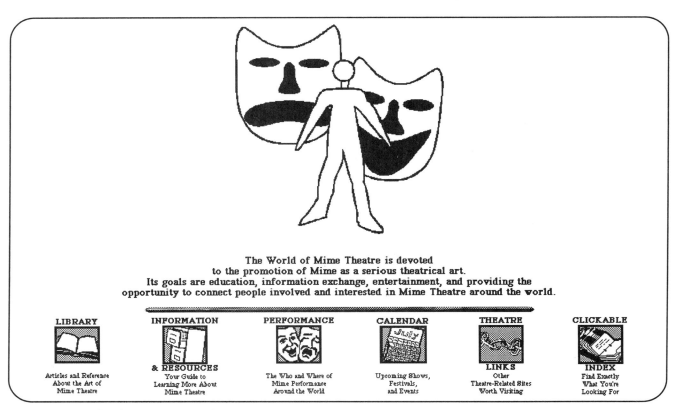

The World of Mime Theatre home page.

Information skills: Locate, organize, and evaluate information; analyze, synthesize, and record information; assemble information in a meaningful manner.

Why Mime?

As a class, students design a survey to help them learn more about becoming a mime, why mimes chose their profession, and so on. Student groups send the survey to a selected mime performer; each group sends the survey to a different performer and identifies the location of the performer on a class map. Student groups chart, discuss, and compare their data with other groups and create a class chart of their findings. (Choose Performance from the main menu, then choose Mime Artists.)

Information skills: Map skills; develop and administer a survey; interpret and chart survey results; assemble and communicate information in a meaningful manner.

Additional Sites for Theater

Children's Theatre Resource Webpage
http://pubweb.acns.nwu.edu/~vjs291/children.html

This site provides links to many children's theater resources, including organizations, publishers, plays, and literature.

The Dramatic Exchange
http://www.dramex.org/

This site archives and distributes scripts.

Internet Resources for the Arts: Drama and Theatre
http://www.wcsu.ctstateu.edu/library/a_drama_theater.html

This site is a collection of links to other sites. Categories include Plays and Playwrights, Stagecraft, Acting and Awards, Music and Theatre, Journals and Discussion Groups, Academic Programs, and more.

Performing Arts Exchange
http://www.geocities.com/Hollywood/Set/2716/lessons.html

This site contains a collection of lesson plans and other ideas related to speech, drama, and theater activities for high school students.

Phantom of the Opera
http://phantom.skywalk.com/

This site is dedicated to the study of *Phantom of the Opera*. Students can access information about the story, sounds, graphics and images, and other related information.

WWW Virtual Library: Theatre and Drama
http://www.brookes.ac.uk/VL/theatre/index.htm

This site contains links to online scripts, journals, articles, and related resources.

GENERAL ART, MUSIC, AND THEATER RESOURCES ON THE WEB

The Internet provides many Web sites for art, music, and theater resources. Many of these sites are designed to be integrated into other areas of the curriculum; hence, several art, music, and theater sites were mentioned in previous chapters. (Consult the index for comprehensive listings of art. music, and theater resources throughout the book.)

Online Magazines and Newsletters

Animation Journal
http://www.chapman.edu/animation/

Animation World Magazine
http://www.awn.com/mag/index.phtml

Filmmaker Magazine
http://www.filmmag.com/

Videomaker Magazine
http://www.videomaker.com/

Other Art, Music, and Theater Sites

The Amazing Picture Machine
http://www.ncrtec.org/picture.htm

The Amazing Picture Machine provides links and a search engine for finding pictures on its site.

Arts and Crafts
http://www.earlychildhood.com/art.html

This is an outstanding resource for arts and crafts resources and ideas. In addition to project ideas and step-by-step instructions, the site features current articles related to early childhood education; an area where teachers can post their own questions, opinions, and success stories; and additional links.

Carnival of Animals
http://busboy.sped.ukans.edu/~music/carnival

This interactive site celebrates Camille Saint-Saens's *Carnival of the Animals*.

Cartoon Mania
http://www.worldchat.com/public/jhish/course.html

Cartoon Mania teaches students how to draw cartoons and offers them the opportunity to post them on the Web.

The Electric Gallery
http://www.egallery.com/

The Electric Gallery features art from all over the world. Artist biographies are also available.

Galaxy Humanity Page
http://galaxy.tradewave.com/galaxy/Humanities/Arts.html

Galaxy provides extensive lists of Web resources by subject area. The Humanities section lists an enormous number of links to art resources, institutions, artists, and more.

Global Show-n-Tell
http://www.telenaut.com/gst/

This site posts students' art and offers links to other sites of interest to kids.

Gupit-Gupit: 3D paper sculptures
http://www.tiac.net/users/gneils/gupit-gupit.html

This site provides information and graphics to help students learn how to make 3-D paper sculptures.

Internet for the Fine Arts: Art Links
http://www.fine-art.com/link.html

This extensive list of art links is categorized by Artists; Galleries and Exhibits; Indices, Search Engines, and Resources; Organizations and Businesses; Museums; and more.

Jogle's Favorite Theatre Related Resources

http://www.artsnet.org/OnBroadway/links/Theatre.html

This site contains an extensive list of links to theater-related sites. Categories include People, Education and Theatre, Stagecraft, Indices, and Newsgroups.

The Judy and David Home Page

http://judyanddavid.com/

The Judy and David Home Page features lyrics to favorite children's songs, miscellaneous art activities, sound clips, and additional links for kids.

Juggling Information Service

http://www.juggling.org/

This site provides many links to juggling resources, information, online magazines, clubs, and much more. The site includes juggling help, multimedia, current news, and links to jugglers' home pages.

Kids' Corner

http://kids.ot.com/

The Kids' Corner provides online activities and includes options to view and submit student art.

The Klingon Language Institute

http://www.kli.org/KLIhome.html

For *Star Trek* fans and performers, this site provides information about speaking and writing Klingon, sound effects, and other Klingon-related information.

The Media History Project

http://www.mediahistory.com/index.html

This site provides many links to information on early, print, electrical, mass, and digital media. It also features a media time line, chat rooms, and online searching.

Medieval Drama Links

http://www.leeds.ac.uk/theatre/emd/links.htm

Medieval Drama Links contains a comprehensive index of links related to medieval drama. Categories include text, set design, props and makeup, costumes, illustrated material, medieval music, and medieval dance.

Museums from A to Z

http://www.vol.it/UK/EN/ARTE/MuseumsfromAtoZ.html

This is an index of online museums.

Origami Page

http://www.datt.co.jp/Origami/

The Origami Page provides information about the history of origami, paper-folding techniques, and many origami projects.

Sites with Audio Clips

http://www.geek-girl.com/audioclips.html

This site provides an index of Internet sites with audio clips. It is an abundant resource for dialog and themes from TV shows, cartoons, and movies. It also includes audio from famous speeches, song clips, radio broadcasts, and celebrity lectures.

The Smithsonian Institution

http://www.si.edu/newstart.htm

This site offers an integrated view of the Smithsonian Institution. It provides links to home pages for all of the institution's museums and many of its offices and research centers.

World of Escher

http://lonestar.texas.net/~escher/

This site provides information about Escher and his many works.

E-MAIL EXCHANGES

Telecommunications is one way to exchange ideas, share projects, and bolster creativity. E-mail is one way to help your students share their creativity.

Hollywood Heroes

Students survey other students around the world to learn their favorite movie, song, actor, actress, commercial, television show, and cartoon. Chart and compare the results by location, age, and gender.

Oh Say, Can You See?

Students research their national anthem and exchange their research with students doing similar research in other countries. Students may research the song's author, meaning, history, and date of publication, as well as reflect on what the anthem means to them. Printouts of the anthems can be attached to the country of origin on a classroom map. Students can also create a time line showing when the anthems were written.

Playing Around

Students exchange class plays with students in other countries. In each class, the students write the play to reflect an average day or week in their lives. Students perform and videotape each other's plays and mail each other copies of the tapes. Students e-mail follow-up questions or comments.

Grade Levels	Information	Research Level
4-12	Illusions	Advanced

Educational Goals

To introduce students to analyzing, comparing, and evaluating information from a variety of sources

To create a biography of a selected performer from the early 1900s.

Procedure

1. Ask students to list as many sources of information that they can and write these on the board (e.g., textbooks, magazines, CD-ROMs, the Internet, television news, newspapers, friends, and so on).

2. Ask students to identify what they consider to be the most reliable sources and to explain their answers. Continue with a discussion on fact and opinion and how to evaluate sources on the Internet.

3. Discuss ways that students can verify information, including the use of multiple sources.

4. Introduce students to the Information Illusions activity sheet, featuring Harry Houdini. Note that many things have been written about Harry Houdini, but that different sources may say different things. Ask students why they think various sources tell different accounts of Harry Houdini's life. How do they know which source to believe? Student pairs complete the activity sheet using three different sources (e.g., the Internet, an encyclopedia, and a book about Houdini).

5. After students complete the activity sheet, they share their findings with the class. Review the importance of gathering information from multiple resources and the importance of evaluating the source of the information itself – whether it is fact or opinion, peer-reviewed, and so on.

6. Students apply what they have learned by using multiple resources to create a biography of a performer of the early 1900s. Students use a format similar to Information Illusions to record and compare their findings.

Extension Activities

1. Students research and report on strongly held beliefs that are no longer true. For example: The earth is flat, the sun revolves around the Earth, and so on.

2. As a class, devise a checklist or chart for evaluating information from the Internet and other sources.

Information Illusions

There are many books and encyclopedias that tell about the life of the famous magician Harry Houdini. CD-ROMs and Web sites also provide information about Harry Houdini. What if, however, different souces say different things? Which is correct and how can you go about checking your findings? To examine this, use three different resources to answer the following questions about Harry Houdini. Use The Houdini Museum (http://www. microserve.net/%7Emagicusa/houdini.html) as one of your sources. Identify your sources below.

1 The Houdini Museum (http://www.microserve.net/%7Emagicusa/houdini.html)

2 _____

3 _____

Where and when was Harry Houdini born?

Source 1	Source 2	Source 3

Where and how did Harry Houdini die?

Source 1	Source 2	Source 3

What was Harry Houdini's real name?

Source 1	Source 2	Source 3

On the back of this sheet, describe any differences in the information that you found and which source you believe is accurate and why. What else can you do to verify your findings?

From *The Internet and Instruction.* © 1998 Libraries Unlimited. (800) 237-6124.

Grade Levels	Composer	Research Level
6-12	Storyboard	Advanced

Educational Goals

To work cooperatively to find facts from a variety of sources and report them in a hypermedia stack

To integrate the use of technology into research methods

To create a flowchart and storyboards to map and illustrate the components of a hypermedia stack

Procedure

1. Students work in groups of four to research information about a selected composer. Each group researches a different composer and presents their findings in a hypermedia format. (If students have not used an authoring program, let them become familiar with the program first.) Groups use a standard storyboard format (see the Composer Storyboard activity sheet). Each group's project will be joined through a main menu designed by the class.

2. Groups research the life of their composer, titles, and digital samples of the composer's music. Students create a bibliography. In addition to books and CD-ROMs, students access information about composers from the following resources: Music History 101 (http://www.ipl.org/exhibit/mushist/index.html), World Wide Web Virtual Library: Classical Music (http://www.gprep.org/classical/index1.html), and the University of Oregon School of Music Information Server (http://music1.uoregon.edu/musres.html).

   Two students in each group research the composer's life, and two students research and find examples of the composer's music. All four students contribute to the bibliography. In addition to music and text, projects should incorporate graphics and digitized pictures that are relevant to the content.

3. After the students have gathered, synthesized, and clustered their information, they create a flowchart to map their hypermedia stack. Next, they make multiple copies of the Composer Storyboard activity sheet. Each group designs its hypermedia project on paper. Textual information goes on the right, and graphics go on the left. The composer's name always appears at the top left-hand corner. *Topic # of #* refers to the user's current location in relationship to the number of cards (screens) for a particular topic (e.g., Music 1 of 3). Students indicate where each button will take the user (Link to: storyboard #). Students indicate special transitions, sounds, animations, and other information under Notes. After groups have completed the storyboard design, members work together to create the final product.

From *The Internet and Instruction.* © 1998 Libraries Unlimited. (800) 237-6124.

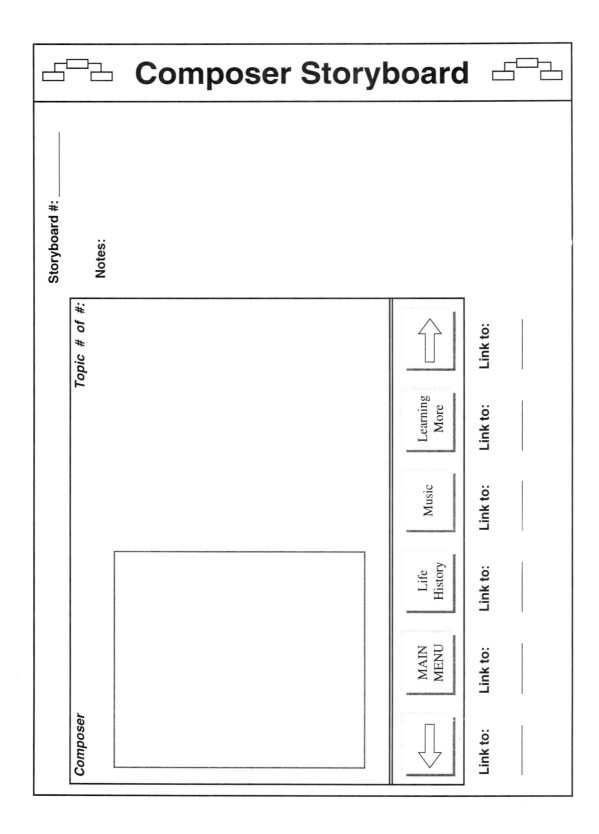

Multicultural Music

Objectives

To work cooperatively to research, synthesize, organize, and present findings from a variety of sources

To identify and compare music from different countries

Grade Levels: 8-12   **Final Product:** Multimedia presentations

Internet Resources

University of Oregon School of Music Information Server (http://music1.uoregon.edu/musres.html)

Yahoo Country and Cultures: Music (http://www.yahoo.com/Entertainment/Music/Countries_and_Cultures/)

Latin and World Music Links (http://www.weltmusik.de/iwalewa/gregor.htm)

Multicultural Choral Music (http://www.asan.com/users/dweber/home.html)

Media History Project (http://www.mediahistory.com/record.html)

Music Education Resource Links (http://www.cs.uop.edu/%7Ecpiper/musiced.html)

Procedure

1. Ask students what they may know about the origins of music, to list and compare different styles of music, and what it is about music that they enjoy.

2. Ask students what they know about music from other cultures. Create a Knowledge Chart with the headings: What I Know, What I Want to Find Out, and What I Learned. Fill in what students know, then ask students to list what they would like to learn about music from different cultures (e.g., what it sounds like, what types of instruments are used, and so on).

3. Place students into groups and have each group research music from another culture. Provide students with the Internet Resources and encourage them to use a search engine to help them find more information about their topic. Each group researches and reports on a different culture. Student groups use a variety of online and offline resources and create a bibliography of their resources.

Multicultural Music (cont.)

Procedure (cont.)

4. Students organize their findings into a multimedia presentation and present their reports to the class.

5. Conclude by filling in the last column of the Knowledge Chart and comparing and discussing students' findings.

Extension Activities

1. Student groups conduct further research on different cultures.

2. Student groups construct a musical instrument related to their topic of study.

3. Student groups draw pictures of instruments related to their topic of study and attach the pictures to a world map to show their origin.

4. Invite local musicians who specialize in multicultural music to be guest speakers in your class.

5. Contact students in other countries to learn more about the music they listen to, who their favorite artists are, and so on. Exchange audio music clips.

6. Create Venn diagrams to compare student groups' findings among cultures.

Learning Through Song

Objectives

To work cooperatively to research, evaluate, and report findings from a variety of sources

To compose a song that teaches a skill or concept

Grade Levels: 4-12   **Final Product:** Class songbook

Internet Resources

SchoolHouse Rock (http://genxtvland.simplenet.com/SchoolHouseRock/)

Muppet Songs (http://www.cs.unc.edu/~arthur/muppet-songs.html)

Children's Music Page (http://www.childrensmusic.org/)

History Happens (http://www.ushistory.com/cool.htm)

Procedure

1. Ask students to identify songs that teach them about or how to do something.

2. Introduce students to the SchoolHouse Rock Web site (http://genxtvland.simplenet.com/SchoolHouseRock/) and demonstrate (download and play) sample songs. Ask what the songs are teaching and why people often use songs to help them remember things or to tell stories.

3. Assign student groups to explore the SchoolHouse Rock, History Happens, and Muppet Songs Web sites listed in Internet Resources and to assemble a list of two to three songs from each site that teach something. Student groups provide a summary of what they learned from reading or hearing the song.

4. After student groups share their findings, discuss songwriting (see the Pipsqueaks link at the Children's Music Page or enter http://www.childrensmusic.org/create.html).

5. Based on your students' ability level, have student groups create a song that teaches about or how to do something. Older students may create their own melodies, while younger students may write the lyrics to a familiar tune (e.g., "Twinkle, Twinkle Little Star").

Learning Through Song (cont.)

Procedure (cont.)

6. Student groups submit and illustrate their song for a class songbook. Student groups perform their songs for the class. Songs may be shared over the Internet, posted on the class Web page, or placed in the school library.

Extension Activities

1. Survey online composers about how they come up with song ideas and melodies, how old they were when they wrote their first song, what they like best and least about writing songs, and so on. See Yahoo Composers (http://www.yahoo.com/ Entertainment/Music/Composition/Composers/) for a list of resources.

2. Student groups research and interpret the meanings of selected song lyrics from the International Lyrics Server (http://www.lyrics.ch/). For example, student groups may research and interpret the lyrics to "American Pie" by Don McLean or Joan Baez's "The Night They Drove Old Dixie Down."

3. Students create an illustrated story songbook by illustrating a song from SchoolHouse Rock or another resource.

4. As a class, students write a musical to perform for other students. The musical may be about saying no to drugs, the results of lying, or other moral issues, or it may be designed to teach students about a famous person, an event, how to do something, etc.

5. Student groups create short, musical puppet shows that tell a story. Student groups design their shows for younger students.

Index

Index of Internet Sites

Bold numbers indicate pages on which addresses are given.